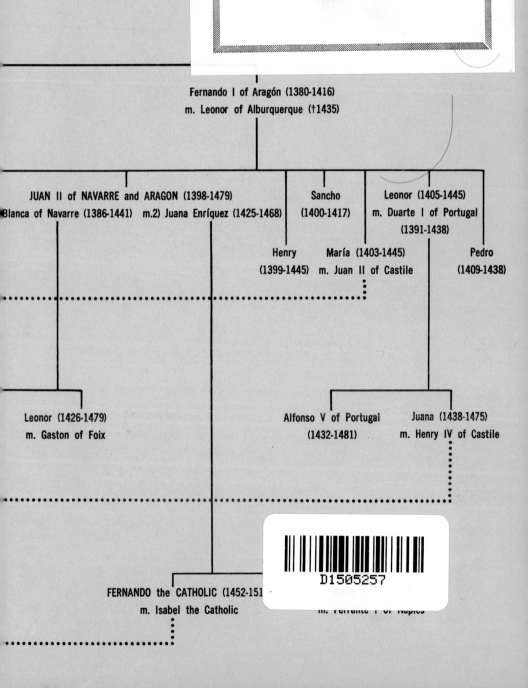

Fernando I of Aragón (1380-1416)
m. Leonor of Alburquerque (†1435)

JUAN II of NAVARRE and ARAGON (1398-1479)
Blanca of Navarre (1386-1441)   m.2) Juana Enríquez (1425-1468)

Sancho
(1400-1417)

Leonor (1405-1445)
m. Duarte I of Portugal
(1391-1438)

Henry
(1399-1445)

María (1403-1445)
m. Juan II of Castile

Pedro
(1409-1438)

Leonor (1426-1479)
m. Gaston of Foix

Alfonso V of Portugal
(1432-1481)

Juana (1438-1475)
m. Henry IV of Castile

FERNANDO the CATHOLIC (1452-151
m. Isabel the Catholic

m. Ferrante I of Naples

❦ Henry IV of Castile

TOWNSEND MILLER was born in St. Louis and educated at Yale, where he received his B.A. and Ph.D. degrees. He has served on the faculties of Yale and the University of Texas. He is the author of *The Castles and the Crown,* a book on Spanish history widely praised by scholars as well as popular critics in both Europe and America. Mr. Miller resides abroad, principally in Mexico and Spain.

Also by Townsend Miller

THE CASTLES AND THE CROWN

Henry IV of Castile

1425-1474

by Townsend Miller

J. B. LIPPINCOTT COMPANY

Philadelphia and New York

1972

U. S. Library of Congress Cataloging in Publication Data

Miller, Townsend.
  Henry IV of Castile, 1425–1474.

  Bibliography: p.

  1. Enrique IV, King of Castile and Leon, 1425–1474.
2. Castile—History—Henry IV, 1454–1474. I. Title.
DP143.M5 1972   946.3'02'0924[B]   70–163226
                ISBN–0–397–00798–1

❀ Prefatory Note

Surprisingly little has been written about a figure of such pivotal importance in Spanish history as Henry IV; the books devoted exclusively to him can be counted on the fingers of one hand. Sitges's volume is a work for specialists. Only the most dedicated will wade through Orestes Ferrara's. Bermejo de la Rica's is a *"vulgarización,"* that word which raises the hair of any author not entirely acquainted with its meaning—"popularization"—in Spanish. Marañón's *Ensayo Biológico* is, as its title indicates, a clinical study, while Lucas-Dubreton's is more a piece of belles-lettres and a general picture of the age than a formal biography. And that is about the lot. Except for Prescott's treatment, that of William Thomas Walsh in his life of Isabel the Catholic, and my own in *The Castles and the Crown*, next to nothing has previously appeared in English.

These facts can no doubt be partly explained by the extraordinary complication of the material. Nor is a writer who undertakes a larger handling of the subject for the first time in the latter language exempt from an added problem, none the less thorny for being minor—the question of nomenclature. Most Spanish names glide easily enough from the English-speaking tongue: Juan, Pedro, Carlos. But with the principal character of this work the case is somewhat altered. His name, of course, was Enrique; so I think of him, so I have called him in my other publications on the period. Yet experience has taught me that the unfamiliar form is apt to occasion hesitance, even embarrassment, for the American or British reader. It is solely to avoid such an obstacle, and with full knowledge of the inconsistencies into which I have thereby fallen, that I here anglicize his name. At least I have not further shackled with his traditional epithet a person of whom I am frankly fond. (The writing of history or biography in a detached and impartial manner affords, in my opinion, small cause for self-congratulation. To be completely "objective" is to have no particular interest in one's subject—and to arouse none in the reader.)

What to call the daughter of Henry's second wife presents a different dilemma. To refer to her simply as "Juana," with so many others of that name among the pages, could only bring confusion. "Princess Juana" is not a valid solution: the title of Princess or Prince was reserved exclusively—indeed jealously, indeed often to the point of bloodshed, as the reader will discover—for the heir apparent, and it would be quite improper to give this unlucky child that designation during the intervals when Henry did not acknowledge her his successor. Conversely, it would be just as wrong to call her "Infanta" at the time when she was, in fact, accepted as the heir. Her popular name of La Beltraneja has seemed to me, in certain places, the best escape from the impasse. Use of it, however, by no means implies that I definitely consider Beltrán de la Cueva to have been her father.

My researches for the volume were greatly facilitated by generous grants from the John Simon Guggenheim Memorial Foundation and from the Del Amo Foundation of Los Angeles. And no one could possibly work in the Castilian fifteenth century without relying heavily upon the investigations and example of the chief current authorities in the field—Professor Juan Torres Fontes of the University of Murcia, Professor Eloy Benito Ruano of the University of Oviedo, Professor (and Rector) Luis Suárez Fernández of the University of Valladolid. To all three of these distinguished scholars I am bound by unrepayable debts of professional gratitude as well as by ties of warm personal friendship. My obligations to a host of Spanish librarians, curators, and archivists who have opened their treasures for me must, on the other hand, and because of their very numbers and dispersion, remain publicly unrecorded.

T. M.

❁ Contents

ILLUSTRATIONS

(following page 120)

Henry IV. A portrait from life
Henry IV. A contemporary miniature, hitherto unreproduced
Juan II of Aragón. A medallion of the day
Seal of Juan II of Aragón
Signature of Henry IV (*"Yo el Rey"*)
Virgen de la Mosca. Painting supposed to contain a portrait
    of Isabel the Catholic
Juan II of Castile. Effigy
Isabel of Portugal. Effigy

※

Part One:
1425–1454

1.

The Uncles

It had been a difficult delivery, and the foreign Queen of Castile lay gushing blood all that icy afternoon in 1425, her moans drowned out by the storm which beat upon the casements: do not expect, should a midwinter journey take you there to Valladolid, a land of sunshine and mild flowers, for the harsh Castilian tableland is raked by snow and sleety tempests now as then. But the son, the heir to the kingdom, had been safely born at last, and while physicians worked at the suffering mother numb hands took up the baby and washed him and wrapped him and deposited him in the wooden cradle painted blue and gold: Henry, the future Henry IV, known by history—with what justice it will be among our aims to examine—as Henry the Impotent.

Born in blood, in hemorrhage: it was the child's inheritance, the dark dower of his House of Trastámara. Indeed, there is much about the occasion that is prophetic, that is almost congealingly apt. One lingers over the weather—cold, cold; all of Henry's life was to be a frozen one, a cold birth and colder death, with half a century of chill misery in between. One finds, too, the air of family disunion, the cleavage and discord, which were to give the boy so deep a wound: it seems that his parents were even then estranged, for why else should the Queen have been inhabiting a borrowed house in the street of Teresa Gil and not the royal palace? We mark, as well, the presence of the Queen's brother—Juan, Prince of Aragón—who came posting fast as he could to bend over the cradle: although there can have been no trace in the sleeping infant of the large, sad, ugly man with the limp hands and broken nose whose abnormalities and weaknesses this Juan of Aragón was ceaselessly to study and exploit, whom he was to hound, harass, and finally bring down, nonetheless one feels safe in saying that the keen mind of the Aragonese uncle already whirred with plots. Much, yes, that is symbolic. But in the crux of suitabilities one fact is glaring awry. That winter Friday was the 5th of January—the Eve of Epiphany, of Reyes, the Feast of Kings. And it is hard to imagine anyone less suited than Henry IV to be a king—especially in the maelstrom of violence, war, and treachery which was medieval Spain.

Spain—we should not use the word, not yet: the nation as we know it did not exist. True, it would be forged before the century was out, and by Henry's own successors the Catholic Monarchs: his half-sister Isabel and Fernando, son of the very Juan of Aragón who stood bemused over the frosty cradle. But in 1425 that splendid pair had not been born, nor the marriages which produced them even contracted, and the Peninsula still lay bruised and sundered in five separate kingdoms: Castile, Aragón, Navarre, Portugal, Moorish Granada. So it had lain for centuries of feudal hatreds and aggressions. So it was to lie through Henry's life, the arid, bone-bleached chessboard on which our bitter game will be played out. Five rival realms, for ever at each others' throats. But it was Castile and Aragón which had perhaps the deepest enmity of all. They were the largest of the kingdoms. Between them ran a long, flat, vulnerable frontier, from the headwaters of the Ebro southeast to Murcia and the Mediterranean. Across that wavering line, for countless generations, their interests had clashed. And by the time of Henry's birth they had a further reason, a very special reason, for contention. We must straightway uncover it; it is the key to much of Peninsular history in the fifteenth century, the strand on which the iron beads of Henry's story will be strung.

The new hostility, in brief, was a dynastic one. Juan I of Castile, who reigned late in the preceding century, had sired two sons. Henry, the elder of them, was a frail fellow; he married Catherine of Lancaster, managed to beget a son upon that burly daughter of John of Gaunt, and came to reign himself as Henry III—El Do-liente, the Sickly or Ailing. His younger brother Fernando, cut off from the crown by what he no doubt considered a mere accident of months, was obliged to mend his fortunes as best he could. He mended them well. For about this Fernando, this second son of Juan I, there was nothing sickly whatsoever. Ambitious, massive, bold, he not only held on like a bulldog to his own considerable inheritance as a Castilian prince but worked ceaselessly to enlarge it. He married the richest heiress in the realm—Leonor of Alburquerque, La Rica Hembra,[1] who could travel all the way from the Aragonese border to that of Portugal without leaving her own lands. He turned to the wars and at Antequera won a great victory over the Moors which gave him his nickname and made him a national hero. At his brother's early death in 1406, he assumed, with his widowed sister-in-law Catherine, the regency for the infant King. High eminence, proud state: it would seem enough to have assuaged even the most frustrated of younger sons. But a yet greater prize awaited Fernando of Antequera. The Aragonese, looking about for someone to wear their crown after the death without issue of their latest sovereign, cast eyes upon the brilliant Castilian prince. Catherine, anxious enough to be free of his interference, had the Cortes put up some fifty millions of *maravedís*[2] to bribe the Aragonese electors. By the Conference of Caspe in 1412 they gave Fernando their vacant crown, although we are free to doubt that it was precisely the one he most wanted—even as King of Aragón he still tried to keep a grip upon Castile and its new sovereign, his young nephew Juan II. But Fernando enjoyed neither Aragonese crown nor Castilian coronet for long. He died in 1416—poisoned, so ran the rumor, by the touchy Catalans, already regretful of their offer. His seven children —two of whom, Henry's mother and her brother Juan, we have just met—were the famous Infantes of Aragón, destined to be the gadflies of Castile for three quarters of the century.

There is no need to sink in a sea of genealogy. The basic situation lies taut and simple: Trastámaras of Aragón aligned against Trastámaras of Castile. On this explosive *mise en scène*, this fizzing bomb of family jealousies and grudges, the stage lights up. Juan II, our Henry's father, is the Castilian King. In Aragón the children of Fernando of Antequera hold sway: a displaced and clannish brood, restless, ambitious, homesick, resentful of the fashion in which they felt their father had been cheated of Castile and determined one day to return to power in it—indeed, by hook or crook, to have its governance.

Well, one might ask, and what was to prevent them? Everything seemed to favor these astute and brilliant Aragonese Infantes in their plots against the coveted, lost realm. One of their sisters was married to its King. They still had huge possessions in Castile— where they had all, in point of fact, been born and bred. Their

mother owned most of Extremadura. Their father left them his own
princely inheritance in his native land, tall castled towns like Peñafiel and Mayorga and Medina del Campo. He had also, long before
he departed to take the crown of Aragón, made sure that some of
the richest Castilian offices—such powerful posts as the grandmas-
terships of the military orders of Santiago and Alcántara—were
bestowed securely in their hands. Together, perhaps their holdings
in Castile outmeasured even its monarch's own—since Trastámaran
kings, for decades, had given away vast ruinous chunks of royal
patrimony to rebellious nobles, in the vain hope of stemming their
revolts. Did not, moreover, those proud Castilian barons work, if for
entirely different reasons, toward the same end as the Infantes—the
diminishment of their King? Insatiable, ruthless, contemptuous of
royal authority and near-monarchs themselves in their craggy citadels, were not these treasonable magnates a tool to hand?

And if the Infantes mined Castile within, without they already
pressed against it, less than ten years after their embittered father's
death, like a crown of thorns. Nothing could be done—or so it had
seemed for centuries—about infidel Granada, on its south. But to
the east stretched Aragón itself, ruled now by Alfonso, the oldest
of the brothers. The Infante Juan—the shrewd watcher in Valladolid, the one who would survive everybody and carry the Aragonese standard long after all the rest of the family were crumbling
into dust beneath smoked Gothic altars—had married the daughter
of Charles the Noble and thus was King Consort of Navarre, that
small but useful country upon Castile's north. And in the west, in
Portugal, the second sister had been betrothed to the Crown Prince
and waited to be Queen. Hedged by the House of Aragón upon
three sides, riven internally with its mounting conflict between
Crown and baronage, ruled—if one may say so—by a lazy, woman-
izing, poetaster King: how did Castile hold out against the aggres-
sors?

But on the question crowds an instant answer. The beleaguered
realm was propped, defended, by one mighty arm—the royal favorite don Alvaro de Luna.

Luna—we must look at him; for all his meager frame, he bestrides
the age like a colossus. Even in his time he was a legend. His control
over his sovereign—and from childhood Juan II of Castile was en-

tirely delivered to him—sent many a rumor stalking, many a whisper in the dark. He was really a demon, some said, in human form. At midnight he turned into a vampire and drank the King's blood in lonely castles: see how that poor monarch went about, all white and listless. He kept a genie in a bottle. Everyone knew the story —and this one happened to be true—of the ring he made Juan wear, to prove his power: the miniature, inside it, of the King kneeling beneath a donkey and doing something vile to it. (The chronicler Alonso de Palencia would substitute Luna himself for the donkey; but in the whole age, a scurrilous and vicious one at that, his is the only charge of an unnatural bond between the two.)

The tales amuse today; it takes no witchcraft to explain how energy pours in to fill a vacuum. But don Alvaro de Luna still puzzles historians. Was he indeed the sterling champion of royal rights whom his admirers make him out—a seer, a harbinger of the absolute monarchism so soon, there in the death throes of the medieval world, to come? Or should we find him just the sharpest-eyed, the cleverest, of the crows? It would be rash to judge. What most disturbs our calculation is the startling way in which his private interests corresponded with the Crown's: working to shore the King, he shored himself. His possessions were enormous; the grants which his weak sovereign showered upon him had made him, beyond all question, the richest man in Castile. He was lord of seventy *villas* and more than twenty thousand vassals. As Constable, he ruled the royal armies. His annual income came to a hundred thousand gold *doblas*, even in modern reckoning some quarter million dollars, and for the age a staggering sum. His mighty castle at Escalona was the marvel of the land.

Such power, such wealth, of course had made Luna universally hated. The Castilian nobles resented and feared him—and why not: every town and title that went to him made one less to go to them. The Infantes of Aragón despised him: he was the chief obstacle between them and the domination, even the dispossession, of their cousin-King. Against that wall their craftiest plottings broke—or were sent, recoiling, back on their own heads. When they kidnaped the King from his bedroom in Tordesillas, Luna hastened to the rescue and saw to it that the third of the Aragonese brothers—the Infante Henry, the hot brash Master of Santiago—was thrown in prison as revenge. When they sent their mother, the Queen Dowager, to weave their ends inside Castile, she found herself shut up on Luna's orders in Santa Clara in that same Tordesillas; one still hears her wails of anguish, there in the Oriental convent on its cliff above the Duero, as the ladder was drawn away beneath her and she was left alone in the dark loft. When their steel-spiked armies broke across the border and took wobbly towns and forts, their own possessions in Castile were promptly confiscated. If three times they used what they trumpeted about as Luna's tyranny to unseat him and force him into exile, three times he used, in turn, the sovereign's helplessness without him to regain the saddle, to come back with even larger dignities and power. If they skeined hidden plots with the discontented Castilian nobles, it was Luna's vigilance that smoked the native traitors out, his expertise that drew them once again to service, if lip service only, of their King: those sleepless eyes saw all too clearly (as we shall see, as we shall find the tragic proof, long years and pages later) that formal coalition of the Castilian magnates and the House of Aragón would spell the utter ruin of the Crown. Checks, stalemates, balances: it is the story of the reign of Henry's father.

But this is not a book about Juan II of Castile—and certainly not about don Alvaro de Luna, although he amply deserves one. Our gaze is for Henry himself, and all we need remember is the paradigm, the dire political equation, which will confront him: the Castilian Crown under incessant siege. With that equation stated, the vultures are assembled; only the prey awaits.

We have, in fact, a splendid chance to bring him forward. In 1430, temporarily blocked in Castile by the frail Treaty of Majano, the Aragonese Infantes left the Peninsula and set out on other, on Italian, exploits: ever since the time of Charlemagne, when Cataluña was his Spanish March, the lands which now made up the Crown of Aragón had felt a pull toward Europe, an eastern itch. It is true that the Mediterranean fruit was no more ripe for the Infantes than the Peninsular, that their conquest of Naples would cost them only slightly less trouble than their long struggle to take possession of Castile; indeed, at a wild defeat upon the boiling summer sea off Ponza, they even found themselves, along with eight thousand of their drenched and seasick followers, dragged from their flaming galleys and hauled away as prisoners. Yet for Castile, at least, their absence brought uneasy respite. And while his uncles languish in brief exile at Italian courts, let us turn—but gently, gently—to the strange, unhappy boy, the inheritor to all this coil of sibling rancors, who was growing up amidst the diamond air and mellow churches of Segovia.

2.

Scenes from Childhood

"My Segovia"—so Henry called it, always: the dreaming city dropped like a bright necklace on its rock at the feet of the snowy Guadarramas. It was his home from earliest childhood; when he was only four his parents, eager to be spared the bother of him, had sent him there to live. And the affinity seems to have been instant: boy, youth, and man, he loved it more than anything—one is tempted to say more than anybody—on the earth. Palencia tells us that persons who sought his favor had first to admire Segovia. The statement stretches out; we must still go there to find him, truly to know him. Wandering those twisted streets one feels him everywhere, comes everywhere, in hidden plazas or decaying walls, upon memorials of him—a *mudéjar* door or window, a palace he restored, a church he gave or soft-eyed Gothic Virgin. Sad that the hurrying visitor sees only the city's two chief curiosities—on the east the Roman aqueduct, whereby the mountain streams, thick with fat trout, sent down their crystal water, and on the west the palace-fortress, the Alcázar, which gives the city much of its profile and almost all its fame.

The boy knew both these monuments; even then they were immensely old. The aqueduct had stood for more than a millennium. Conundrum to an age unversed in history and thought to be a work of Beelzebub, it was much in ruin at the time: thirty-six of its soaring arches had been pulled down during a Moslem raid in 1072, and the structure as we see it today was not restored until the end of the century, by Isabel the Catholic. On the triangular crag above the confluence of the Eresma and the Clamores where the Alcázar springs skyward, superb defensive site, a polyglot of races trailing back into antiquity had perched their citadels. The dark Iberians walled themselves from prehistoric bison and stone-axed raiders high upon it. There rose the Roman fortress, then the Visigothic, then the Moorish. For three hundred years the present castle had been abuilding, eyrie of Castilian kings; *sala* by painted *sala* they had enlarged it, turret on turret, tunnel on rocky tunnel, a honey-colored maze. It was, in fact, still piling: throughout Henry's boyhood the Torre del Homenaje, the huge oblong tower which first greets and stuns the visitor, was going up. That tower, today, affords the best view of the city. And it is much the same view Henry would have seen, had he climbed among the sweating masons and the din of hammers. The medieval cathedral (it stood just down below, in front of the castle's drawbridge) now is gone. But all the rest is little changed: the huddle of ancient houses, the square blunt towers of noble mansions and Romanesque churches rising above them, the circling golden wall. And the broader view, of course, as the eye lifts, has altered not a trace: off to the east the silent mountains with their flanks of thick black pines, on every other side, level to aching distance, the empty plains of High Castile.

Yet it is hard to imagine Henry as the sort of boy who would have gone clambering about on planks and scaffolds. He seems, from the first, to have been introverted, uncommunicative, painfully retired. Our pictures of his earliest youth are scarce; the chroniclers, like everybody else, were too intent on Luna's struggle against baronage and Aragón to waste much time upon the far, unwanted boy. But somehow those few we have already cast an air of ill fortune, of abandonment and rue: it is impossible not to think of him when one sees in Segovia's present cathedral the touching effigy, with bangs and little jerkin and crossed still hands, of another luckless royal child: Pedro, son of Henry II, who was dropped by his nurse—so runs tradition—from a dizzy window of the Alcázar and smashed on the rocks below.

When Henry had his own childhood accident which broke and flattened his nose and made him look, seen from the side, as if something had been torn from his face ("like a monkey,"[1] adds Palencia, with accustomed charity), we do not know: surely while very young—a lifelong wound, inside and out. It is not until he was six that the first recorded glimpse of him, however fleeting, comes. There was an earthquake in Segovia that year. (We shall feel others; all through the age even the ground shifted and shook.) Henry was in a tower of the Alcázar, bent to his lessons, when the *temblor* struck. We are told it was Lope Barrientos, his Dominican tutor,

who rushed in and scooped him up and carried him down to safety
in the open patio. Lope Barrientos—one would look far, incidentally, to find a less suitable mentor for such a child: staunch mon-
archist, admittedly, one of the precious few, but abrupt, short-tem-
pered, outspoken, and his constant fulmination that his young
charge would be the "perdition"[2] of the realm can hardly have done
much to bolster the self-confidence, minimal at best, of a shrinking
and unattractive boy.

Brief views, dry mentions among documents which the patient
hand of History must flesh out and frame. We have another the year
after the earthquake, in 1432: the child was dragged off to Zamora,
upon the western borders, to be sworn as heir by the Galician
magnates—significantly, it had taken Luna seven years to bring
those outland Grandes to such obeisance. The mists part fleetingly
again in 1434, when Henry was nine. That was a bitter winter in
Castile. It began to snow the last day of November and never ceased
till February (once more the cold, the cold). The walls of Valladolid
split open; the creaking mills around Medina del Campo were
stopped, and "for more than forty days"[3] there was no food except
boiled wheat; cattle lay dead in the fields with stiff legs upward to
the leaden sky. Perhaps to spare the frozen lad such rigors, and in
a casual moment of concern, his father, with don Alvaro de Luna,
took him south. Luna stayed over at Toledo to inspect the funerary
chapel he was having built for himself behind the high altar in the
cathedral. But King and Prince went on to Extremadura, to the vast
Jeronymite monastery of Guadalupe. There Henry had Sunday
dinner in the refectory with the whole cowled Chapter, seated at a
table apart between his father and the Prior—all unaware that he
would be buried within those same gray walls, but miserable and
self-conscious enough, even so. In 1435 there was a famous tournament in Segovia—some wandering German knights sought armed
adventure, the King came with his whole court, the lists were
drawn in a level place beneath the Alcázar—and we know Henry
saw it: the chronicle records, in passing, that the combatants "made
reverence"[4] to him with the fierce tips of their lances. Saw, perhaps,
rather than watched. Display and pomp were always foreign to
Henry's modest nature, he hated any kind of violence and bloodshed, and one imagines that he followed with far more interest the
work of those unfortunate Segovian jewelers who worked like mad-

men, four whole days and nights, to produce the twenty-two gold chains of Castile's great Order of Escama which the Germans had the nerve to ask for.

Such is about the sum of it: all we have ever known of Henry's childhood. The day of the Segovian tournament that childhood, anyway, was almost over—like the realm's brief peace. For in the next year the marauding Aragonese uncles were back in the Peninsula. And their arrival brought large changes for the lonely boy.

Not all of the Infantes returned from across the water. Alfonso, their King, had fallen in love with the Italian Renaissance and stayed on—the rest of his life, in point of fact; we shall see little of him. Of the two youngest brothers, one had already died from natural causes and the other was about to be removed, at the siege of Naples, by a cannon ball which bounced three times in front of him and then sheared off his head. It was only Juan, all wiles and chilly smiles (not for nothing was he to be Fernando the Catholic's father), and the firebrand Infante Henry who set foot again on Spanish soil that springtime day of 1436. They came, ostensibly, to take hold of the swinging helm in Aragón: their mother, the Dowager Queen and Regent, had died from shock when she heard the news of Ponza and the wholesale capture of her tribe. But Juan's shrewd head englobed a wider plan as he rode westward to Castile. Henry, that curious nephew off in Segovia, was growing up. He would soon be old enough for marriage—and what more to the interests of the House of Aragón than to provide his wife? That would ensure continuance, when Henry came to reign, of the useful plan whereby one of their family shared the rival throne. Better yet, any child of such a union would inherit all Castile.

And Juan had just the proper bride in mind. The Queen of Navarre had given him three children: Carlos, Blanca, Leonor. Inevitably, he disliked and feared them: their mother was Queen Proprietress of Navarre, where Juan himself was only the King Consort, and as her true and legal heirs they formed a constant threat to the total rule which he was determined to have in the Pyrenean kingdom. But at least these obstructive children made good marriage fodder. Blanca, the older of the two daughters, was Henry's age, and it was toward a match of this poor girl with the young Prince that Juan, once he had reached the Castilian court, began to press.

He met resistance: the sources speak of "*muy grandes alteracio-nes,*"[5] great arguments, during the autumn parleys on the subject in Toledo. The opposition came, of course, from Luna, whose diplomacy leaned always to rapport with Portugal. But Luna, at the moment, was more closely hemmed than usual by the jealous Castilian nobles: he felt himself obliged to buy the Infantes off. At that, he wrenched some humiliating concessions out of Juan: the brothers never again would enter Castile without its King's permission; they took a token pittance, a "misery"[6] of florins, as pay for their appropriated lands. But Juan was ever the kind who could bear short deprivations for long ends, no doubt he was abetted by Henry's mother, always more helpful to her brothers than to her spouse, and the upshot of the sessions in Toledo was a document, "sealed with a seal of purest crimson wax,"[7] giving him what he wanted most of all—Henry's hand for the young Blanca. Even the place and date of the *esponsales*, the legal engagement, were safely set: Alfaro, up by the Navarrese border, and at the start of spring, as soon as the winter was over and travel was possible again.

This chaffering at Toledo, earliest among many in which Henry was to be the helpless victim, brings us our first full picture of the youth: three chroniclers describe the engagement ceremony the following March. And once more a sense of the forlorn hangs over the accounts. Neither father nor mother showed sufficient heart to accompany the timid boy; Luna was left to take him to Alfaro. The backdrop, again, is winter; there had been miscalculation in the weather (why—unless for Juan's haste to get the matter settled—one does not know; those lands of Soria through which they went are high and bleak, released to spring only in late May or June), and a squad of two hundred peons had to flounder ahead to clear the mountain passes of their snow. In Alfaro itself there was a nervous delay; the fat Queen of Navarre was obliged to travel slowly, and her arrivals were often late. But at last the tinkly Navarrese cavalcade came down along the Ebro: the Queen, Blanca, her older brother Carlos—all of them led by the Constable of Navarre, Pierres de Peralta (he will be Juan's hatchet man throughout). The two constables advanced and made their formal greeting. Then Henry and Blanca were nudged forward on their ponies. They met, dismounted. The Bishop of Osma—Pedro the Cruel's grandson and thus Henry's only kin, if exceedingly remote, among the Castilian party—joined their hands and pronounced them, at least officially, man and wife. Rich presents were exchanged—rings, jeweled brooches, chains, fine horses, bolts of cut velvet and cloth of gold. They do not much catch the eye. It is the two young *novios*, left alone together for a moment after the ceremony, confused and blushing, who linger most in the mind. We need not waste sentimental tears on their short age (they both were twelve); such was the universal practice, in a time when life expectancy was less than thirty everything had to be accelerated, anybody not married by sixteen was considered either a freak or a saint. Yet to one who knows the long and special torture which lay ahead of them, there is something uncommonly sad, something almost inexpressibly touching, about this glimpse across the ages of the two mute, bashful children—pale girl and knobby boy—standing in a cold field beside the silent Ebro, hand in hand.

Knobby, but not yet grown. Henry, at twelve, seems still to have been quite small: when he returned from Alfaro and met his father, who sat on horseback, Luna—a slight man himself—was able to lift him in his arms to receive the perfunctory royal kiss. It must have been soon afterward, however, soon after he was safe again in Segovia, that his clumsy and hulking body (always so strange a repository for his gentle heart) began to shoot up. All accounts of Henry agree that he was large, and his mummy, even after five hundred years, measures a full six feet. Marañón finds in his ungainly frame—the huge hands, the thick teeth, the oversized head and bulky limbs—a telling example of the incipient "gigantism"[8] which always, in his learned opinion, denotes some abnormality, some inner jangle, something deep amiss. What the great endocrinologist failed to observe, although it would have added a fine touch to his portrait of Henry as the classic introvert, is the imperfection, the slight "corruption,"[9] of general health to which his official scribe Castillo refers: debility of constitution can hardly have failed to heighten the boy's sense of insecurity and slant, his disinclination to exert or to compete. And perhaps most significantly, most chillingly of all, it is these same years of early adolescence—when he was beginning to be free from the primacy of nurses and more able to pursue an unencumbered bent—which bring the first evidence of his gravitation, destined to work him such

damage, toward base and hardened company, toward an element of
the jostling world around him yet so much outside him which we
well might call, without putting too fine a point upon it, trash.

This predilection of the heir for culls and ruffians, striking even
then, gave pause to everybody—his tutor Barrientos, his father,
Luna. To Luna, in all likelihood, especially, with his constant efforts
to maintain the state and dignity of the Crown; his ruminations on
the future must have included some gloomy thoughts about the very
unroyal habits of the Prince upon whose head that imperiled object
would one day devolve. It was bad enough that the young fellow
wore those drab and ratty clothes (plain stuffs, dark colors—almost
as if he wanted to disappear, to blot himself from sight), that he used
the humble *"vos"* even with children and servants and let no one
kiss his hand, that when there was a court gala at the Alcázar or an
audience or a procession he was never to be found. But what on
earth possessed him to spend his time—when he sought human
society at all, rather than that of animals—with stableboys and
thugs and wrestlers? It was "unsuitable," the quality abhorrent
above all else to Castilians. Nobody understood it. It still confuses
historians. Yet is it really so difficult? We can, perhaps, reflect a little
further than busy Luna. The complex seek the simple, the low in
their own eyes the even lower, and surely these careless, tangible
clods to whom Henry was always so fatally attracted gave him a
welcome outlet, one of the few he ever had, from his whorled and
troubled thoughts. Reflexes of a strained, unsimple mind, they come
and go throughout his life: a periphery, a faceless, nameless, ever-
changing chorus. They need not detain us. We would do better to
meet some of the principal figures of our gathering cast. Already,
here in the closing years of Henry's boyhood, several of those
emerge.

Let us look first, and with an initial shudder, at Juan Pacheco—
soon to be Marqués of Villena, in time Henry's chief minister, and
always a tireless architect of his doom. History has its fashions, but
it seems safe to say that no one will ever try to rehabilitate this
Marqués of Villena: the verdict remains unanimous against him. He
arrived in Segovia, placed in the small princely retinue by Luna, as
little more than a stripling himself—although it is hard to think of
Villena as anything but born old, born a politician: from the start
he had a hand of ice in a glove of velvet, he neither raised his voice

nor lowered his guard, in a saw of the day he never spoke ill or acted well. Seven years Henry's senior, he sank his fangs at once into the passive boy; he kept them there for forty years. Little of Villena's person has survived to us. The effigy on his cluttered tomb at Segovia's Monastery of El Parral is much posterior, and the one physical detail we have of him is the strange quaver in his voice (Pulgar tells us that it came from an illness, and indeed throat infections seem to have been congenital to him—to his whole family, in fact). But his repellent mind we do know, all too well. There will be more than enough occasion to see it at work. Here we need only state its outlines. His motives are midday-clear—riches and power. Even his method, now, is not too hard to grasp: divide and rule, set everybody at odds and then offer himself as peacemaker—of course at a stiff price. That in the process he had to plunge both Henry and the kingdom into chaos mattered, to this ambitious crook, less than a bean. Mariana, in the next century, called Villena "the chief author of the tragedy."[10] One must differ with the great Jesuit; that role, as we shall see, belongs to Juan of Aragón. But Villena certainly did more than his fair share to bring about Henry's ruin. And the worst of the whole performance, the thing that in the end makes him so despicable, is that he wrought his damage under the guise of a friend and a protector: Judas, Janus, adder at the trusting breast.

It is a relief to turn from Villena to Diego Arias, another of the early Segovian circle who will play a major part in Henry's world. With Arias the picture lightens, grows almost droll. He was a converted Jew, a *marrano*, from Avila. He had begun as a traveling salesman, a hawker of spices. To draw his crowds he juggled and sang Moorish songs. Down on his luck in Segovia, he caught the young Prince's sympathy; Jews, Negroes, Moslems—Henry warmed to outcasts of any sort. He gave a job to the raffish prestidigitator—as tax collector, one thankless then as it is today. The peasants in his rounds spat on him, slammed their doors in his face, even tried to beat him up. But Arias persisted. He developed a knack for getting away on his spavined horse, the sorry beast "of miserable aspect and cheapest price"[11] which gives Palencia such caustic merriment: he acquired a nickname—Diego Volador, Diego the Flyer. Yet he was not always to be a figure of fun. Soon he became one of the palace secretaries, later chief purchaser for the youthful court. In the end he had charge of all Henry's finances. He handled them deftly, sharply, as cleverly as he had ever juggled balls. Of course he feathered his own nest in the process (not that Henry cared): the great square tower behind the *casas reales* in Segovia is part of his mansion. Diego Arias Dávila: a rising figure, fast shedding his Jewish gabardine and salesman's pouch. One of his sons came to be Bishop of Segovia; the other broke Henry's heart.

Nor can we find much cause for laughter—on the contrary, there is much for tears—in Miguel Lucas. For early, too, in this wan Segovian dawning, we encounter that tangled lad. He was Henry's age—first in a long, long line of dubious young companions, and the only one of them who could ever be called an honest friend. Villena brought him up to the princely household; he came from Belmonte, one of Villena's towns in Cuenca—a farmer's son, a frivolous, good-hearted, charming boy. Once, on a boring ride, he caught hares and tied them with bells and let them run ahead to leap and tinkle and amuse his listless master. He shared Henry's fondness for music; he loved the dance, the sheen and torchlit strut of the emerging theater. Yet with all his passion for masques and balls and mummery and *haute couture*, there was an odd vein in Lucas of the moralist, almost of the prude: "a young man most observant of religious rules."[12] Not a happy combination, this play of the pious and the mundane. Tension already crackled in the youth. Later it was to explode in a paroxysm of guilt and self-horror which ended his career. And even after he tried to reform, even after he finally married, there are signs that the strain, the pressure, continued: he slept in the same bed with his wife for over a year before he touched her. "O excellent virtue!"[13] cries his chronicler. Perhaps; perhaps not. The "Coplas del Provincial," in one of their foulest stanzas, have something far less flattering to say about his sexual bent.

But Lucas's wedding lies far in the future; Henry's looms. He turned fifteen in 1440. In that same year the Castilian nobles again unseated Luna and drove him from the court. Juan of Aragón found the coincidence too happy to let pass. Was not the time ideal for the church wedding of Blanca and Henry, pledged in the chilly fields of Alfaro three years before, which meant so much to his long-range plans? Luna, who frowned on it, was out of the way. The Prince had come ripe for breeding. Nor could Juan afford to dawdle: these forced retirements of the Constable were apt to be disappointingly brief. Either with or without that permission he had promised to obtain, he made his way back into Castile, up through the passes of the Guadarramas and out on the gaunt tableland, to Valladolid and the King. There the Queen, as well, awaited: she seems by then to have been living permanently apart from her philandering husband (and no better than she should be, herself, Mariana tells us), but a project so important as the one to which her brother had alerted her was worth a reunion. Between them, the rudderless King proved easy enough to heel about. The wedding date was fixed—September, and why not there in Valladolid? To Navarre went one of Juan's usual cool orders from his delicate, well-groomed hand: let Blanca and her mother prepare for the nuptial journey. (Carlos, the Prince of Viana, was this time not to accompany them: already Juan's hatred of that oldest child had become a settled thing.) A tone as Aragonese as possible had to be arranged for the approaching event: the second sister, now Queen of Portugal, could hardly be hoped to reach Valladolid in time for the ceremony, and their own King, Alfonso, was even farther away in Italy, but another of Juan's messengers rode south to the younger brother, the Infante Henry —he would do well to suspend for the moment his ill-masked plots against Castile down around Murcia and get on up. The Castilian sovereigns sent off some couriers of their own. Those dusty horsemen with the lions and castles on their saddlebags bore invitations to the Grandes: soon, in drafty towers and arrased chambers all over the realm, great leathern chests were being dragged about and opened, armor was being polished, finery dusted off. And of course Henry, if almost incidentally, had to be told.

Of the melancholy youth's reaction to such sonorous tidings we are not informed. Surely he realized that his boyhood, the days of hiding his shy heart and homely face in murky churches, of riding alone in silent forests or sitting in sunny windows watching the reddled sheep wind over the vast plain, had drawn to a sudden end. What he did not know—or at that age can only have dimly guessed, can only have touched fearfully and bewilderedly and perhaps explored in fumbling whispers with young Lucas and then shrunk back from, ashamed, unwilling, unequipped to face it—was that the cruelest wound he yet had borne, would ever bear, was about to fall upon him.

3.

A Wedding in Valladolid

Most of the storks are gone from High Castile by the end of August, but any one of those great flapping creatures which chanced still to be lumbering around in the warm air above Briviesca that early September day of 1440 would have peered down at a curious sight. Two processions were drawn up on the ocherous wastes outside the town. A slim girl and a fat lady stood at the head of the smaller of them. The other, aglitter with tabards and poised trumpets and the pendons of guilds, was obviously in galas of reception; a man with a noble's mien and flowing robe waited politely at the front of it. Yet what gave the little scene its special piquancy was a group of Jews and Moslems, kneeling in the dust before the slender child and holding up to her the Torah and the Koran. For the girl was Blanca of Navarre, and the strange dusky figures in their outlandish garments were observing an ancient and picturesque custom, that of offering the symbols of their faiths as tribute to "sovereigns new-come to reign in foreign parts":[1] they had no reason to suppose, that far-off autumn afternoon, that Blanca would never be Queen of Castile—or of anything else. Neither, fortunately, did she. Hesitantly she leaned forward; she reached out and touched the unintelligible scrolls. And with that the tableau broke up, sprang into life. Trumpets blared, mummers and jugglers leaped, everybody remounted and rode on, bright rivers joined, into the city, with waving banners and shrilling flutes and pounding drums. No doubt the perspiring Queen, as she jarred in under the gate, already smacked her lips: she liked parties and (all too evidently) lots of food, the noble in the furred robe was nobody less than Pedro Fernández de Velasco, the mighty Count of Haro, and the Velascos, who had been *camareros mayores* to Castilian kings for over a century and owned most of these northern regions of the realm, could be expected to lay on with lavish hand.

She was not disappointed. Briviesca was the Velascos' family seat, and they all went at once to the ancestral palace. A banquet stood ready, with musicians to enliven it and seneschals and troops of liveried squires waiting to serve; arrayed on Gothic sideboards were huge vessels of gilt and silver, the Velasco plate which generations of rapacity and sharp practice had built up. Long tables, swagged with gorgeous hangings, stretched out for the knights and ladies. A smaller one, on a dais, was set for mother and daughter. There the Queen affably insisted that Haro's Countess join them. As the three took their seats, an endless succession of "roasts, fowl, fish, pastries, and fruits"[2] began to be brought in. The minstrels played, slowly the sun dropped down among the flashing bowls and ewers on the sideboards, they ate and ate.

And that was only the beginning. The scribe who recorded these brilliant fiestas at Briviesca wrote in pop-eyed wonder. They do, in truth, afford a splendid example of the baronial pride and power so central, so disastrous, in our tale. Haro grandly decreed that nobody, neither foreigners nor natives, was to spend a penny during the visit; his storerooms and pantries were thrown open, and in a ground-floor *sala* he set up a fountain of pure silver which gushed, available to anyone, his Riojan lands' incomparable red wine. Less crass delights were offered to the gentlefolk. Their days went by in masques, in bullfights, in the mock jousts with hollow harmless lances so popular in the age. Each night there was another banquet and a ball afterward: towering headdresses, clank of medieval jewels, swish of miniver and ermine.

It was not until the fourth day, however, that Haro really surpassed himself. A large field stretched beside the palace, probably to insulate it from the rabble, and this empty expanse an army of laborers had turned to a wonderland. Part of it was now covered by a transplanted forest, where puzzled boars and bears and stags with branchy antlers roamed. Close by glittered a man-made lake, stocked with trout and pike. Above these sylvan marvels, and to feast upon, had been erected a great tribune made of twenty levels, all carpeted with green sod laid so close and cunningly together "that it seemed sprouted there."[3] (Where did Haro get it? There is not that much grass in all Castile.) Out to this *fête champêtre* the whole company trailed, late that fourth afternoon. Flowered tables stood along the twenty levels—royalty's on the topmost, and with a canopy of crimson silk. They ascended, found their places; they goggled and applauded; they sat down. A troop of two-score knights, before they ate, rode out and entertained them with a tourney. During the banquet fifty hunters, arrayed in Haro livery and leading bloodhounds, beat about in the fake forest killing its helpless game; fishermen skimmed the lake and brought their silvery prey, wriggling and thumping, up to the silver girl under the red brocade. When darkness fell, a thousand torches were lighted, so many and so bright "that it seemed like blazing noon."[4] In the effulgence, once the gorging was over, they danced on the precious grass. They danced the greater part of the night. And breakfast, served "almost at daybreak,"[5] brought fresh pleasures, fresh surprise: each of the ladies found at her place a golden ring set with a diamond or a ruby or an emerald. But with that it was finally all over, Haro distributed two gunnysacks of coins among the exhausted musicians, and everybody stumbled off to bed.

For mother and daughter, at least, the repose was brief: obviously such a party could not be outdone, it was time to be getting on to Valladolid. They were up and off by tierce the following morning. We know very little about Blanca; she is substantially a cipher in the dreadful story (and how pitifully apt her name!). But it is to be hoped—as she rode along the Arlanzón to Burgos, then south beside the Pisuerga, winding with her destiny on its own way to join the Duero—that she had enjoyed herself. For her childhood, like Henry's, was nearly over, and the rest of her life, all down to the prison and the poison, was to be unmitigated hell.

Valladolid, the ancient central city, awaited in nuptial array. The Crown could hardly be expected to mount anything half so magnificent as the Velascos, but what was possible it had done. Tapestries hung from the windows, oxen were stalled, *salas* had been swept and perfumed and fresh rushes laid. The royal blood of both Castile and Aragón was gathered in: the Castilian King and Queen, their quarrels and mutual suspicions temporarily on leash; Juan, far more eager for his daughter's arrival than for that of his mountainous wife; Juan's brother the Aragonese Infante Henry, Master of Santiago, ridden up sweat-streaked and barely in time from Imperial Toledo; the tricky but unavoidable cousin don Fadrique Enríquez, Admiral of Castile, of whom we shall see so much. For days, to clot with this *realeza*, the noble clans had been pouring in, opening their local palaces, getting ready for the parties—Stúñigas from off in arid Extremadura, Mendozas from Guadalajara, Pimentels from their walled cities in the great wheatfields, the Tierra de Campos. Who of Henry's friends were asked over from Segovia is not recorded: apparently none—Pimentels and Mendozas would not be caught dead in the same house with people like Arias and Miguel Lucas— and thus once more it is lonely amidst a crowd, surrounded by the very class with whom he always felt least comfortable, that we see Henry riding up the river, once everything in Valladolid was ready, to greet his Princess. They met the bridal party two miles past Santovenia. In waning light, with trumpets and flambeaux, they brought it into town, straight to Juan's *posada*. There they dismounted, took refreshment, had the first family reunion.

Oddly, the Castilian King was not on hand for it. Neither courtesy nor curiosity (he had never seen Blanca) seems to have been enough to bring him: a commentable absence, one that caused a certain strain. The Castilian Queen, however, was even too much in evidence. She quizzed, aspersed as usual, made her own cynical assessments. Blanca, under analysis, could hardly have failed to freeze, and of course Henry never contributed anything, always sat dumb as a stone. The Master of Santiago's talk was apt to run to battles down around Murcia which interested nobody—except his brother Juan, who knew all about them anyway. Such attempts at gaiety as were produced by the jolly Queen of Navarre fell heavy as lead—especially on her husband. Juan of Aragón has been called many things over the past five centuries, but "jolly" is not among them, and as he sat there shading his weak eyes against the torchlight and listening to this loud and impossible woman whom he had been obliged to marry to possess the crown of Navarre, surely he was congratulating himself that he had managed to keep so long away from her and fervently hoping that once the wedding was over he would never see her again. (He very nearly got his wish.)

It was not, perhaps, the most cheerful beginning for a round of festivity. And once things had begun to go sour, they went rapidly worse; indeed, an air of doom hangs over these wedding celebrations of Henry and Blanca like a prophetic miasma. Even the welcoming tournament, staged by the *mayordomo mayor* Ruy Díaz de Mendoza and calculated to strike a joyous note of pomp and glamour, quite failed of its intent. For some reason Mendoza decided to hold it in full panoply of war, *a la alemana*, with combat lances: no pretty games with wands, with hollow *cañas*, here. Such murderous weapons soon took the toll which more judicious planning might have anticipated. An unlucky knight from Toro, his skull split open by a lance that pierced the eye slit of his visor, pitched from his horse and died in a wallow of blood, red as the high red town downriver to which he would never return. Another had his right arm torn off. The Count of Castro's nephew was skewered through the pelvis, and the Admiral's brother had his forearm snapped in two. The King (this event, at least, he had deigned to attend) finally found the carnage too much. Irritably he threw down that great staff on which he had latterly been leaning—perhaps for lack of don Alvaro de Luna—and called the whole thing off.

Nor did the ugly affair of Sancho de Reynoso, of the Admiral's household, do much to help. For reasons not divulged by the sources, this hotheaded young brute chose the occasion to kidnap his stepfather, who lived with the Count of Castro; he set upon him in a dark alley, trussed him up, then carried him off to the neighboring castle of Villoria. Castro demanded justice, and the King ordered Henry to get over to Villoria and handle the matter. Henry: of all people. Was there malice in the choice? In any event it was certainly a boy sent on a man's work, and the dangerous mission proved even more painful, more trying, than the diffident fifteen-year-old lad could have guessed. When he drew up at the castle, the gate was flung shut against him and noisily barred. He sat there a moment, not a very commanding figure, on one of those little Arabian horses he so perversely preferred to the impressive war steeds on which the House Royal was expected to go about, then raised his voice as best he could and stammered a feeble summons. Sancho appeared on the battlements. He looked down, gave tongue to a string of mean and derogatory remarks, contemptuously withdrew. He did not return, and Henry was left helpless in front of the closed gate: a new humiliation, a further proof—and this a public one—of his incompetence, his inability to cope. The epilogue is scarcely less unattractive. When others of more thew finally were sent, they bore a pardon for Sancho if he would give himself up. But no sooner was he in custody back in Valladolid than the King, perfidious man, ordered his execution; instead of another party, the court found itself treated to a gory beheading in the plaza.

And as if these mishaps were not enough to cast a pall on every-thing, suddenly people began to die like late-summer flies. The Prior of San Juan was the first to go. San Juan was a powerful Order, its head a person of consequence. But hardly was this digni-tary cold in his burial robes when he was followed to the grave by an even more important figure—Pedro Manrique, Adelantado of León, head of the vast and mighty Manrique clan. Don Pedro's origins were gnarled with the roots of time, either birth or marriage connected him with almost everybody in the realm (the Admiral was his half-brother and the Count of Haro his son-in-law; his mother had been a Mendoza; his wife was cousin to the Queen of Navarre), and his death put the greater part of the court into instant mourning. The sovereigns themselves had to show fitting grief. It is true that the entire Manrique family despised the Crown: they had been bitter and set on vengeance ever since the King, at Luna's bidding and for either real or imagined plotting, had seized don Pedro three years before and thrown him into prison (an incarcera-tion which Manrique's fifteen children, crowded at once into the garlanded throne room for a terse and sarcastic audience, were not slow to point out as the ruin of his health and the chief cause of his demise). But appearances were appearances; the garlands had to come down and royal parties be canceled. Nor had the autumnal scythe finished its swinging: suddenly the Count of Benavente, the great Alonso Pimentel, dropped dead. Benavente, too, was intri-cately related, and his passing plunged those few nobles who had not been kinsmen of Manrique into weeds of commemorative serge.

Mourning, blood, funeral chants: such was Henry's wedding march. For no matter how many the contretemps or how inauspi-cious the atmosphere, the central fact, the marriage "so desired by everybody"[6] (for "everybody" read the House of Aragón), had to be brought off. On Wednesday, September 14, between nine and eleven at night, a little procession wound down through the cobbled streets toward Juan's *posada*. Juan himself headed it, followed by the dispirited Prince and the Castilian Admiral don Fadrique, selected to serve next day as Henry's best man—a choice surely of Juan's contrivance, for that meddlesome and myopic royal cousin, who could no more be kept from mischief "than the hen from pecking,"[7] was already deeply committed to the Infantes' cause. They dismounted in the courtyard, entered the *sala*. There Blanca, decked for the sacrifice in bridal white and Navarrese crown jewels, stood waiting for them, close to her mother's side. Everyone bowed; untasted sweets were served; forced compliments exchanged. Then they all went back to the courtyard and the procession reformed. Blanca mounted her pretty palfrey; the Queen was hoisted on a good stout mule; off they rode to the royal palace behind San Pablo. Again it was the Queen of Castile, alone, who received them. Again there were refreshments and stiff civilities. At God knows what hour the bride and her mother were taken to a richly adorned bedchamber and left there to spend the remainder of Blanca's last unmarried night in such qualms and maternal counsel—all of it wasted breath—as we cannot say.

What we can say, and clearly, is that the ceremony next morning had been reduced, given the doleful ambiance, to bare essentials. A great church wedding with assembled court and billowing choir was out of the question; instead, an altar had been set up in the palace for a private Mass. Juan rose early and arrived betimes: it was his precise and cautious way. Close on his heels, in purple, came the Cardinal of San Pedro, appointed to do the knot. When the lazy King was finally up and ready, he and the Queen and Juan went for Blanca and her mother. Through the rushed halls they escorted her, out in the *sala* with its tapestries and gleaming candles. At least for this occasion, one supposes, Henry had been persuaded, or commanded, to bathe (*"inscius balneorum,"*[8] Rodrigo Sánchez de Arévalo calls him—"unfamiliar with washing") and put on royal garb. Whatever he wore, he stood there near the altar, with the testy little Admiral at his side. The Cardinal received them; they knelt; the Mass began. And suddenly the bell had jingled and the Wafer been imparted and it was all over, suddenly everybody was standing again and staring at each other: what to do till night? For the long state banquet which usually arcs that trying gap was equally impossible, and the best anyone could think of was a small family dinner in the chambers of the Castilian Queen.

Even this private observance took place in malaise, in blight: Henry's father refused to attend. No one knows why. The language reporting his surly act is ambiguous: *"se sentía enojado."*[9] "He was feeling"—what? *"Enojado"* has two meaning in Spanish: "angry" or "ill." One judges by the context. Unfortunately there is no context here; "The King was feeling *enojado* and went to his room,"[10] the chronicler baldly states. Had something happened at the ceremony —perhaps a further *gaffe* on the part of Henry—to set his temper off? Or was he merely suffering from one of those excesses, so common with him and so harmful to his flabby constitution, at table or in bed? We can take our choice. And it may not be of much importance. All that really matters is that away he stalked, Henry was left stinging from the slap, and in a new atmosphere of tension and constraint what remained of the family went in to make their feast.

It seems to have been a pretty thin affair. Newlyweds themselves are seldom at their best on that occasion. The toasts were not partaken of by Henry, who never in all his life touched wine ("*nunca jamás,*"[11] his chaplain Castillo tells us—"absolutely never"; here, at least, the language is plain). Banquets were the last thing that interested Juan of Aragón: he was vegetarian. And matters were hardly helped by the presence of a remote, decrepit Portuguese connection, the Infanta Beatriz, who happened to be in town and whom nobody knew. Even the Queen of Navarre found her spirits damped. But finally the long, golden, awful afternoon had worn away and the last of the platters were gone and the tables cleared and taken up, finally the gold had faded into silver and the silver into black, finally compline had rung in San Pablo across the way and it was full night and they could be about the business.

They rose. Down vaulted corridors, with cressets, they trailed to the nuptial chamber, long prepared. Heralds stood at the door, ready to sound a fanfare when the bloodied sheets were handed out. They went past them, in. The great bed glimmered, and the three notaries required by law beside it—to attest the first moan of joy or pain that would prove the royal bride a virgin, and royally pierced —were waiting at their posts. The family found all in order, then withdrew. Servants stripped Blanca of her snowy gown. They laid her on satin pillows and in turn departed. Henry, presumably, undressed himself; he disliked to be touched. Perhaps he lingered a moment on the edge of the bed, dangling the dainty feet which were such a curious contrast to his large, ungainly frame. But at last he got in and drew the curtains. The notaries took their place.

One feels sorry for those notaries as they sat on and on in the silent room upon their hard wooden bench while the torches guttered out: already by mid-September the nights on the high *meseta* are turning sharp. One even feels a little sorry for Juan of Aragón, pacing the drafty corridor beyond the door for hours of mounting anxiety before he finally gave up, before he went away and left the nodding trumpeters to drowse alone. For after all he had done— after all the scheming and maneuvering and waiting, all the delays and misadventures and journeys down dusty roads—nothing whatever happened in the bedroom. No spotted sheets came forth; the groom—and it is for him, of course, and for the girl who shared his desperate struggle behind the curtain, that one feels sorrier than for anybody else—had been unable to fulfill his function.

There is something cold and clinical (to end a cold story) in the court chronicler's reporting of the disaster. "The Princess"—so he said it, and, in truth, what more was there to say?—"remained exactly as she had been born."[12]

4.

The King Is Captive

Young Henry's anguish at his failure as a husband need not be labored; now he knew why he felt so much at home upon the desert, why he had always stood in such awe and helpless admiration before bulls and hairy athletes and swollen young grooms. The nature of the political dilemma which later would confront him may still have been veiled from his incurious eyes. But already he realized with brutal clarity his private problem: whether he would ever be able to conquer his impediment, to make himself like others and prove himself a man.

Juan of Aragón's reaction to the fiasco calls for more comment. The less said about his feelings for Blanca the better; never paternal, they now were permanently curdled by her disgraceful incapacity—his mind was not generous or tuned on psychological finesse—to arouse the sluggish Prince. What does concern us is an almost immediate change in Aragonese policy: rather, the return to a policy laid aside. For three years the Infantes had placed their hopes upon this marriage. Well, it had not worked out, had not come, in what really mattered, to anything. And Juan was already certain, unlike Henry, that it never would; the autumn went by with Blanca still a virgin, and it grew increasingly apparent that the first disappointment was not a simple thing of fright and nerves. Why go on beating that dead horse? Some day the chance might occur again to breed an heir for the rival throne. At the moment, however, they had wasted their ammunition. And to Juan's lights there was nothing for it but to write off this slanted move and get back to methods more familiar, more direct: force, seizures, threats, new bargains with the Castilian nobles. The decision at once displayed itself. Suddenly the temperature in Valladolid dropped like the expiring year's, the thin mask of family consonance fell

off; suddenly, on one excuse or another, people began to clear out
of the unlucky city in droves.

Henry, oddly, was among the earliest to depart. Moreover, it
looks as if he went alone. How he managed we do not know. But
he cared nothing for convention or appearances, and whatever his
fashion of achieving it he was back in Segovia for Christmas—an
event which he always made Samsonian efforts to hold in that dear
place. Soon afterward went his uncle the Infante Henry, bold Master of Santiago. One day on a frosty hunt he asked the King's
permission to visit his Order's seat at Ocaña, but his real prey
proved to be Toledo; he rode straight there and took possession of
it. Juan deployed the queens of Navarre and Castile in Arévalo;
Blanca seems to have accompanied them. Then he summoned the
other sister, the Portuguese Queen. She might be helpful—or anyway of more use than where she sat, for the King of Portugal was
dead and his brother had appropriated both the realm and the
eight-year-old heir. The Castilian King himself moved down to
Avila and the stout refuge of its walls. In short, the rival factions
were assuming position for that renewal of hostilities, that fresh
outbreak of the old "debates and scandals,"[1] which everyone could
plainly see was coming.

It did not long delay. Toledo was only thirty miles from Escalona,
the castle-fortress where don Alvaro de Luna pined in restless exile,
and it soon became evident that the Master of Santiago had commandeered the Imperial city as a base for immobilizing, perhaps
even for capturing, the favorite: the Infantes' constant nightmare
was a reunion of Luna with the King. Early in the year he called
the Admiral and the new Count of Benavente to his side. With these
willing troublemakers he began to inch toward Escalona. They
subdued and leveled the interposing castle of Olivos, which it took
"all the laborers of the area"[2] to pull down. They moved closer and
reduced Torrijos. When they reached Maqueda they were only six
miles from Escalona, almost in sight of the huge citadel that soared
above the Alberche. Luna had a bad moment, the next day, as he
looked out across the shallow river from his battlements and saw the
six hundred horse of the Infante appear glittering from nowhere
and begin to set their camp amidst the dusty olive groves for siege.
But by then something was happening up toward the north. The
King, in Avila, had finally come to life.

It is true that the Crown, as usual, had little with which to retaliate against these new depredations of the Infantes. Almost the only noble of real consequence at the royal side was the Count of Alba, a fairly slippery customer himself. But with Juan II of Castile guile could always make up for any lack of sinew; he began devious negotiations with chief persons of Medina del Campo, one of the Infantes' strongholds, and when he found them favorably received he moved out of Avila. After a pause in Cantalapiedra, where he exchanged some sulfurous remarks about "fire and blood"[3] with a herald of Juan of Aragón whom he happened to meet in front of the church, he rode on to Medina. There the "fire and blood" turned out, thanks to his bribery, to be a peaceable reception; the gates were opened to him and he took up residence in the palace on the *plaza mayor*.

The loss of Medina fell like a bomb upon Juan of Aragón. The town belonged to him (he had been born there); moreover, it constituted one of the great "keys to Castile" and its gigantic and well-nigh impregnable castle of La Mota was among the most formidable in the whole realm. Reconquest of this prize seemed to Juan worth almost any cost; from Arévalo, where he had been masterminding the rebels' movements, he sent a swift order to his brother to drop the investment of Escalona and hurry north. Early in June the armed clans of Aragón, grown to a host of almost two thousand by the addition of the Admiral's brother and the Castilian counts of Ledesma and Castro and Valencia de don Juan, were assembled in Olmedo and poised for striking at the confiscated city. But help, as well, was on its way to the King. The same idea had occurred to the sovereign—that the perilous situation warranted anything, even the breaking of his word (at best a friable commodity) to keep the favorite in exile; he, too, sent messengers to Escalona, and Luna, relieved of siege, set forth, picked up his half-brother the Archbishop of Toledo and the Master of Alcántara, and rode over the mountains. Although neither side knew it, the same day the Infantes marched west across the ten miles of rippling wheatfields between Olmedo and Medina, Luna was fast approaching from the south. The Infantes made their camp before Medina's gate of Santiago. Luna slipped in by back ways the following midnight, and his arrival brought the royal forces inside the city to three thousand horse. Obviously something big was about to happen.

Just what, unfortunately, has never been quite clear. A half hour before dawn on Peter and Paul, a segment of Medina's wall was opened from within; the Infantes, apparently, had done a little palm-greasing of their own. At the same time they made a frontal assault upon the Santiago gate. The King, loose in his bed, was awakened by the tumult. He started up in terror, threw on some armor, witlessly grabbed his stick. In the patio he took the first mount he could find, a sleepy mare, and in this unmartial array, followed by his standard-bearer and a page who had the presence of mind to collect the royal lance and shield and helmet, got out into the plaza. There his retainers, inexplicably shrunken to a thousand, joined him. Accounts of that wild dawn, no doubt like the occasion itself, are utter chaos. The enemy—miraculously, too, now turned five thousand—poured in from every side: down the street of San Francisco, down the Rua. If the hysterical figures can be believed, the royal force was hopelessly outnumbered. In any case, the King himself so saw it. He ordered Luna, whose sword was already bloodied with the gathering fray, to escape while time remained. According to Gonzalo Chacón, Luna resisted this strange behest and obeyed it only when it was repeated "two or three times"[4]—even then, so adds the loyal amanuensis, more to save the Archbishop and the Master of Alcántara than with any thought for himself. The King's chronicler, conversely, has the Constable accede with alacrity at the first hint. Reluctant or no, he went. The three of them cut their way through the melee, got out under the Arcillo gate, and the King was left in the middle of the plaza with little more than his mare and standard and overburdened page when the Infantes came and took him.

Took him—there is nothing else it can be called. However matters may have fallen out that early summer dawn in Medina del Campo, the result, at least, is clear: the sovereign, for all the hypocritical kneeling and hand-kissing which ensued, had at last been forcibly seized by the Infantes. And once securely in the saddle, they bore down hard. A drastic Sentence was drawn up. Luna, by its humiliating terms, had to be banished for six years instead of six months, and this time not to Escalona but to Riaza or Valdeiglesias, two of his other possessions: a wry choice, since both were *villas abiertas* where he would be unable to shut himself up and wax strong and return to the King's defense. Neither he nor his brother the Archbishop could maintain a force of more than fifty men of arms. Royal correspondence on affairs of state had to be eliminated, and that of a private nature subjected to scrutiny. In a word, the King was a virtual captive, and not until Henry's own reign shall we see the Castilian Crown sunk to worse depths of impotence and disgrace.

With its sovereign in foreign custody and the favorite in his straitest exile ever, the realm flamed to ruinous disorder. In the deep south there was fresh trouble between the two proud families who had a stranglehold on most of Christian Andalucía—the Guzmáns, then counts of Niebla but fast clawing their way up to the dukedom of Medina Sidonia, and the Ponce de Leóns, well on their own rise to the marquesate of Cádiz. Off in the west, in Extremadura, the Stúñigas got their hands upon Plasencia. In the far north, perhaps, the confusion was at its worst. In the Basque province of Guipúz-coa, an angry proletariat rose on the Crown's chief fiscal agent, its *merino mayor*, and seized his lands. In the north, too, in Durango, there was even an outbreak of heresy, that ultimate horror; it was finally contained (most of the guilty were arrested and burnt up in Valladolid and Santo Domingo de la Calzada), but the mere fact that it had happened showed that ecclesiastical as well as civil authority was on the point of total collapse.

No one who knows that canny family will be surprised by the consummate skill with which the Infantes exploited this turbulence for their own ends. They forced their helpless victim to convene his Cortes at Toro early in 1442—and to present so pathetic a picture of the realm's necessities that the *procuradores* voted him eighty millions of *maravedís* to help relieve them; most of the millions, one hardly has to add, went straight into the Infantes' pockets. When news arrived that the Master of Calatrava lay dying, they saw to it that a bastard son of Juan was named his successor. Control of the lands of Calatrava, which linked on the east with those of Santiago and on the west with the ancestral holdings in Extremadura inher-ited from their mother, gave the Infantes a wide solid band across the whole south-central portion of Castile. Indeed, when they began to assemble an army for the conquest of Portugal, under guise of restoring their exiled sister, it looked as if their lifelong ambition—hegemony of the Peninsula—was about to be realized. Only the God impugned in Durango knows what might have happened had they not, finally, overreached themselves at Rámaga. For in that obscure town, in the summer of 1443, after two years of leading their brother-in-law around by the nose and forcing him to do their bidding and feign it his own, they decided to drop all pretense, to assume the robe, the seal, of majesty itself. On the night of July 9, in a sudden coup, they dismissed the King's last personal retainers and locked him up in a small room with armed guards both inside it and at the door: a common prisoner.

It was too much even for a supine realm. Little as the Castilians had for which to thank their Juan II, some deep and atavistic revulsion at this outrage, some buried loyalty perhaps more to the ancient crown than to the man who wore it, began to ferment, to rise. And the hand which most stirred it up and brought it to expression, the one Castilian brain which still had wit and nerve to plan at this disastrous juncture, belonged to Lope Barrientos.

The reader will remember Barrientos: Dominican friar, Henry's tutor, the gruff guardian who had carried a frightened child to safety in the Segovian earthquake. Barrientos, with the years, had inevitably prospered: his long relations with the royal family were of the most intimate sort, and he was widely and deservedly known as an *"hombre de buen consejo,"*[5] a "man of good counsel." The passage of time, in fact, had made him Bishop of Segovia. But it had also deepened his despair over the young Prince and the shady associates with whom he surrounded himself. Anyone like Barrientos was bound to have constant friction with Diego Arias, who by then was a past master in peculation and had, in addition, married a barmaid from Madrid; the two sons of this sordid union, already Henry's cronies, seemed little better; flighty ephebes such as Miguel Lucas, with their chatter of hair-dos and the dance, were simply too much for the episcopal stomach. Chiefly to get out of this soiled and ambiguous atmosphere he had exchanged, shortly before the events which we now chronicle, the miter of Segovia for that of Avila. But wherever he lived or whatever his office, Barrientos remained a staunch supporter of the Crown. He had watched with increasing anxiety Castile's prostration and dismemberment. And with the Infantes' really appalling stroke at Rámaga he finally decided to act, to do what he could to stop the ebb of the kingdom's blood while there was yet some hope.

His mind made up, he went first to see Henry. The visit must have cost him, but he was prepared to swallow private feelings if he could bring about the plan he had conceived. At any event, he rode over to Segovia, and one winter day he sat down in the Alcázar face to face with the glum and awkward Prince—no longer a boy but a grown, slouchy, unshaven husband (for all the good it did him) of nineteen—and gave him some plain talk.

Henry needed it. His role in the broils of the past three years was anything but admirable. He had lent himself as one of the principal instruments in bringing about his father's shame. He had been in intermittent but open cooperation with his uncles and his mother as they wove their tightening web around the sovereign. He had pacted with traitorous nobles. He had even been a signer of the disgraceful Sentence of Medina del Campo. It is impossible to exonerate him. But extenuations can, and should, be found. He was still very young, still stunned and disoriented by a private discovery, a tremendous shock. He had always been malleable, been pitifully eager to please, to make himself liked and wanted—and the accumulated pressures to join the conspiracy put on him by his mother's family were immense. Above all, he was by then completely under the thumb of Juan Pacheco, the future Marqués of Villena. And Villena's tactics were always, as we have seen, to stir up troubles which only he could solve. Nobody even at the time had any illusions about the large part Villena played, or the motive behind it, in sowing discord between Henry and his father. "Ever"—so writes a contemporary—"he urged the Prince to drive the King into necessity . . . for thus he thought to increase his own estate."[6]

Barrientos, of course, knew all of this when he sat down to talk with Henry. But he was much too familiar with Henry's stubborn loyalty toward the people he had chosen as his friends to criticize Villena; that only stiffened Henry's resistance. Instead, and taking a former teacher's privilege, he plied him with some direct and sharp-edged queries. Was it not time to end this lamentable division? What right had the mere branch to healthful life without the paternal trunk which put it forth? Did not their long study of homilies together prove that no greater sin existed than for the child to dishonor the father? Had he no natural instincts? (This was always an unfortunate question with Henry, one sure to make him wince, and the Bishop quickly shifted to firmer ground.) Was it not sheer folly, anyway, to subvert and chip the very crown which he would some day inherit? How could he hope for loyalty in his own time if he himself, while Prince, set such an example?

Considerably to his credit, Henry listened. His instincts were always good. No doubt he was worn out with the uncongenial game in which he had been made a constant shuttlecock, and probably a little ashamed at the duplicity into which he could now see, under the Bishop's unsparing exegesis of the circumstances, he had been sucked. Yes, he agreed, it was time to mend the breach. He was ready, Villena or no Villena, for a reconciliation with his father. And grasping that promise, a thing he had never known Henry to go back on, Barrientos left Segovia and set out on a second visit— now to the King.

Access to the guarded sovereign was not easy to obtain, but a priest had certain rights. The prisoner in that season lay at Tordesillas, and there the Bishop straightway went. He rode over the Roman bridge across the Duero, up the steep cliff, stalked into the ancient palace on its brink. Ruy Díaz de Mendoza, the chief jailer, was dubious, but Barrientos brushed him aside. He found the King in his chamber; he drew him into a corner and came at once to the point. "My lord," he announced, "our words must be brief, and substantial." The King gazed back at him plaintively. "Bishop," he asked, "how does this state in which they have me look to you?" "Bad," said the Bishop. "And what is the remedy for it?" "Sire, the Prince will be your remedy."[7] Then, in episcopal susurrations, he quickly sketched his scheme. The King must pretend to be down with a raging cold (illness, with him, was never a difficult pose). Henry would come to condole. Taken with "attack of catarrhs,"[8] the King would clutch his hand for comfort, and in that ancient and binding posture for feudal homage the son would swear himself the father's faithful vassal.

It worked out well, this famous little scene of cloak and dagger. Henry arrived; all *sotto voce*, and "so fast and secret"[9] that neither Mendoza nor the guards guessed what was going on, the oaths were given and parchments to confirm them unobtrusively exchanged. The first two pieces of Barrientos's patriotic puzzle were securely in place: sovereign and heir were reconciled. All that remained was to make it a triumvirate—to bring in Luna.

The Constable, however, proved rather more difficult. Not that he had much compunction about the ethics of breaking out of exile; fire had to be fought with fire. But he put up several objections. He doubted whether his force and the Prince's were strong enough to defeat the Infantes. Besides, he had never had much confidence in Henry, and less in Villena. Above all, and here he spoke bluntly, he strongly suspected that the whole thing was not really the Bishop's plan but some indecipherable trick of Juan of Aragón. Barrientos swore on assorted relics that it was not so, argued back with all his dialectical skill as a one-time professor at Salamanca, and Luna, in the end, let himself be convinced. Give him a few weeks, he said, to gather his armies. One final question, though. The King happened to be a prisoner. What about that? Don't worry, said the Bishop; he would find an answer.

And so he did. With mounting hope and confidence he rode again to Tordesillas. There he discovered that the sovereign was soon to be moved, under surveillance of the Count of Castro, to the castle of Portillo, not far from Valladolid. He had another whispery visit with the *malade imaginaire*, gave quick instructions, and set some dates. Then he sent trusted messengers to Henry and Luna. Henry raised banners for his father and marched west to Magaz. There Luna joined him, with five hundred horse. In Portillo itself, on the morning of July 15, the King rose unwontedly early. He announced that he felt better and would like to go hunting—a leaf from the Infante Henry's book. Castro of course went along. At noon they were near Mojados, where they found—surprise—Barrientos's friend the Cardinal of San Pedro. Would it not be polite to dine with this dignitary? They ate. The tables cleared, the King looked coolly at Castro. He would not, he said, be going back to Portillo. The Count started up. Then he sat down again, abruptly; the Cardinal's suite, their disguises thrown off, turned out to be loyal soldiers from Valladolid. Castro departed alone for his empty citadel. The King, with his liberators, went on to Valladolid. He slept that night in the familiar city. The next morning, "with happy face"[10] and a great blowing of trumpets, he rode up along the Pisuerga. Henry and Luna rode down it from Magaz. Halfway, at Dueñas, they met. The King and Luna embraced. Blushing and inarticulate, and not the sort into whose arms people were accustomed to falling, Henry stood by and watched. Barrientos hung in the background, all abeam. He had brought it off. The King was free, and safely reunited with both his Constable and the heir. Just how would the Infantes cope with that?

Astonishingly, they did not even try. The dreaded coalition—to say nothing of its army of seven thousand—was, it appeared, too much for them. Anyway, they fled the realm. Their allies among the Castilian nobles "enrocked" themselves in their fortresses. Swiftly, almost miraculously, everything had reversed. The usurpers were gone, their grip had been broken, for the first time in nearly a decade Castile could breathe again. The rest of the summer and into autumn the King marched merrily about in the baked basin of the Duero, heart of Juan's Castilian dominions, appropriating the towns and citadels of that decamped tormentor. Nor did the lands of the Infante Henry fare much better. Down toward Murcia, down through the dry riverbeds with their pink oleanders, rode Luna and the Prince to confiscate his holdings as Master of Santiago. By early winter the mopping up had been completed. Henry was home in Segovia, Luna once more in charge of the great seal, the King in lazy ease among his pneumatic blondes, his lutes and sonnets.

And then, as suddenly as it had come, the respite was over. In January, just when matters seemed finally settled, the snows and tempests brought an even colder notice. The Infantes were back. Far off in the east the Count of Medinaceli, Luis de la Cerda, had betrayed the bastion town of Atienza into their hands, and they were swarming across the frontier in heavy array. Everything had been an illusion. They had not given up at all. They had gone to Aragón only to regroup, to gather armies for a fresh invasion.

It threw the King in a rage. Oh those hateful De la Cerdas: for two centuries, ever since the time of Alfonso the Wise, whose stock they were, they had bedeviled the Crown. Oh those even more hateful brothers-in-law: now the whole horrible business would have to be faced again. Barrientos was chopfallen—so much riding in vain, so much persuading and prodding and smoothing of ruffled feathers. Henry, safe in peace—in hiding—at Segovia, was equally downcast. He had done as he was told. By happy chance, there had not been a war. But now the effusion of blood, so alien to his nature, loomed anew.

Of all the battered Castilians, Luna alone was not dashed. On the contrary, his spirits rose. For thirty years he had sought to bring the

Infantes to open battle. Always they had glanced off, negotiated, evaded; perhaps he alone had felt no jubilation at their departure the preceding summer. This time, however, from the size of the army with which wild westward-running rumors said they were pouring in, it looked as if, at last, they too were ready for a military show-down. If only he could force them to a critical encounter; if only he could smash, once and for all, the full armed might of Aragón. Luna was, for all his other talents, at heart a commander, and not for fourteen years, not since 1431 when he smote the turbaned Moors at La Higueruela in the Granadine *vega*, had he fought a pitched battle, a *batalla campal*. Perhaps this was his chance. In brio and flush he turned to mobilizing the kingdom for what he hoped—and sensed, now that the royal ranks were joined and the Infantes in admitted panoply of war—would be a final and decisive conflict. Nor was he mistaken. With an almost terrible speed, with mounting fatality, the pieces began to fall in place for the great battle of Olmedo.

5.
The Plains of Olmedo

Luna's strategy in the events which now rush in upon us is amply clear: to meet and destroy the Aragonese invaders before they reached High Castile, where they surely planned to make junction with the seditious Castilian nobles. How much time he would have to prepare he did not know. Some, anyway; the foe was still in the eastern marches and would have to wait for the levies of the Infante Henry to come up from Murcia—a long ride. He set about welding the royal army with characteristic dispatch. El Espinar, on the western slope of the Guadarramas, was picked as rendezvous. There, all through the icy February of 1445, troops clattered in. The small town burst its seams; bivouacs sprang up in the rocky fields around—thin tents against the wind, steeds pawing the frozen earth, red forges clanging in the crystal air. But Luna worked ceaselessly on, organizing, billeting, provisioning. Nothing could stop him, not even the startling news at the end of the month. For there, too, in El Espinar, came the large tidings—both the Queen of Castile and the Queen of Portugal were dead.

There is much of the strange about these sudden deaths. They happened almost simultaneously. The symptoms were identical: four days of violent headache, then the eruption of lavender welts all over the body and instant demise. Was it plague? Was it poison? Luna fell under wide suspicion of having them done in with "herbs,"[1] but there has never been a shred of proof. Perhaps the oddest feature of it all, however, is the King's behavior. We know nothing of Juan of Aragón's reaction to the news, off in the east, although one feels safe in supposing it profound: his two sisters, constant allies in the family plans, had been eliminated from the game. But Juan of Castile's was recorded. It is not attractive. He could hardly have been expected to do much about Leonor; she was only his sister-in-law, and Toledo, where she expired, lay far away.

Yet Villacastín, the seat of his wife's passion, is very close to El Espinar. Messengers surely came over, during four days, to tell of the illness. But he never bothered to ride the ten miles to visit her and see if he could ease her suffering. Nor did he attend the funeral —perhaps his shabbiest conduct in all his heartless years with his cousin-wife.

And if the King himself showed no concern, there was far less reason for Luna to break off his tasks for any official show of grief. Besides, fresh news, the last of that fateful month, had just arrived —news much more important, to him, than the death of queens. The Infantes, their musters united, were driving west. They had already crossed—freely—the domain of Medinaceli. Even now, so ran the ominous announcement, they were in lands of the Mendozas and threatening Guadalajara. Alcalá de Henares and Torija and Santorcaz had fallen. His reprieve had run out. He must move at once. Henry, groaning in spirit at this new test but true to his word, rode in from Segovia with his *mesnadas* and that private bodyguard of Moors to which he was so inappropriately attached. Early in cruel March the whole host struck camp, raised standards, and started over the sierra.

They came down its eastern flank and approached Madrid, not much of a place at the time. There they spent an excited night. The next morning they pushed on: scouts had reported that the Infantes were massed at Alcalá de Henares, less than twenty miles along. Nearing the town, and in high anticipation, Luna fanned out the army in battle order. But when they arrived, it looked as if there was to be no encounter. In fact, it looked as if there was no enemy. Luna stopped, surveyed the empty fields with his piercing eyes, and bit his lip. Where were they?

Where they were, it transpired on closer inspection, was extraordinarily well hidden. At Alcalá the banks of the Henares break up in steep ravines; deep in these pockets, these gullies, the Infantes lay entrenched. It was a fine defensive position, and Luna knew so at once. His cavalry, under the circumstances, would be useless. Yet there they were, stopped, cornered, intercepted almost within his grasp. What should be done? The days went by in stagnance, in futile conference with his captains. He sent forth parties of skirmishers, closer and closer, hoping to lure the enemy out. Still nothing happened.

There were also, in point of fact, some arguments in the gullies. The Infante Henry, like Luna, itched for immediate battle. Hotheaded, high-hearted, impetuous, he always had one aim: strike, rush in. What did it matter if they were outnumbered? Let them risk everything at once. Juan listened patiently, smiling the thin smile that showed his pointed little terrier teeth. They could not risk it, he said. They must wait until Olmedo. Then things would be different; there the Castilian barons were appointed to meet them. Somehow they had to leave this cul-de-sac, to get across the mountains, out on the *meseta*. And Juan's calmer head prevailed. One night in stealth and silence, with cloak of moonless darkness, they slipped away.

Luna, the gulches empty, was in unconcealed distress. This came of dawdling; his quarry had escaped him. But he knew where they had gone; armies, in dry Castile, do not march without leaving traces. All he could do was pursue them and hope again for a pitched battle—now they were in the open and on the run. The chase would be difficult. The enemy had a twelve-hour advantage. Their lighter forces could make better time (to speed the invasion, they had brought no infantry). But it was his one course.

In haste he reordered the army and turned back west. They were in Madrid by night. The next morning, Palm Sunday, they pressed relentlessly on, relentlessly higher. At dark they rode into the village of Guadarrama, almost on the crest of the sierra: thirty-six miles that day, a stupendous march. Even so, they were too late: the *aposentadores*, those household officials always sent ahead to prepare the royal quarters, swarmed round them with babbled talk—on their own arrival that morning they had glimpsed the rear guard of the Infantes' army, cold sunlight on their lance tips, vanishing up through the pass of La Tablada. Luna ordered only the briefest repose. By dawn they were on the march again, crowding their own way through the snowy pass, coming out in full sight of the long, bare horizons, the Campos de Castilla, the High Plains. Bare indeed: the foe was nowhere to be seen. But they raced on north; they might still have time. Nothing more clearly shows the desperate pressure on both pursued and pursuers than the date: people simply did not march in Holy Week, let alone fight. By Wednesday, Vigil of Maundy Thursday and the three *Días Santos*, the Sacred Days, even Luna had to halt. They were near Arévalo. They occupied it.

And there they learned the tidings. That very day the Infantes had reached Olmedo, taken it after short resistance, and shut themselves in. The race was lost.

The race, but not the battle. Luna still hoped for that. He could not know that the Infantes too, on arriving at Olmedo, had met some disagreeable surprises: their Castilian allies were not at hand, and they had been obliged to send off couriers with urgent messages —what was the matter, gird yourselves, come at once. All he did know was that he had the enemy stopped, fourteen miles north. And this time they must not escape him. As soon as Easter was over he marched his host from Arévalo, moved it along the bank of the Adaja, and set up camp in the pine grove of Almenara, six miles to Olmedo's southwest. The King thought it a pretty place. But Luna was still not satisfied; he wanted to be closer, ever closer. Scarcely were the *reales* made at Almenara when he broke them up again. He went further along the Adaja. Three miles due west of Olmedo, on the river's far bank, he found terrain he liked. There, he announced, they would establish themselves. Three miles: the net had truly drawn in, drawn tight.

This final campsite of the Castilian army is not hard to identify. The sources tell us it was bounded on the east by the Adaja and to the north by "the great ditch that comes from Medina to empty in the river,"[2] and a very modest amount of tramping will find the ditch, choked up and overgrown though it now is. Secure in this angle of ditch and river, Luna placed his tents. He pitched them, so says his chronicler, unusually close, whether for greater safety or to deceive the Infantes about his army's size we do not know. On the south he dug new ditches. (Behind them, west toward Medina, there was no danger.) He worked, we are also told, with tireless speed. And when it was all set up, all ready, he strode to the riverbank. Impatiently he stood—bald, scrawny, short, but Jupiter with his thunderbolt—and peered across the waiting Olmedan fields of wheat and poppies, those fields which the smocked peasant who binds his sheaves or digs potatoes there today still calls, without the faintest notion why, Los Estragales—the Fields of the Disaster, the Damages.

Waiting: for there were yet to be delays, the thunderbolt must still not fall. The Infantes parleyed: it was always Juan's technique. Besides, they needed time—for their allies to come up. On the plain between the *reales* and Olmedo, slightly nearer the town than the river, rises a small hill; there they sent spokesmen. Alba and Barrientos and Luna himself came out to meet them. Stale grievances were aired. Had the King no shame—stealing the Infantes' ancestral possessions? Would he not restore them? No, he would not. Had they no shame themselves, breaking in like this, violating their oaths, taunting their overlord? To and fro the discussion went—and meanwhile the traitorous nobles arrived: the Count of Benavente and Pedro de Quiñones, the scrappy little Admiral and his brother.

But by then the royalists, too, had motive to hold off. Word reached the camp that the Master of Alcántara, with six hundred horse, was coming to join them. That, even Luna agreed, was worth a wait. How long would the Master be? Six days? Six days, said Barrientos; he could promise nine. He went back to the hill: more haggling, more threats and recriminations, more Salmantine dialectics. Behind this verbal smoke screen, the Master of Alcántara slipped into the royal camp. The Count of Haro, as well, conveniently appeared. Haro himself, cross-eyed and apt to ride in the wrong direction, was not of much use in a battle. He brought, however, the skilled Velasco troops. And close after them came further news: the Portuguese Constable had set out from Lisbon to their aid.

At that, however, Luna drew the line. Lisbon was weeks away. He was sick of waiting. The occasion would never be riper, his forces never readier. Twice he marshaled the army and led it east, to Olmedo's very walls. Both times the Infantes refused to come forth and fight: Juan was still arguing for politics, for maneuver. Luna returned to the river and fretted anew in his pavilion. Ascension passed, and Pentecost. The wheat grew hip high, then heavy with bristling head. The poppies among it nodded. Hawks hung in the empty sky. Again, as at Alcalá de Henares, it looked as if nothing would happen.

But the hour was there, was coming; soon those green fields would run with brighter red than poppies ever knew. And in the end it was not Luna at all who brought on the battle but—ironically, almost incredibly—Henry himself.

That historic 19th of May, the day of Armageddon, dawned close and warm—unseasonably so, for the full lash of summer does not strike the Castilian heartland until late June. The morning, we gather from shreds of internal evidence, was one of *claros*, those bursts of great white Spanish light which fall through parting clouds in spring. It had been uneventful. So too, it seemed, would be the afternoon. At three o'clock the world was still. The clouds had burned off by then; it was really hot. Olmedo lay like a dusty topaz in the sun. (True, there came an occasional flash of armor under its walls. But that was only a troop of the Count of Castro, charged with the day's guard of the crops, the *huerta*.) The wheatfields stretched unstirred. Across them, off on the far side of the river, the royal encampment drowsed: its tents with pennons limp, mounts tethered and arms put by. In all that hushed immensity there was but one small movement. Out on the plain, near the low hill, a little group of horsemen darted and wheeled. It was Henry and a few of his household.

Odd exhibition, this, and typical of its quirksome leader. The hour—siesta, when any good Spaniard should be out of sight. The mode—*a la jineta*, on graceful little jennets, lightly armed and with short stirrups and knees drawn high: Moslem, in brief, and totally wrong for a prince of Castile. But Henry liked these random *chevauchées* in the wide air; he had made them almost daily. They helped to relieve his tensions. A few times they had even brought a rival group out from Olmedo for quick skirmishes—and those he liked best of all: no blood was shed, they were really only games, only tests of horsemanship, to see who could ride the fastest, come the closest, skim aside the latest.

Perhaps it was in hope of stirring up just such a challenge that he suddenly turned, this sleepy afternoon, and headed for the hill: the Infantes seemed to consider it, like everything else in the neighborhood, their private property. Whatever his motives or lack of them ("sheer imprudence,"[3] growls Palencia), he led his hot companions straight up the slope. They reached the top and paused, to ease their horses—while Fate moved at last, while eyes in Olmedo's watchtower took in his maneuver and sent word of it down to the council table and a swift order from the Count of Castro went out. They sat there on the hill, restlessly, some quarter hour. They were just about to leave when Henry glimpsed it—the puff of dust. A small group like themselves, *jinetes*, had left Olmedo: sport.

He called his men around him. They galloped down the slope,

back to the plain. They started east, bent low, toward their advancing kind. But then they saw the trick. The others, halfway there, came on no longer. Instead, they fanned away to either side. Behind them rode, like thunder, the whole guard of the Count of Castro—mighty-mounted, armed cap-a-pie with battle lance and sword and iron mace.

For all his dislike of war, Henry was certainly no coward; he bore with fortitude, and uncomplaining, trials which would drive the most heroic mad. But it must have been a terrible thing for him, for anyone in the Middle Ages, to see a troop of men of arms—those human arsenals, those sometime tanks—come charging down. Luna's chronicle says that there were a hundred of them; the Chief Falconer of the Castilian King left record only that they were "a thick battalion."[4] In any event, they were too many and too much for Henry's little band. He and his companions reined in hard. They hesitated a moment, motionless in their own dust. But there was only one thing they could do. Abruptly they pulled their horses' heads around and streaked away, westward, for the safety of the Castilian camp.

They won; why else that style of mount? Sweating and breathless, they spurred across the river, beyond harm's reach. And a messenger ran to the royal tent with news of what had happened.

The King was furious. He had been roused from his nap. And to make matters worse the thwarted pursuers, when they did reach the riverbank, had stayed for a while, leering out of crossbow range, before they too wheeled around and started back toward Olmedo. The chroniclers try hard to invest Juan II with stature at this point, to drape him in noble speech about his resolve to uphold the Crown's honor and chastise the affront of Aragón to his son. But his own subsequent account of the day's events gives probably the real truth of what occurred: as he had done all his life when he was in trouble, he sent at once for Luna.

Luna himself was anything but angry. If the Infantes were willing to commit so large a troop of men of arms, he might now be able, finally, to tempt them out with their whole force. The afternoon, unfortunately, was wearing on: far behind them the great square tower of La Mota already was in shadow; off to Olmedo's east the castle of Iscar stood in full sun upon its rocky butte. Yet if he hurried there could still be time. He told the King to arm, to summon the royal standard. He strode off to rouse his soldiers and gather his captains. In moments the whole encampment was astir. Trumpets rang out, commands called back and forth, bright banners were unfurled.

All the accounts agree upon the speed with which Luna marshaled the royal army and got it across the river. The entire operation could hardly have taken more than half an hour; although the nearby bridge was not commodious, the Adaja is never much of a stream, and less in May. We know their numbers, too—some 2,800 horse. (The foot is less certain; they had perhaps 2,000, but many were left in camp.) And once on the other side, they deployed with equal speed into the order for their march against Olmedo.

Luna, as Constable, took the center, the van. He had 1,000 cavalry: 600 in his *gruesa batalla*, his main force, including all his personal retinue, and wings of 200 each—one of them in the command of Alonso Carrillo, then Bishop of Sigüenza but soon to be Archbishop of Toledo, that pugnacious cleric who will play so large a role in our developing story. Considerably behind Luna, and a little to the right, came Alba and Iñigo López de Mendoza with a troop of 200 more. Henry lay off on the left, and less behind, with his own household: 450 mounts, led by himself and Villena. Behind Henry, the large *batalla*—550—of the Master of Alcántara. And to the rear of all, as *retaguardia*, the King, with a spate of loyal counts and prelates: 600 horse, and no doubt such foot as they had brought.

So formed a Castilian host at the end of the Middle Ages. Let the eye scan it briefly—as they sit there ready, lances aloft, their horses fetlock deep in wheat and poppies—and then fall upon the one man who could set them into final motion, the King himself. He spoke to his standard-bearer, and his red lions and castles went up. He signaled another squire, and the great double war drums, the *atabales*, began to beat. He loosened his rein, his horse stepped forward. And with him the whole army moved—pacing and then at canter and finally at gallop, out, on, east toward Olmedo.

The chronicler Chacón, who rode among them, outdoes himself in his description of that gorgeous tide; his page bursts into flame, it blazes and glitters. All the years after, what he most remembered was the light; he was a true son of his age, and light and beauty were synonymous to the medieval mind. "For the sun fell athwart them," he cries in ecstasy, "and their armor was freshly polished, and their weapons shone, and it was glorious to see."[5] Their shields were richly chiseled "with strange figures and inventions."[6] Some had short capes of silk or velvet, stiff with silver and gold. Some wore their ladies' scarves, some curious wings of painted feathers that streamed out behind. Their helmets shamed the day: the crests were savage beasts or castle towers in gilt and bronze, the visors thick with pearls and all afire with precious stones. The mounts, too, went adorned—silk hangings on their flanks, plumes on their heads, their throats encased in steel and hung with golden chains, with golden bells. The lance tips coruscated. The hooves, across that stone-strewn plain, flashed crimson sparks.

It must, in truth, have been a splendid sight, this latter fanfare of a world so soon to pass. Yet it seemed, when they reached Olmedo and drew up before it, that they had come in vain: much cry and little wool. The mighty walls stared back at them, silent and empty. The gates were shut.

They waited there a while, "*un grand espacio,*"[7] frustrated, angry, hot inside their armor. They waited longer: a half hour, three quarters. The sun was plunging. Squires began to ride back and forth among the Castilian commanders. Their gage, it seemed again, was not to be picked up. They could not wait for ever. Finally, around five thirty[8] (we are told that there were still two hours of sun, and it set that day in Olmedo at half past seven), the order went out: turn, go back, once more, to the camp.

They faced about, hearts heavy—except, perhaps, for Henry's. Slowly they rode away. As the King had brought up the rear in the advance, so now he had the lead in the return. He was almost to the river when it happened.

That messenger who galloped westward must have come in foam, with bloody spurs. He sought the royal standard, reined in, cried Luna's message. The Infantes were coming out. Pouring out, in fact —"*sus batallas ordenadas,*"[9] in full fighting order (the Infante Henry had finally won the argument, Juan had given in, the decision was made for battle). They must all turn back. An engagement was inevitable.

Now History heaves and wakes; the hour postponed for decades had struck at last. The King put on his helmet. He unsheathed his sword; he sent word that he was coming and that the cry should be

"Castilla! Castilla!" Luna, far over the fields to the east, was riding up and down his line; he had stopped and wheeled about just west of the hill. Surely he was not speaking the high-flown speech which we read in his chronicle. He did not have time: the whole force of the enemy was out by then, and driving across the plain.

They came in two huge waves, all cavalry. The one on their left, to the south, was of 1,500; the Infante Henry led it, with the Admiral and Pedro de Quiñones and the Count of Benavente and Rodrigo Manrique, Count of Paredes. Juan himself, with the counts of Castro and Medinaceli, commanded the other, of 1,000. Luna's battalion would face the first, Henry's the second—and it is clear that both of them were outnumbered.

Luna saw that, too. But Mendoza and Alba, not far to his right, would come to his aid—just as the Master of Alcántara would join the Prince. There was nothing to do but prepare—to hold their line and rein the horses close and wait until the enemy was far enough advanced for an attack. They sat there briefly, plumes fluttering. And then the trumpets sounded, the great lances came down into position, the whole line surged out.

They met the rebels just beside the hill, lance against shield and helmet, splinter, reel, fall. They drove on through. And quick behind them, with the foe still stunned, came the charge of Alba and Mendoza. All of them had been carried far past by their momentum. They swung around; so did the enemy. Once more the lances leveled, once more the gallop and crash. And this time they closed in.

Such were *"los primeros golpes,"*[10] the first blows. They had been bad enough: Luna's right thigh was torn open, and the Infante Henry already bore a vicious wound—a gash in the left wrist and all up his inner arm. But they were far from the last. "And with the lances shattered, they drew their swords, and laid about them with stout strokes. And the ones who had fallen and could still get up stabbed at the horses of those who brought them down, and all did all they knew, and the more the blood flowed forth the more they raged."[11] Helmets fell off, some wrenched loose with glaived hands, some struck away by swords. The horses reared and screamed and ran about with dragging bowels. Those who were down indeed (chain mail had long gone out of style, and plate armor weighed like stone) were killed by flailing hooves—trampled and battered, ground into the roil of guts and poppies and silk and ruined wheat.

Much the same thing was happening on the other front, to the north: the charge and shock, the ping and thump of arrows, the whistle of swords. But all agree that the battle was fiercer—*"muy más áspera"*[12]—on the Castilian right, where Luna and the Infante Henry met; they were the greatest captains of the age, and both had much at stake. By then they were fighting in a pall of dust—red dust, for the sun was setting, adding new blood. It seems to have been to escape it, to get above it, that they took to the hill, with its firmer soil. There, up and down that slope, the full storm came. There Luna's banner fell, his crescent moon, dropped by his stricken ensign—but snatched and raised again by loyal hands and borne in furious vengeance to a last assault. For there, as well, the tide of battle turned. The Infante Henry's forces could no longer bear those "huge and terrible blows."[13] They gave their backs, they fled. The rebels' other wing, off on the twilit plain, seems to have broken just at the same time. It was all over. It had lasted little more than an hour. "The great high God of Battles and the Apostle Santiago chose that the King of Navarre and the Infante Henry be defeated."[14]

There will, perhaps, be those who seek less pious reasons for the Castilian victory. And they exist, in plenty. The Infantes had been at serious disadvantage in the initial charge: since they rode westward, the dropping sun fell straight into their eyes. Their right wing was much weakened by the defection, early in the battle, of the Count of Medinaceli; he seems to have been stung by conscience for his betrayal of Atienza and to have come over, with all his troops, to the Castilians. Their lack of foot cost the invaders dear, while the royal infantry apparently moved up swiftly from the King and played a major role by bringing down, with swords and javelins and arrows, the enemy's horses. (The King's own part in the engagement is obscure; both his Official Version and Palencia have him take his cavalry to aid the Prince, but in Luna's chronicle he seems to hang behind, sending foot and advice. Of Henry himself nobody says a word.) Too, general laws obtain. Any force which chose, like the Infantes', to fight so close to its base had an unpleasant truth with which to reckon: the cowards among them, with refuge near, were tempted to run. Valera cynically observes that all armies have more of the craven in them than of the valiant, and we know, in fact, that many fled here on both sides. The fugitives among the rebels skipped into the town and were out of the way. But the Castilians who ran only met their advancing rear and were caught up amidst them and carried straight back to the fray. The Castilian sovereign's own chronicle tells us—and how bitterly the word rings!—that by the end of the battle there were far more "left"[15] with the royal ranks than with the rebels.

However this may have been, the victory was complete; it and Toro, thirty years later, are the two most decisive battles of the Spanish fifteenth century. Long after night had fallen the rout went on—the flight and hot pursuit across the plain, the taking of prisoners, *"los últimos horrores del combate."*[16] Almost every rebel standard had been captured: the Infante Henry's, the Count of Benavente's, Manrique's, the Admiral's. Among the hundreds of prisoners were the Count of Castro, the Admiral's brother and two of his nephews, the son of the Navarrese Constable Pierres de Peralta, "and other knights and persons of importance."[17]

One by one, with mounting triumph, these great prizes were brought back to the Castilian camp, to Luna's tent: the seized standards set up outside, the noble captives led sullenly in. For there, in the high May night, in the dancing torchlight, the victory conclave was held—Luna had hidden his wound all during the battle, but now he was down, too hurt to move, and with the surgeons at him. Everyone crowded around, "marveled by how he had borne so long so fierce a pain."[18] The royal secretaries were already at work on letters announcing the victory to all the kingdom. Sentences of death, of banishment, were being dictated.

We are told that the King went into another rage when the Admiral's brother was brought before him. It seems to have been the "resplendent armor"[19] of that traitorous cousin which somehow set him off. He leaped up "possessed by fury";[20] he shouted that the prisoner must be killed at once. Luna, grimacing under the surgeons, calmed him down. The Admiral hated the Crown quite enough, as it was. Now if they had been able to hold on to that archconspirator himself. . . .

But the Admiral had got away. He was, it is true, taken with the rest—by Pedro de Carrera, one of Luna's men. Yet as his captor led him, on foot, across the dark fields toward the royal camp, his dark mind worked. Valera says that what he offered Carrera was vassals

and money and even a *"donzella"*[21] of his house. According to Palencia, Carrera turned out, in those rip tides of loyalties, to be one
of the Admiral's former retainers. In any case, before they reached
the river, the prisoner had his horse and sword again. He veered off
and rode toward the north, to his great castle at Torrelobatón, to
future bale. Had he fallen that day, Spain's history might have
changed.

Quiñones, too, escaped. "Squire," he announced to the proud
youth who had captured him, "Squire, I am badly hurt. I beg you,
remove this helmet from my head—I cannot bear it."[22] The squire,
poor gullible lad, turned over his own sword to free his hands for
the job; Quiñones suddenly raised it and slashed it down through
the boy's face, then galloped across the plain.

And of course the greatest fish of all had slipped through the net
—the two Infantes. They managed to get back inside Olmedo. But
they knew they dared not stay. In the morning, perhaps before, the
victors would be at them. They must be away, at once, with cover
of dark; there was scant time even to stanch the Infante Henry's
wound, and none to dress it properly. Their frenzy to escape, that
ruinous night, rings through the chronicles: the running, the shouting, the search for fresh horses, the stuffing of saddlebags and
throwing them down again. For in the end they abandoned everything—arms, luggage, servants. Just before midnight the two of
them were off, clattering under Olmedo's eastern gate, then close
against their horses' necks and spurring toward Aragón.

It was a wild ride, a terrible ride, for the fleeing brothers: almost
two hundred miles. The Infante Henry's arm grew steadily worse
—swelled, blackened, burned. But they stopped only to change
mounts: off one and up to another and driving on. And finally they
made it. Finally they foamed into Calatayud, safe across Aragón's
border. The Infante Henry pitched from his horse, collapsing.
Physicians were summoned.

They could do nothing. It was too late; the gangrene had gone too
far. His fever soared. He began to rave—perhaps of clanging
charges along the Segura, through the hot fields of Murcia. Then
suddenly—"for his charm, grace, courage, and dash," says Palencia,
always partial to Aragón, "the best man of the age"[23]—he gasped
and died. They did not have his great white mantle of Santiago with
which to wrap him. In his dented armor they brought him down

from Calatayud's tall Moorish castle and into the city of tiled domes and minarets below. They laid him before the altar of San Pedro Mártir. And there, in the murk and silence after the Requiem, with everything done and everybody gone, Juan—left to himself for the first time in those dreadful days—stood on by the corpse in the most cruel trance of his forty-seven years.

Aragón, beyond any question, would never make armed assault upon Castile again. Its troops were scattered. Its general, its greatest warrior, lay dead before him. The alliance with the Castilian barons was broken; they, too, must be in full flight. No, Juan realized, war could no longer be the answer to the family dream. Henceforth their efforts to have the Castilian crown must take a different cast: through politics, at angle, from afar. And the entire burden would now fall on him. How rapidly the clan had been wiped out: three deaths among them in as many months! Of all the seven only two remained: he and Alfonso, the King—and what good was Alfonso, twined and bewitched in Neapolitan garlands?

Grave, grave, the situation. The way seemed closed all round. Yet nothing, to Juan, was ever completely hopeless. In time, he might reknit his coalition with the neighboring barons. The Castilian King's own health was none too good. Henry had produced no children, and perhaps when he succeeded his father a whole new plan could be constructed on that useful—that permanent?—incapacity. He had always found some way to carry on, even in deepest dark. He would find one again; he could, he must.

So Juan of Navarre and Aragón beside his brother's corpse, among the mortuary tapers of San Pedro Mártir: a cold man in a cold circumstance, alone, defeated, bayed—but with a will of iron.

6.

Two Marriages

The booty of Olmedo was enormous; for weeks and months after the battle it was still being doled out. The dead Infante's grandmastership of Santiago, with its immense income and perquisites, went —deservedly—to Luna. Villena had his marquesate and even managed to worm in his wretched brother, Pedro Girón, as Master of the Order of Calatrava. Alonso Carrillo, the blustery bishop whom we have just met, soon rose to the primacy, the miter of Toledo. Mendoza was created Marqués of Santillana. Henry himself did not come off too badly: the King gave him Cáceres, Logroño, Ciudad Rodrigo, Jaén.

But the moody Prince did not await this division of the spoils. A few days after the victory, while the royal army lay encamped at Simancas on its march north to seize the towns and castles of the defeated Castilian nobles, he broke away. Again during siesta, and as usual with no word to anyone, he took to horse and galloped off. His absence discovered, the King sent after him—there was never much doubt of where Henry would head—with orders to bring him back either by persuasion or by force. But he outstripped his pursuers. He paused briefly in Santa María de Nieva for a fresh mount. Then he drove on the twenty more miles to Segovia: haven, heaven. One breathes his sense of relief, of escape from unwelcome entanglements, as he rode east, his large legs bouncing against his little horse, through the blue cornflowers and yellow broom that springtime day. The ordeal of arms, of forced association with people whom he did not like and who he knew did not like him, was over. Hs was going home, back to the only things he ever really wanted or understood: seclusion, peace, anonymity, the barred door and the silent forests and the undemanding sun.

Now, indeed and at last, begins his full and visible identification with Segovia. He was grown and a free agent. Moreover, for the first time in his life he had money, plenty of money: his dead mother's inheritance, the rents of the rich towns he had just been given, his six million a year as Prince of Asturias—a title bestowed on him soon before Olmedo. In short, he could finally do quite as he pleased with the beloved city; his generous heart could repay its debt of gratitude to the one place on earth where he found himself at ease, where he could go about unremarked and accepted and making shy overtures of friendship, where he always considered himself—so Colmenares tells us, and Colmenares, that other loyal Segovian, should certainly have known—"more a citizen than a sovereign."[1]

Many were the garlands which Henry offered to Segovia through the rest of his life, and he began to weave them in just these years. Now start the grants and *mercedes*, the string of favors, which he was never to leave off. No one, reading of Segovia's wealth and glory in the latter Middle Ages, can fail to see Henry's nurturing hand. One of his first privileges to the city was the freedom from paying, at its Thursday market, taxes on anything but wine and meat; in time its dwellers were exempted from all tribute to the Crown. He fed its economic life. He encouraged the wool trade, the weaving. He established its two great fairs, in late winter and early summer, and gave them the added bait that no one who came to them could be arrested for debt while away from home. He made an annual grant for education. He even provided the citizens with two public scales. But above all he now began to build, to beautify. As a more normal man would deck a mistress, so he adorned the town.

Much of its present architectural splendor is his work. He finished the Alcázar's Torre del Homenaje; he decorated—in the *mudéjar* style, the Moorish, to which he was so drawn—its throne room and the gorgeous Hall of the Pineapples, with its countless gold stalactites of that exotic fruit. To live among such opulence, however, was not for his modest tastes; he put up simpler *casas reales* at the other end of town, behind the church of San Martín. No doubt because they were simpler they have lasted less well: one finds only the *zaguán*, and two windows with gessoed arabesques, and the den for his lions. East of the city and near the start of the aqueduct he built another retreat, today the Convent of San Antonio el Real, where the ceiling of gilded and woven wood still steals the breath. El Parral, too, the Jeronymite monastery just across the Eresma, is from his hand: Villena had founded it but typically left the expense to Henry—although it is Villena's blazon above the door (a stewpot and a chessboard: what apter arms!).

Yet the place he loved the most, enriched the most, was the cathedral, old and decayed and constricted though it was. He always wanted to build a new one on an ampler site. In fact he gave seventeen millions for that purpose—most of which went into the Ariases' bag. He did remake the cloister; when the present cathedral was constructed, in the next century, it was moved there stone by stone. He presented the Chapter with twenty sumptuous copes and endowed the great organ, one of the most famous in Spain. Another of his gifts is the revered image of Nuestra Señora de la Paz (an advocation which must have appealed to him)—gaudied up in the eighteenth century with nearly a hundred pounds of rococo silver and placed in a Bourbon *fauteuil,* but still with the same serene medieval face on which Henry so often must have gazed.

Often, since he seems to have visited those dusky cathedral precincts almost daily. It was his habit to slip in quietly; he would show by a sign that he was not to be acknowledged and then shrink back into a stall and sit for hours. He did not go for devotions: Henry's battered mind ran to the skeptical, even the radical, and it was one of his chief misfortunes, both personal and public, that he set little store by Holy Church. What took him, beside the darkness and seclusion, was the music. Always that was his major solace. He played the lute expertly. He spent what harder men considered scandalous sums upon his private choir. At times he sang with them himself. Marañón would have him a tenor: a plain guess. But whatever the timbre, we do know the taste. "He loved sad songs,"[2] his chaplain tells us: the Castilian sadness, the sadness of space and crumbling rock and lonely sky, the mournful airs one hears today on shepherds' flutes high in the *serranías* of Segovia—as Henry heard them so many times himself, and stopped to listen, on his long mountain rides.

For there, upon the slopes of the Guadarramas, is his other favorite haunt—the forest of Balsaín. It is terrible in winter: the fogs, the hush, the branches bowed with snow. Even in August the light falls pale, a gloaming, through those tall back pines. Summer or winter, however, Henry loved it. He kept his animals there—boars, bears, stags, chamois, his fierce favorite bull. He kept them well: this shuttered man felt most at home with beasts and trees. To hold them safely in, he made a high thick wall. To hold intruders out, he stationed fearsome guards before the gates—Ethiopians and hideous dwarfs. Deep in the heart of this remote preserve he built a lodge. There he would bury himself, for days and nights, with Miguel Lucas and clots of their roughneck friends. Nobody knows what went on. Nobody knew even then, although people endlessly conjectured (Blanca, who seems to have been living in painful retirement at Olmedo, surely among them). One thing alone is certain: these bachelor weekends did Henry's reputation—were always to do it—immeasurable harm.

Characteristically, he paid no heed to that. He was restless, still sick with the knowledge of his dereliction as a spouse. He needed relief, however he got it, from his private cross. One cannot begrudge him his hidden years after Olmedo. One can, on the contrary, be glad he had them: they were his last of any peace. Not that, even so, his withdrawal was as successful, as nearly total, as he might have wished; he remained the heir, the object of veiled or open machinations, and inevitably he was drawn back from time to time into noisier events. We glimpse him, and probably here with more reluctance than ever, at the fruitless siege of Blanca's brother, the Prince of Viana, in Estella. He was dragged into the fateful arrest, near Tordesillas, of the plotting Grandes (Alba now gone over to them): many of them had fled abroad after their defeat at Olmedo, but they were filtering home and at their seditious work again. We see him in the shocking mess at Toledo (its revolt against the Crown; the King outside the Bisagra gate demanding submission, with the cannon ball lobbed at his feet—"Catch that orange!";[3] Henry pushed in by Villena, who hoped for gain from the disorder, but growing tired of the unintelligible negotiations and wandering off in the midst of them to seek a strange huge pig which had swum the Tajo). Yet he always returned to Segovia as soon as he could after these interludes, to the pines and the quiet sunlight and the sheltering cloisters.

He did not, in fact, even attend his father's second wedding. For while the *mudéjar* ceilings went up in Segovia and the deer browsed at Balsaín and Henry sat listening alone to plainsong, his widowed father was taking a new wife. That marriage had vast consequences not only for Henry but for everyone else with whom we deal, and we must examine it. It brought Henry a sister and a brother. It sent Luna to the scaffold—and finished the King.

Luna himself, as one would expect, was the chief architect of this second match of Juan II of Castile; for almost forty years he had managed the sovereign's life. Predictable, too, that it should have been—or so Luna thought—a marriage of mere political convenience. For once more the Constable was beginning to feel uneasy. The euphoria of Olmedo had worn off, and it became increasingly apparent to him that in spite of the great military victory all might still not be well with the realm. The nobles, as we have seen, were again in effervescence. Above all, Luna knew Juan of Aragón far too well to think that he would ever really give up.

True, that archfoe's fortunes were clearly near their nadir at the time. He was notoriously hard pressed for money: the economic health of the Crown of Aragón, so abundant in the fourteenth century, was all at once in precipitous decline. His wife, not long after Blanca's wedding, had finally eaten herself to death at Santa María de Nieva, but his own efforts to remarry—with Juana Enríquez, the brilliant young daughter of the Castilian Admiral—still were meeting, thanks to the objections of her sovereign, with no success. He and Carlos of Viana had reached the breaking point: the dead Queen's testament, which unrealistically asked that the son and legal heir never call himself King of Navarre during the father's lifetime, had made their relations intolerable, since Juan was no more disposed to have the title without the power than Carlos the power without the title. The Catalans, always a prickly and ungovernable tribe, were giving him endless trouble. Low ebb, indeed, as anyone could see. Yet even in his extremity, Juan was causing what trouble he could. Already he was pushing again at weak spots on the Castilian border. From Torija and Atienza, the last two of his holdings in Castile which had not been confiscated, he mounted raids on cattle. There was evidence that he had pacted with the Moors to strike up from the south. And it was precisely in observing these moves that Luna once more took alarm. In a word, he saw that the hydra of Aragón, however prostrate, was beginning to grow new heads, and that he should at once seek ways of containing the fresh menace before it had time to mature.

How better, he reasoned, and the logic at least was unassailable, to meet a resurgent threat from the east than by a tightened alliance with Portugal, on the west? And what surer means to such end than a Portuguese marriage for the widowed King? Since the Aragonese Queen of Portugal was also dead, her opposition no longer needed to be feared. Its youthful new King, her son Alfonso V, had a fourteen-year-old cousin, Isabel, who would make a suitable bride. And having conceived his plan, Luna moved quickly. The charming boy-Constable of Portugal had not reached Castile in time for the battle of Olmedo. But once there he lingered on for the victory celebrations. He too was the Portuguese Infanta's first cousin, and before he returned to Lisbon Luna engaged him in some useful Constabulary talk.

The King, if one is to believe his chronicle, had other ideas about a second wife: he yearned for the French Régine, daughter of Charles VII and a famous beauty. Historians generally take this trans-Pyrenean passion for fantasy. Yet there may have been something in it. Shortly before Olmedo, the King privately commanded the chronicler Valera to seek her out. But when Valera went to pick up the money for his journey, the Treasurer discovered everything —and told Luna. Luna countermanded the order and pressed on with his Portuguese negotiations. The Pope gave a dispensation of consanguinity; the marriage contract was signed in April of 1446 at Avila, then by the Portuguese six months later in Evora. The Infanta Isabel, the beautiful girl with the *"ollos pretos,"*[4] the dark eyes, set out for Castile. The King and court went down to Madrigal de las Altas Torres to meet her. And there on July 22, 1447—just nine days after Juan of Aragón did finally marry the Admiral's daughter in Calatayud, a match which was to have results of almost equal moment—the wedding took place.

It held surprises for everyone. The musky King was bewitched by his supple young bride; Madame Régine flew out of his head. The new Queen's discoveries were less pleasant. Of course she had heard of Luna's dominion over the King. But she had never dreamed, until she was actually exposed to it, that his dictates extended even into the bedroom. It was bad enough to have an old friend of her husband constantly underfoot; it was really insufferable that he should try to set, on pretext of the doughy monarch's health, the hours and limits of their couplings. Everything we know about Isabel of Portugal tells us that she was jealous, ambitious, possessive, no woman to share a husband, let alone a throne. There can be little doubt that she conceived an almost instant resentment against Luna, that a determination soon took root in her to break his power. Nor is there much that Luna soon realized his error, soon saw that his long ascendancy was challenged, that he had brought a rival instead of an ally: "the knife"—it is the same Valera speaking—"that cut off his own head."[5]

So came about that portentous contest between wife and favorite which is the central act of Castile's mid-century, but which we cannot pause here to do more than sketch. It is dreadful to follow —the Queen all smiles for the man she was beginning to despise, the sovereign mazed in old affection and new passion, Luna himself swinging between cold doubt and lifelong confidence in his own power. For of course the victor of Olmedo and La Higueruela fought back, fought to maintain his footing; he had been faced by heavy odds before.

But this was a new kind of enemy, one which a forthright man like Luna was ill equipped to understand: caresses, warm thighs, a whispered plea in bed. Everywhere, as the relentless duel wore on, there are signs that the King was slowly yielding to those amorous persuasions, was turning against the friend. Everywhere there is fresh proof that Luna, for all his efforts, steadily lost ground. He asked to be given sole command of the siege of Estella "but could in no wise draw or incline the King to what he requested."[6] He urged the monarch to retire for a while to the convent of Las Huelgas, "where there was a large group of gracious and noble nuns, and other well-connected and high-born and handsome and cultivated ladies . . . who know how to do many and diverse and most agreeable things"[7]—a transparent enough suggestion, and one which met with a denial both emphatic and of an inspiration equally obvious. At the rain-drenched siege of Palenzuela, raised to revolt by the Admiral from afar, he was able to control neither the King nor his own troops.

And before long the Queen had a new weapon, one which even Luna must have realized would drive his fortunes further down: she bore a child. They gave the girl the name of Isabel, after her mother. History has enlarged it—to Isabel the Catholic.

The young wife fell strangely ill with that tremendous birth; she plunged into *"profunda tristeza,"*[8] she shut herself up, she sat motionless and staring. Palencia charges that Luna had poisoned her. But Palencia, as he saw sodomy behind every bush, found venom in every cup. What seems more likely is that the wrench of child- birth first exposed the latent seeds of her insanity—the curse she brought upon the Spanish royal line. We are told that in her vapors she would speak with no one but the King. It is not hard to sound the conversation: she had proved her love, he his autumn virility (so different from that useless Henry); they were a family now; they needed no one else. The eye of Destiny, to be sure, had not yet opened: nobody could have guessed the exalted role which lay ahead for the child there in the cradle between them—any more than Juan of Aragón could have surmised (although one imagines his ceaseless mind already at its calculations) the large future of that infant son, Fernando, whom his own young wife had borne him, during a hailstorm, a few months later. But surely the proud Portuguese mother used to the full her new-found hold. In any event, she at last decided to strike at her hated rival. And the weapon she selected was a man named Alonso Pérez de Vivero.

This toad, this creature with the "viperous tongue"[9] and the black heart, had been a pensioner of Luna's, raised from nothing; it was Luna himself who had put him in the position he then held, of *contador mayor* to the Crown. Having hopped so high, he thought to go even higher by pleasing the sovereigns. And they needed an arm; if the King was finally disposed to liquidate Luna, he had neither the valor nor the decency to do it on his own.

The instrument was well chosen: if anything was calculated to unsettle Luna, to goad him to some mistake, it was ingratitude. Yet for a while he managed to maintain his calm. With reason and telling logic, when Pérez deliberately offended him, he turned the insults aside. Even when words were given up for action, even when traps were set for him in dark places, he still was nimble enough to elude the peril. Three times he escaped armed ambush. But with two whole years of that, his nerves were raveling. They snapped at last in Burgos, the Good Friday afternoon of 1453. He was on an open tower that day with Pérez. Letters arranging for an occasion to kill him, at the next meeting of the Council, had just come to his hands. He thrust one of them at Pérez. "Whose writing is this?" he demanded. "The King's," said Pérez. He held out an- other. "And this?" he asked. "Mine,"[10] Pérez answered. And Luna could control himself no longer. As Pérez hurtled down, an abutment of the tower broke open his skull. A squire who stood watering a horse in the street below was spattered with brains.

Murder, plain murder: Luna had finally blundered. The Queen worked a last persuasion. Stammering upon a bench beside a brazier in the Burgalese *casas reales*, half undressed for bed and half crazy at what he was doing, the King wrote out an order of arrest. In the dawn the Crown's chief bailiff, with two hundred troops, rode down from the castle and surrounded Luna's *posada*. Almost unbelieveably, Luna first tried to run; he borrowed a peon's cloak and set out down a dark alley. But somewhere near the tanneries his pride returned to him. What was he doing, skulking through alleys and sewers in peasant's clothing—a man who had aided Joan of Arc, who had routed Moors, "the greatest lord without a crown Castile had ever known"?[11] He stopped and swung around; he would run no more. "The hunters," writes Chacón, "when they wish to catch the ermines, dig up the earth around them and throw water on it and make it mud. The ermines seek to flee. But when they think they are safe, they find that ring of mud. And not to soil their splendid whiteness they turn back, they put themselves in the power of the hunters and the dogs. Thus are they taken and killed."[12]

Thus was the great don Alvaro de Luna taken: in the patio of his *posada* with the broad doors thrown open, sitting upon his finest war horse and wearing the silver armor a king of France had given him, his standard raised, his sword unsheathed to surrender, his squires about him, sobbing, on their knees. Thus was he killed: in Valladolid, upon a public platform, his thumbs bound tight together but with no blindfold, the executioner straddled tall and black above him. We are told that a vast moan rose from the watching crowd there in the Plaza of the Ochavo when the bald, wise old head was hacked all off at last and held dripping up. And well might Castile have lamented: the Crown's best bulwark, the stout shield which had stood between it and its foes both foreign and domestic for nearly half a century, was irretrievably gone.

But that, for all its resonance, is schoolbook platitude. What most concerns us in Luna's destruction is, as always, Henry. Did he have any part in the dark rune of blood and vengeance? (For that matter, did Juan of Aragón? No document yet hints it, although he had much to gain.) Apparently not; apparently he held aloof, and uncommitted, while the titan fell. The reason usually given is Villena: he saw that Luna's removal, so essential to his own rise, could well be brought about by other hands. But there is a much simpler explanation. All through those closing months of Luna's tragedy, Henry was far too deeply plunged in a grave problem of his own to think of anything else. He, also, had made up his mind to seek a new wife. Even as the noose tightened around Luna, in February or early March of 1453, he rode down to Extremadura for an exploratory talk with his young cousin, Alfonso of Portugal, about the possibility of a match for himself with that monarch's sister Juana.

The meeting was secret—understandably so, the suitor being married. We learn of it only by accident, from a letter of Alfonso to the Count of Benavente, who was still in refuge in Portugal. We do, however, know its outcome. Alfonso, for reasons which we shall shortly consider, gave his approval. As soon as Henry reached home he sent his attorney to make representations before Luis de Acuña, Suffragan Bishop of Segovia, for a divorce from Blanca. The wheels turned fast. In the small town of Alcazarén, on May 11, while Luna sat cramped in his prisoner's cage a few miles off at Portillo awaiting his final removal to Valladolid, Acuña dissolved the marriage of Henry and Blanca, on the plain and perfectly valid grounds that it had never been consummated.

7.

A Divorce

Henry's divorce is one of the knottiest and most grievous problems that can confront a Spanish historian. Yet it has to be unwound. It throws flat upon the table the question of Henry's sexuality—and raises, in so doing, issues which are basic not only to his whole personality and reign but also to the reign of his successors, the Catholic Monarchs.

Let it be stated at the outset that Acuña's procedure in the difficult negotiations—despite the fact that he was a kinsman of Alonso Carrillo, Archbishop of Toledo, at that point still an adherent of the Crown—was a model of correctness. Whatever his private opinions and affiliations, he listened impartially to the opening statements of the two attorneys. Henry's, Alfonso de la Fuente, requested a divorce on the basis that in more than three years (the period required by law) of repeated and determined efforts, and even with "devout prayers"[1] and all kinds of other "remedies,"[2] Henry had never achieved "*cópula carnal*" with the Princess. He added that this failure was undoubtedly the result of some supernatural "*spell*" or "*legamiento,*" since Henry was not similarly incapacitated—a vital point—with other women. Blanca's attorney did not contest. On the contrary, he corroborated everything De la Fuente claimed, both about the futile attempts and the existence of a *legamiento,* and also asked for a separation.

Much ill-informed and condescending laughter has been directed at this matter of the "hex" or "spell" to which Henry's impotence with Blanca was attributed. How childish of the petitioners! we are told. How droll (or how dishonest) of the Bishop to lend himself to such a transparent device. Not so. The age was full of daemons: hands reached out of heaven, spirits barked or neighed or swam. The mind of medieval men was profoundly pictorial, ineradicably symbolic. And who shall say that they were wrong? Perhaps they were only seeking concrete identification for strange states and forces which we call differently, call more abstractly, now: escape mechanisms, traumas, psychological blocks. The whole matter is one of terminology. The only thing remarkable about it is that a mind as basically modern as Henry's should have fallen in, on this occasion, with a medieval practice—or that the Bishop, who was surely under pressure for a decision which would be both speedy and favorable to Henry, should have done so conscientious a job.

For he was nothing if not thorough, once he had heard the original pleas. To avoid any "fraud or collusion" by the attorneys, he required them to give a solemn oath that they were acting in good faith, that to the best of their knowledge all they said was true. Then he dismissed them and sent for the principals themselves. Henry, questioned apart and apparently with considerable closeness, swore "by his estate and royal lineage" that the facts were as represented: total effort and "operation" on his part, and total failure; he bore down heavily on the claim that no malefic influence similarly impeded him in his relations with other women. Blanca, in her sad turn, took an oath "upon God and the Cross" (a detail interestingly omitted in the case of Henry) to the truth of the statements—and added, when pressed by the Bishop on an important aspect, that she had never offered the slightest *"estorbo"* or hindrance to the marital act. By way of bolstering the procedure and observing a further legal nicety, he also asked for character witnesses, people who could attest to their veracity, from both the Prince and the Princess. Henry sent him "seven notable persons," high clerics of the realm and officials of the royal household. Blanca—"since she had no kinsmen in these lands," touching note in a dry bag of legal bones —was obliged to offer her chaplain and confessor and "some other honest gentlemen."

All fair, all proper. Yet in a question of such gravity it was not enough. The crux of the matter was of course whether the Princess had been deflowered. Many oaths were already taken to the effect that she had not. But in a sense all that was mere allegation. The law needed facts. And there was, in the end, only one possible way to obtain clear and convincing proof: a physical examination of Blanca. For that purpose, the Bishop appointed a pair of "honorable ladies, decent and of high standing and conscience, married matrons expert *in ópere nuptiali"* to wait upon her. Blanca, who one would think had already suffered enough, went through the humiliating exploration. The matrons' pronouncement: she was still virgin, "whole as the day she was born."

It seemed to be sufficient. Acuña could have signed an annulment then and there: proof that there had been no intercourse was all that was needed either in civil or in canon law. But—to the despair of historians—he did not stop with that. A final doubt assailed him. Two constant claims had been presented: that Blanca was a virgin, and that Henry was potent with other women. Of the first, he had obtained clear physical proof. Now, to be scrupulously fair and unassailably thorough, should he not seek physical proof of the second? Would not such proof, if it could be found, add conclusive weight to the theory of a spell, a *legamiento?* Yet how to go about it? A sexual examination of the male offered certain problems, in fact was on all counts less practicable than that of the female. But at last Acuña thought of a possible solution. There was a rumor— which surely the object of it at least did nothing to silence—that Henry sometimes visited the brothels of Segovia. Might it not be wise to seek information in those establishments? A new call went out to a confidential agent, now a man, a priest, a colleague.

There is something unattractive, even repulsive, about the picture of this "good, chaste, honorable, ecclesiastical person" (he has had the luck to remain anonymous) slipping off to the stews for enlightenment on the sexual habits of the son of his King. But the age was not squeamish or noted for delicacy of sentiment, and he went and came back with a report. The tough *filles de joie* whom he consulted had not minced matters. They seem to have responded with alacrity, almost with relish, and while the crudeness of their language makes direct quotation inadvisable, one perhaps needs only say that it left no doubts whatsoever as to the frequency or completeness of Henry's demonstrations of sexual prowess among them.

What are we to think of this vivid and uncompromising statement about his virility—buried for centuries in the bill of divorcement itself? Is it true? Or was it a bald lie, bought from accommodating harlots by Henry's agents both to save his face and to add plausibility to the new marriage with Juana of Portugal which was already being arranged? Scholars who have written since the document became available are in complete disaccord. Sitges, Henry's first modern defender, takes it for full disproof of the long tradition of his impotence. Orestes Ferrara, in his contentious book on the subject, entirely agrees. Others are either scornful or dubious. Marañón, Spain's great scholar-physician, casts a wary eye upon women who, if they would sell their bodies, would probably sell anything —yet comes to his famous conclusion (alas, none too helpful) that although Henry was basically an *"auténtico e indudable eunocoide"*[3] he might still, upon occasion and with effort, have been sporadically capable of the full sexual act. The general reader may feel that they are all straining at a gnat. Not so, again. The issue is one of the highest importance in any book upon the period: if the statement of the prostitutes is true, then the whole thesis of Henry's impotence falls apart, and much of subsequent Spanish history—especially Isabel the Catholic's right to the throne—must, as the reader will become increasingly aware, be re-examined, be examined in an entirely new and rather chilly light.

Our trend, like Marañón's, is one of grave reservation. It is certainly true that Henry felt most at ease in low company; these women are the counterpart of the rough or humble men he made his intimates, and it is quite possible that with them he found himself less inhibited, less frozen, than with his aristocratic wife. But two facts, usually ignored in their bearing upon the issue, jar violently against the prostitutes' assertion.

The first of them is that we have, by chance, a clinical description of Henry's genitals. It was left by a German visitor, Hieronymus Münzer (these accounts by foreigners who had no stakes in the local squabbles are of utmost value), and although customarily printed in the original Latin it had best, in this instance, be set down plainly: "His penis was thin and weak at the base, but huge at the head, with the result that he could not have an erection."[4] One cannot deny that this was written twenty years after Henry's death, and at the court of Isabel and Fernando, a place where the stories of Henry's impotence had taken firm hold and it was to everyone's advantage to foster the belief in his abnormality. Yet it does have a convincing ring. Münzer was a physician, a distinguished one, a graduate of the University of Pavia; surely he engaged in professional talk with his Spanish colleagues, just as there were surely some of them still alive who had either attended Henry or known the morphological facts of the case.

And the second piece of contradicting evidence, too, comes from a doctor. Years later, when the full scandal had broken over Henry, he sought confirmation of his masculinity from Juan Fernández, who had been one of his household physicians from the time he was born. Fernández obliged with the information that Henry at the age of twelve had suffered some sort of accident (*"ocasión"*[5]—the word is maddeningly vague) which disabled him for intercourse in his marriage with Blanca, but from which he in later years recovered. Writers set on making Henry the father of his second wife's child have seized upon this statement with such joy that they have entirely overlooked its corollary: if Henry was sexually disabled for the duration of his marriage with Blanca—and the language makes Fernandez's assertion quite clear that he recovered only afterward, *"después"*[6]—then the claim of the prostitutes obviously will not stand.

In sum, with Blanca proved a virgin and Henry's exploits in the brothels at least under heavy doubt, the case for his virility even now looks rather frail. But let us be just, let us try to be thorough, let us emulate the good Bishop. A final consideration, a very large consideration, is dictated by common sense—that voice so often drowned out in the cannonades of academic debate. Henry was seeking a new wife. If he knew that he was impotent, then why this second match? The question cries out for answer. And only one affords itself. Although the evidence indicates strongly that at twenty-eight Henry had not proved himself a man, it shows as well that he had not yet given up. Surely he still had hopes, still felt that perhaps under different circumstances and stimulations he could conquer his obstruction and thus get rid of that grinding sense of failure and abnormality which we see so clearly—and which he may have dimly sensed—as the chief root of all his shames and insecurities. No other hypothesis will explain so much: the tension and anxiety with which we shall watch him approach his second marriage bed, the ultimate (and surely reluctant) decision of a kind man to repudiate a wife who had never done him any harm, his acceptance of the onerous conditions laid down for the marriage with Juana by her brother Alfonso of Portugal.

For it may also have occurred to the reader to wonder just where Alfonso stood in this whole matter. What did he know of Henry's private life? Probably, almost inevitably, a great deal. The extent to which Henry's sexual gaps and tangents were general knowledge by 1453 is a moot point, although it is difficult not to agree with most of the annalists that even then he was all too familiar with the suppressed sneers of courtiers and the invitations and obscene gestures of ambitious boys in the streets: what passes off more or less unnoticed at fifteen is not so easy to conceal when one is approaching thirty. But at royal levels his incapacity at least with Blanca could hardly be hidden, and certainly Alfonso was aware of it. He was nephew by blood to Juan of Aragón and by marriage to the King of Castile, and thus first cousin to both Henry and Blanca. Carrillo, as Primate, had to review Acuña's decree, and anything known by the tactless and garrulous Archbishop was known to everyone in high circles sooner or later. Why, then, did he countenance the match for his sister? Palencia has something to offer on the subject: "Don Alfonso . . . nonetheless, easily persuaded himself that this farce of a marriage could enlarge his territory, instead of reflecting that what it more probably would bring was nothing but misfortune . . . and when he thought the moment was ripe it is said that with much impatience he required his sister to state whether she would accept a barren marriage and be content with the mere name of Queen—and that she responded, among other answers, that she would rather have such title in a great realm than children with another husband."[7]

This seems a little too brutal, even for Palencia. Yet it is true, documentally true, that Alfonso took a strong and cautious hand in all the matrimonial negotiations. A sense of having the suitor at disadvantage hangs over the contracts, mingled with a vague fear of some sort of *desaire* or embarrassment to the Portuguese House and a determination to come off well rewarded financially, anyway, if things went wrong. Juana, he stipulated, must go with no dowry. Before even the preliminary agreements were signed, Henry had to make her an outright gift of one hundred thousand gold florins, unreturnable under whatever circumstance and payable in cash (Juana's attorney went to Medina del Campo to see the money counted out and safely delivered "in three big canvas bags");[8] this donation by Henry has looked, to many, suspiciously like a bribe. The groom had also to give her a wedding present of twenty thousand more florins, "which will stay with the said *señora Infanta* in any case, whether children are born to them or not."[9] Olmedo was to be turned over to her, and an annual allowance of a million and a half *maravedís* on Crown revenues provided. Hard terms indeed, and they create an almost irresistible impression of polite blackmail. But Henry accepted them all, "content with the lady only."[10]

Acuña had signed the divorce, "having God before his eyes."[11] Blanca, the inevitable sacrifice, went off to Aragón and to fresh martyrdom at the hands of her foiled and angry father. Capitulations with Portugal were signed. The way at last seemed clear for the new marriage, for Henry to press forward to the critical experiment. Yet the knowledge which he sought was still withheld: the wedding, after all, had to be postponed. For other events, enormous events, thrust in—thrust everything else, even the Portuguese alliance, temporarily aside.

We are told by Chacón that from the day of Luna's execution the courtiers of the Castilian King had often come upon him weeping, "in bitterness for the death of his loyal Master."[12] It seems more likely that the feeble monarch's swift decay sprang from a cause less noble than the "gnawing worm of conscience"[13] to which Chacón attributes it. Luna had braked his appetites—especially those lustful twinings with his second wife which seemed so harmful, so inappropriate, to a man of his age and constitution. The watchful eye removed, he went back to them—"daily delivered," says Palencia, "to the embraces of a young and beautiful bride."[14] One outcome of this indulgence was the birth, on December 17, 1453, of little Isabel's brother Alfonso, a new piece on the political chessboard. Another, apparently, was the final collapse of the sovereign's health. Whatever the reasons, he came already *"mal dispuesto"*[15] from Escalona, where he had appropriated the dead favorite's castle. He continued to feel ill as the court moved north through Avila, through Medina del Campo. At Valladolid, which they reached the first week in June, he grew steadily worse. The middle of July he took to his bed. It was clear that he was dying; Henry was hastily summoned from Segovia. And on July 22, 1454, in the palace behind the Monastery of San Pablo, the sorry life of Juan II of Castile came to an end.

Henry was King. The immense responsibilities which he so dreaded and disliked, which he knew himself so poorly equipped to handle, were full upon him.

❀

Part Two:
1454–1465

8.

Southern Games

Henry's own twenty-year reign has been traditionally divided into two contrasting decades—one of power and eminence, the other of disgrace. But the juxtaposition is much too pat. What candid eye will fail to perceive that his first ten years as King were as fraught with perils and failures, in kind if not in degree, as the *via crucis* of his second? He came to the crown already hobbled and marked: suspect himself, the Throne exposed and quaking with Luna gone, relentless foes inside the realm and out. It is true that mighty men curried his favor in the first half of the reign—monarchs, dukes regnant, popes; we shall even see him offered a foreign diadem. But only the most naïve can think that such tributes were sincere or disinterested, that the bouquets were not poisoned, that these advances were not, in most of the cases, dark political gambits of their own, gauged to enmesh him and to bring him down. The dice were loaded against him from the start. Indeed, the suspense of Henry's story springs not so much from whether he would win out over his enemies (given himself, given them, how could he hope to succeed?) as from the particularly subtle and vicious way in which he was destroyed. And the seeds of his ruin were already planted, even astir, that summer morning of 1454 in Valladolid when his father died.

Nevertheless, his proclamation as King was sufficiently splendid (not since the twelfth century had sovereigns of Castile been formally crowned), and for once in his life Henry comes before us almost with *élan*, with dash. As soon as the dead monarch's body had been deposited before the altar of San Pablo, a brilliant procession formed. All of Henry's retinue took part in it, and all the heralds and trumpets then attendant on the court. He rode himself at its front, accompanied by a king of arms dressed in the royal tabard and crying, at intervals, "Castile! Castile for King Henry!"[1] People and tapestries hung from the windows; curiosity, if nothing else, would have brought a crowd to look at this man who had kept himself so hidden from the public eye. Throughout the ancient city the cavalcade wound: past the great house of the Admiral (that one, significantly, empty), past the churches of San Miguel and San Benito and the two Santa Marías, through the plaza where Luna's bloody scaffold had stood a year before, on by the Monastery of San Francisco, no doubt up the street of Henry's birthplace, Teresa Gil. Then they went back to the palace, and Henry put on mourning and awaited the arrival of the Grandes.

They came, perforce: down from their sun-baked castles, across the glittering plains. They knelt and did him homage, God knows with what private thoughts. On this occasion, at least, Henry could not withhold his hand from kissing. Nor could he, by his kindly nature, refuse the terrified pleas of the dead King's retainers; beset by the usual visions of personal disaster, they crowded around him and begged not to lose their posts. Let them not worry, Henry reassured them; they could join the new household, there was room for all. Of course, in the higher echelons, a few changes did have to be made. Ruy Díaz de Mendoza had long been the royal *mayordomo mayor*, and Villena despised and feared the powerful Mendozas: suddenly Ruy Díaz found himself in the street and Villena possessed of his important office. Arias, too, saw an opening. Why should he not be rewarded? Why, in fact, should he not be made a *contador mayor?* There were, to be sure, already two of those financial dignitaries, the number prescribed by custom. But a lapse here and there might pass ignored in the current excitement. Why be conventional, anyway? Henry, approached from such angle, was never hard to persuade; from that time dates the triple *contaduría mayor* in the Spanish Crown.

Accord in the court, in the kingdom—at least for the moment. And the new sense of peace, of well-being, must be pushed out beyond the frontiers. Portugal: the coming marriage would take care of that. France: ambassadors went north to reaffirm the Franco-Castilian alliance which had stood for almost a century—the Trastámaras had come to power in the first place through French aid. Aragón: Alfonso the Magnanimous was the only one of Henry's uncles who had ever been able to abide him, and the envoys who sailed off to Naples were ornately received and assured of friendship and sent home provided with a *"scriptura"* of peace in which the name of Henry, as "trunk" of the whole "royal line of the Goths of Spain,"[2] was graciously allowed to go first. But Alfonso, everyone knew, was only a figurehead in Aragón. The real power there, as in Navarre, belonged to Juan himself. And Juan was a very different matter from his easy-going brother; the tendrils of his discontent clung far too fast to be swept aside by ambassadorial flourishes.

Yet even in the vexing issue of Juan, a solution was thought up. The heart of his rancor against Castile—or so it was felt—lay in his lost properties. And Henry, with his accession, was enormously rich: from the paternal inheritance now added to the maternal, from the reincorporation to the Crown of Luna's treasure, from the vast rents of the masterships of Santiago and Alcántara, both vacant then and in the Throne's administration. Perhaps some of that wealth could be put to immediate use; perhaps, with a monarch so impoverished as Juan, cash could do more than compliments. In sum, perhaps his sequestered Castilian holdings could be officially bought.

They could be, and were (at least on paper; the money, as we shall see, was never paid). A treaty blithely called of "perpetual peace and friendship"[3] between Juan and Henry was signed early in October at Agreda, up near their common border. For an annual payment of three and a half million *maravedís*, Juan renounced all claim to his family possessions in Castile. A half million was to go to the son of the dead Infante Henry, and for a similar amount Juan's bastard Alfonso gave up his pretensions to the title of Master of Calatrava, which he had stubbornly been trying to regain ever since Villena contrived to get it snatched away from him and bestowed on Pedro Girón. But Juan, still spinning long and devious strands, slipped in a condition: pardon of the Castilian Admiral don Fadrique Enríquez from his sentence of banishment and the restitution of his lands.

Henry should of course never have allowed the Admiral to return to Castile: his family had been inflicting trouble on the Crown for generations, he had stood with the rebels at Olmedo, the fact that he was now Juan's father-in-law left little doubt as to where his interests lay. To Henry's credit, there is evidence that he at first opposed this stipulation. But he was eager to make a favorable impression, to ingratiate himself with his new subjects as widely as possible (the Admiral was related to half of Castile), and he soon

gave his consent. A similar desire to please, to irradiate good will
and clemency, led him to two more pardons which were to prove
almost as calamitous. Diego Manrique, Count of Treviño, was
released from imprisonment—and we have seen that the whole
Manrique family was unalterably hostile to the Crown. Freed, too,
at the persuasion of his close Mendozan kinsman Santillana, was the
Count of Alba, still in custody at Segovia for his plots against the
dead sovereign. But in Alba's case there was a cogent reason: his
military experience along the Moorish frontier. For Henry—crest
of the wave—had decided to renew the war upon Granada.

Why so confirmed a pacifist as Henry should have chosen to open
his reign with a martial move seems to call for explanations—and
they have never been lacking. Palencia throws the decision onto
Villena: a scheme to distract public attention from his own chi-
canery at home. The role of Arias, as well, has not been overlooked.
That mercenary mind was quick to point out how pleased the Pope
would be—alarmed as he was by the fall of Constantinople the year
before and the general indifference of Europe to the infidel menace
—and how the money raised through papal cooperation need not all
be spent on the war (Calixtus's Bulls of Crusade ultimately brought
in more than a million ducats; even young Isabel, packed off soon
after the accession with her widowed and embittered mother to live
at Arévalo, scraped up the price of an indulgence—two hundred
maravedís, about a dollar). For those who find such explanations too
cynical, there are others. Henry, for all his lack of interest in politics, well knew the menace of the nobles, and perhaps a good way
to forestall any thrusts on their part would be to unite the nation
again in the ancient cause of the Reconquest—not for two centuries,
not since the fall of western Andalucía to San Fernando, had any
real inroads been made on the Moorish realm. Or perhaps, once
more, his motives were more private; perhaps by stepping forward
as leader of the Holy War he hoped to remove some of the tarnish
which already touched his name.

Explain it as one will, he announced his startling intention to the
Cortes of Cuéllar, the first of the reign. The reaction of the cities,
which were to be called upon for sixty-one millions, we are not told.
But the barons were openly delighted. For centuries the great families had swelled and battened on Moslem conquests, and now all at

once bright visions of new spoils began to crowd their heads. There was, it is true, a slight edge of skepticism in the answering speech of the Marqués of Santillana, entrusted with their response. Almost as if he sensed what was coming, he warned Henry that "so arduous a business" as war upon Granada must be undertaken with seriousness and vigor, and no "lightness" or "laziness"[4] allowed to creep in. But Santillana was a poet, a phrasemaker, notoriously fond of the sound of his own voice; his jarring note was forgotten. A spring rendezvous was set for Córdoba, and the Cortes rose in an atmosphere of exhilaration. The nobles departed to ride about their rocky domains and gather their *mesnadas*. Henry was even able to be back in Segovia for Christmas with Lucas and the grooms and wrestlers and his thirtieth birthday early in January.

But it was a busy winter for him. Final arrangements about the Portuguese marriage had to be made; to speed things up and save distances, it was agreed that Juana should come to him while he was on campaign in the south. Regents during his absence were appointed—the Count of Haro and the Archbishop of Toledo, Alonso Carrillo; Henry told them to take such care of matters that he would not be followed, be hounded and "distressed,"[5] by the administrative affairs from which Castillo tells us plainly he always "fled."[6] And in the midst of all his activity Alica—the son of that fallen and exiled King of Granada, Ariza, whom Henry fancied to be his vassal —arrived at Segovia for a visit. Moreover, the dusky Prince came with a retinue of almost four hundred. Of course Henry for years had kept a large Moorish bodyguard, those "flatterers and ruffians"[7] and specialists in abnormal Eastern vices who had already caused so much resentment and gossip. But he welcomed the new contingent and took it into his household and ordered that they be provided with silks, fine woolens, good gold Castilian *doblas*, and whatever else they wanted. Strange preparation, one observes, for a war upon Moslems. Yet everything about it was to be strange.

Henry set out for Granada late in March of 1455 with his ill-assorted train. They rode fast: over the snow-packed Guadarramas, across New Castile and La Mancha, down to the bursting southern spring. The nobles were waiting impatiently in Córdoba. They joined forces and marched east. Unopposed, they entered the Moorish kingdom between Alcalá la Real and Moclín. They pushed on past Pinos Puente and into Granada's broad green Vega. There, in sight of the capital itself, they at last drew up.

The numbers of this army are variously estimated. Palencia sets the total at twenty thousand, Castillo at forty thousand; other sources range in between. On the cavalry there is general agreement —some ten thousand. The trouble seems to be with the peonage, the infantry,[8] raised chiefly, and no doubt fluidly, from the southern towns. But perhaps all that needs really concern us is one clear and startling fact: the size of the forces, whatever it may have been, was entirely out of proportion with the result. For it at once became apparent that Henry meant to do little against the enemy, or nothing at all.

See, with the astounded army, his curious behavior. He sat for four whole days there in the Granadine Vega—"more as if to admire the city than to attack it,"[9] muses Palencia. And indeed it must have been a ravishing sight to him, to that artist's soul shut up and mangled in his coarse and clumsy body: the heaven-hung Arabian eyrie, the dream of pink towers, the rose garland dropped on the slope of the glistening mountain. Like Segovia, in a way: like a warmer and softer Segovia. It was far too beautiful to destroy, even to touch. When the Moors came out in array, he allowed no sword to be drawn, no battle to be loosed. Why not? his bewildered captains asked him; that was what they had come for. Leave be, he answered quietly: life was so precious, "it could not be bought or retrieved,"[10] to expose it to danger was a terrible thing. But the nobles could not be curbed; with or without consent they must have some sort of action, the pressure must be relieved. They went off on their own in the environs, to engage the foe. And although they lost few in these skirmishes, Henry was nonetheless angry. Well then, they replied in despair, let them at least get on with the *tala* —the traditional destruction of the crops. But even in the *tala* Henry proved difficult. Only the grain could be ravaged, he commanded. All trees (his lifelong love of trees!) must be respected— particularly the olives, which were so slow to fruit: whoever cut one down would have his own ears lopped off. The whole of Granada would someday be his, he added cryptically; so why lay it waste?

Odd tactics for a war. Odd man, to prize Moslem olives more than Catholic ears. And what was, in effect, Henry's real intention in these Granadine campaigns? The question is much debated. Castillo sets down his version: "to harry the land for three years and put them in great hunger, then to lay siege and be at them until he took them."[11] Many have found Castillo convincing; a modern authority goes so far as to call the entire operation conceived in a "logical" manner, as a "slow battle of attrition."[12] Yet this fits but poorly with Henry's promise to the Cortes of Cuéllar to "destroy the enemies who persecute our Faith," to "give battle to the Moors who usurp our territory," and then to "return with honor."[13] Palencia goes to the other extreme; he insists that the Moors were hopelessly divided, that they already suffered from hunger and problems of supply, that Henry could easily have overthrown them had he really gone about it. Cooler minds have reasoned that if it took Isabel and Fernando ten years to conquer Granada, with Spain united and the barons tamed, then Henry can hardly be expected to have done it overnight. But with that, one is back where one started. If the job was impossible, and known to be impossible, why did he use such unequivocal language about being able to bring it off?

Be all that as it may, the nobles were furious. They had polished their armor and honed their lances and readied their battle-axes—and for what? To sit idly about in fields of asphodel and be forbidden to attack, there with the enemy right in front of them? They had been to enormous expense; they had brought themselves and their armies half across the Peninsula. Where was to be their reward? The visions of booty faded. They caviled, complained, argued with their *roi fainéant*—to no avail. If Henry really had some plan of slow "attrition" and economic warfare, it was quite beyond their comprehension. Nor were the rank and file hard to arouse, to disaffect: they had been obliged to bring their own provisions—and probably had skimped, with an eye upon the *tala*. The grumblings gathered and swelled. All sorts of ugly rumors began to spread through the camp. Henry had never intended to fight. He had led them there only to ruin and humiliate them. He was even—oh worst and ugliest of all—in secret league with the Moslems, their ancient and unalterable foe.

Unalterable: yes. Historians make far too much of the friendly relations, the peaceful coexistence, of Moslems and Spaniards in the Middle Ages. It is true that many Moors lived among Christians and many Christians among Moors, and that with hundreds of years of being thrown together in the same peninsula there was bound to be a certain rubbing off of arts, business methods, language. But this is, in the end, superficial. Familiarity hardly means approval, and it is even truer that under the surface accommodations a black hatred, a congenital fear and resentment, ran. How could it fail to be so—between stubborn patriots, colliding and uncompromising faiths? From time beyond memory, brown babies in Moorish cradles had been scared out of their wits by threats of hairy blond giants swooping down from the north with icicles in their beards to gobble them up. Generations of Castilian warriors had ridden home from their conquests with bagfuls of Moorish heads which they tossed to the boys in the villages for playthings. Cross and Crescent, North and South, white and dark: the world does not greatly change, and this particular bad blood had been running for seven centuries.

Placed against such a context, Henry's fondness for everything Moslem stands in jagged relief. And there can be no question about that fondness. He sat on the floor (so did most, in a chairless age—but never a king). We do not need Palencia to tell us that he took his meals "reclining":[14] a foreign visitor, Tetzel, recorded that "he eats and drinks"[15] in the heathen manner. We have often seen him riding *a la jineta*, and accompanied by the Moslem guard which was now an anomaly indeed. His penchant for Moorish clothing is common knowledge; he even had himself depicted wearing a turban for the great frieze of portraits of kings in the Alcázar at Segovia. San Fernando, admittedly, appeared there in the same attire. But San Fernando stood on the opposite wall from Pelayo, and since the frieze ran all around the room Henry, as latest of the sovereigns, wound up next to that first of them, that mighty victor of Covadonga—a contrast most viewers considered unfortunate to a degree. Besides, with Henry the matter clearly went deeper than costume or table manners. Villena once said that royal influence had been put on both him and his brother Girón to embrace the faith of Islam. This was probably a lie: Villena made the accusation in a moment when he was particulary agitated and hard pressed. But like most slanders, it may have had its grain of truth. Many aspects of Mohammedanism could hardly have failed to appeal to someone like Henry; his lethargic and passive nature was perhaps not ideally suited to the rigors, the sterner mandates, of the Catholic faith.

Palencia hammers incessantly at his "hate for all Christian cults"[16] and brands him again and again *"aficionado a la secta de Mahoma. "*[17] Tetzel himself (once more, an impartial source) says that he was "an enemy of Christians"[18] and adds to the list of Henry's infidel habits the baffling statement that he even prayed like one: *"und betet alls auf den heidnischen sitten. "*[19] All this is not to suggest that Henry was a practicing Moslem. But we would do well to realize that his religion was almost as doubtful as his sex, to take into large account these flirtations with Islam—especially at such a time. What had been merely impolitic at home became, in the field against Granada, an outrage, an open scandal.

It was, therefore, both as Christians and as knights that the nobles were wounded by Henry's conduct of the war. And the same sort of thing continued, grew even worse, as the campaign went on. The march upon the capital having come to nothing, the host turned westward. Camped outside Antequera, where Juan's father Fernando of Aragón had won his famous victory over the Moors, even Henry knew that some commemorative show of force was called for. He would take Archidona, he promised; they could scale its walls by darkness. But for some reason he was slow in arriving, the tepid Andalusian dawn had already broken, the plan had to be abandoned; instead, Henry went off into the forest to search for "certain swine and deer."[20] They moved on south toward Málaga, the second city of the Moorish realm. They camped at Alora, in its lovely valley between two streams. They camped four miles from Málaga, then only two.

But again in the sight of a tempting prize, the army again found itself leashed: in the Moors' own internecine troubles, Málaga was for the moment loyal to Ariza, and Henry felt any damage to lands leagued with his official vassal quite out of the question. Some of the noble captains did, once more, slip off; they pillaged and burned Pupiana, an act "which much annoyed the King."[21] Chiefly, however, they were obliged to sit in their tents and stare at their weapons while Henry fraternized. For it developed that Ariza was actually in residence in the city. First he sent presents to Henry: fowl, figs, raisins, butter (it was rumored throughout the camp that at the bottoms of the baskets, under the dewy leaves, lay gifts of a harder and shinier nature—bribes). Then he decided to come himself, to visit his son, who was still in Henry's train. Soon enough Ariza would turn traitor, but Henry suspected nothing and received him graciously; he would not even allow him to uncover, to throw back his white burnoose, for the salutation. They got on so well at dinner that Ariza was invited, with his retinue, to stay the night. Unwise enough, if well intentioned. But in time—again before Granada itself—this same sort of unseemly dalliance led to a near disaster. Henry had found a summerhouse in the Vega which caught his fancy; he commandeered it and ate in its garden, with Lucas, every day. The King of Granada, knowing their tastes, sent out his *"menes-triles"*[22] to distract them, to lull them. And there, while they sat chained a long summer afternoon by the wailing music and the slim-hipped dancing, the picked band of Moslem marauders broke in upon them. They came within an eyelash of taking Henry—and of course for the King to be captured would have meant the instant termination of the war.

Such a state of affairs could clearly not go on. The atmosphere was too tense, the army's resentment and disappointment were building too high. And suddenly, ominously, the first faint thunder spoke: the barons decided to act.

The whole of this initial conspiracy against Henry is vague, oblique. And perhaps it had to be so. The nobles were still far from organized or confident; the dreadful lessons of Olmedo and Luna's execution were much too fresh in their minds. Moreover, as yet they had no real platform to put forward, no *point d'appui*. Unready to strike on their own, they looked about for a cover—and fixed upon their sons. Many of those new scions of the ancient families had come along on the expedition, "eager to do doughty deeds"[23] and "to emulate the olden knighthood."[24] Might not their muscular young idealism be put to use, be flexed to rebellion? If a plot came off well, the Grandes could take the credit themselves. If it came off badly, they could always throw the blame on juvenile high spirits.

It may seem a bit unfair to have put the lads in the middle. But it was certainly canny: to such marksmen, Henry offered a perfect target. And the choice of ringleader—Pedro de Velasco, the son of the Count of Haro—was little short of inspired: his father, back in Valladolid as regent, could reach out no restraining hand. Young Velasco proved easily inflamed. He gathered his friends in a secret conclave and took the floor. "What species of madness," he asked them, "could bring us to honor, to obey, a man so steeped since childhood in unspeakable vices, a man who not only dares to relax the warlike discipline of our noble forebears but even in his dressing and riding and eating—to say nothing of his hidden and filthier sins —prefers Moorish customs to those of our Christian religion, of which"—the adolescent syntax here grows somewhat garbled—"he displays not the slightest trace, but rather all manner of crimes against honor, to the shame of the Church, the vituperation of his own name, the disgust of his subjects, and the perversion of all mankind?"[25]

How many of the older magnates attended this rally we do not know—apparently Alba (so much for Henry's generosity in releasing him from prison), probably Girón and Rodrigo Manrique, Count of Paredes. It is not even clear what they finally decided to do. To take Henry and force him to their martial wishes? Palencia's statement that they actually planned to kill what young Velasco had raved on to call the "execrable monster"[26] seems a little unrealistic: things had not yet come, would be long in coming, to that. Whatever it was, the entire affair fell through, this first small fruit of revolt failed to mature: on the day set for the plot, Henry was somewhere else. Even when he did learn of it, shortly after, he forgave everybody concerned—both young and old. Perhaps at the time it all struck him as being faintly foolish. Or perhaps he was too distracted by a fresh development. For suddenly word arrived which drove everything else from his mind, word which broke off the campaign at once and headed the court and army back toward Córdoba.

Juana had left Lisbon. The new bride who meant so much, who might prove so much, was on her way.

9.

New Faces

The Portuguese escort brought their Infanta as far as Badajoz, just across the border. There she was taken in charge by Medina Sidonia, whom Henry sent to meet her. The great southern Duke—he had now reached that eminence, only the second Castilian not of royal blood to achieve it—led her slowly, detained her with the lavish festivities of which she was reported to be so fond. Henry, during the progress, rode rapidly up. Near Posadas, twenty miles from Córdoba on the Guadalquivir, the two groups almost converged. There Henry reined in. But he could not rein his curiosity. Disguised, and with four companions, he broke away and galloped on. He found the pretty procession: Juana upon a palfrey, sixteen, beautiful (for all the rocks slung at her, no one has questioned that), dark with the darkness that ran through the House of Aviz, and surrounded by her twelve young Portuguese maids of honor—inappropriate phrase. But he did not join it. He hovered along beside and at a distance—conjecturing, hoping, peering between tamarisks as they all rode down the muddy wide river to their horrible destiny.

This roadside espial is perhaps not quite the example of nervous voyeurism which some have found it. Such royal inspection of arriving brides was frequent, was little short of a tradition, in the Middle Ages. But there was tension enough in the actual meeting a few hours later. Juana put up in Posadas; so did Henry, and decided to make an official call, to reveal himself. Yet even then he went more as to an execution than toward a lovers' encounter. "His look was not one of fiestas,"[1] Palencia tells us, and Palencia, who was already Henry's Latin Secretary, may well have been there or had an immediate account. He seems to have taken pains to wear his drabbest clothes. His blond hair—his one good feature—he concealed under a tight *bonete*, which he pulled far down on his brow.

He set out almost muffled, in a heavy black cape. "Perspicacious portrait," says Marañón about this famous description, of "sexual timidity"[2] on the eve of marriage. Of the interview itself we have no report at all. Sitges, determined to prove Henry's masculinity at any cost, suggests that they may have mated then and there. A hail of ridicule has beaten upon this unlucky remark since the day when it first saw print. And it does seem wildly astray: Henry was scarcely the person to ignite at first touch. All we do know for a fact is that he arrived around midnight and stayed four hours, and that afterward he went off on a long ride, as he always did to relieve his pressures.

That is no place to observe them—the squalid hot village in the middle of the night. We can see them better in the formal welcome at Córdoba. Henry had hurried ahead to arrange the reception, and Juana rode in on the 20th of May. When he learned she had passed the gate, he went down to the door of the palace. Flanked by the French ambassadors (they had come to acknowledge his own, to sign the new treaty of friendship), he stood and waited. Juana rounded the corner, trotted up and dismounted. He went to meet her; he summoned his courage and kissed her upon the cheek. As they turned to face the public, there in the merciless eye of the Cordobese sun, he reached down and took her hand.

We, too, might try to be kind to Juana of Portugal. She has suffered much from the moralists. Her sins—and we shall not deny them—changed the whole course of Spain. But let reason, if not sweet charity, assess the cruel position where she—where the couple—was thrown. She had no depths, no extensions, no acuities; small chance, in fact none at all, of her unraveling anyone so intricate as Henry. What could she possibly have made of the big ugly man with the teeth like organ keys and the smashed nose who was supposed to be her companion for the rest of her life? One looks in vain for a single trait they had in common. She was dainty and fastidious and finicky—he sloppy and seldom clean. She bought perfume by the jugful; he relished (strange trait even for him) all manner of nauseous smells: rot, burning leather, horse hooves, "and others still more foul."[3] If she was party-mad and obsessed with finery, he had the social and sartorial instincts of a troglodyte. His defects—his taciturnity, his indecision, his lack of self-confidence—must have driven her frantic. His virtues—his modesty, his tolerance, his patience—were precisely the sort which a frivolous young girl could be least expected to esteem. It was, in short, and from the very beginning, the kind of hopeless mismatch of age, habit, and character which only one thing can hold together: the bond of passion.

And what about that?

A Spanish marriage, especially a royal one, comes by slow stages. The contracts themselves had taken almost two years to put into shape. The *esponsales*, the wedding by proxy, were performed in Lisbon, with Fernán López de la Orden standing for Henry: lying, rather, for the two, according to custom, had to be stretched out together on a bed. And even with Juana in Córdoba, there still were frustrating delays. The *desposorios*—the civil union and joint signing of contracts, from which there could be no drawing back—took place the night of Juana's arrival. Palencia and Valera say that the Archbishop of Tours, head of the French delegation, officiated at this ceremony; Castillo has it Alonso de Fonseca, the flighty Archbishop of Sevilla. Palencia goes on to claim that no papal waiving of consanguinity had been obtained (the *novios* were first cousins, children of sisters). Both points, at the climax of our story, will be of the utmost importance. But for the moment let us press on, like Henry, to the heart of the matter. Three days later the Nuptial Mass was said privately in the palace. This time there can be little doubt about the celebrant—Alonso de Peleas, Bishop Elect of Mondoñedo, whom we shall also meet again in his due turn. They went from that to a public High Mass in the cathedral. Then they returned to the palace for the banquet. Henry, wound to his highest pitch of anxiety, dined on a dais with Juana and the ambassadors. Night came. The chamber stood ready. The crucial moment, the great experiment, was at hand.

He had done everything possible. He did, unlike most contemporary sovereigns, go sober to the test; we have seen that he never drank. But the whole hot store of La Celestina was there to fortify him: broth of bull's testicles, salves of the libidinous Italians, powder of porcupine quills. He had even suspended the ancient law about notaries at the bedside. None of that, he decreed; things were difficult enough already. And no traditional showing of sheets, the custom which had brought him such humiliation on his wedding night with Blanca.

Yet all of it was in vain: once more he could do nothing, the full blow fell. "And the King and the Queen slept in the same bed, and the Queen remained intact as she arrived."[4]

Some scholars look askance at this statement of Valera's and refuse to accept the second sexual disaster unless they have documentary proof. They do not find it. One doubts that they ever will: it is hardly the sort of thing to appear in official records. Yet there is abundant evidence of a different—and even more telling—nature. For suddenly, violently, Henry's life goes all askew. Everything about his behavior in the weeks and even months after the wedding in Córdoba reveals a man unstrung, dismembered, almost in a state of shock.

We note the upheaval at once, in the ceremonial visit to Sevilla which he and Juana proceeded to make. When they neared the city and Henry learned of the crowds, the "pomp,"[5] that awaited him at the gate, a panic gripped him. Those new whispers, those winks, those knowing and now irrepressible smirks—he was unable to face it. He broke free from the cavalcade, rode alone cross-country, skirted the walls until he found a postern, and then slipped through it, like the criminal which he probably felt himself, and into the Alcázar unobserved.

But of course this time he could not really flee, however great his suffering, his compulsion to hide. No longer was he a prince, to canter off and nurse his latest wound in quiet Segovia. Now he was King, and he had to come out from those shaded patios of the southern palace and confront the royal blaze. Somehow he got through the Sevillan balls and audiences and tourneys. Somehow he bore the famous barb of Gonzalo de Guzmán: three things, that local wit announced, were of so little worth he would not stoop to pick them from the street—Villena's enunciation, the Archbishop Fonseca's gravity, Henry's virility. He endured Sevilla's relief to see him go, the last feeble spurts of the expiring campaign, the break-up of the army, and the nobles' sullen departure for their lands. And soon he was to have an even crueler humiliation—the open laughter at his brief, vain pose as a don Juan. For scarcely had autumn come and the southern experiment been put aside and the court gone north again to High Castile for the winter when he flung himself upon that odd and desperate course.

Nothing in Henry's whole story is more pitiable—just as nothing could show more clearly a new exacerbation of his nerves—than this strange feint of amorous intrigue on which he now so frantically lashed out; it is pure *cri du coeur.* Yet the setting, at least, was ideal for it—games, gadding, palaver. The Queen and her Portuguese nymphs had turned the court quite upside down. *"Desenvueltas,"*⁶ Castillo calls Juana's attendants; he used the word in its moral sense, but its literal meaning—"unwrapped"—is fully as accurate. They went about with their breasts uncovered—and more, "to below the navel."⁷ They painted their legs and their thighs, for the benefit of the young men who helped them on or from their palfreys. They lay late abed; they primped and sighed and reeled off scented missives. And most of them got what they asked for: in the contracts with Portugal they had all been promised proper husbands, but soon enough they became *mancebas,* lights of love, instead. Ready ripe fruit, why go to the bother of marrying them? The Mendozas, especially, plucked with free hands: Isabel Enríquez went to Santillana, Leonor de Quirós to Pedro Hurtado, Mencia de Castro to Pedro González, already Bishop of Calahorra and on the dizzy rise which would bring him the Cardinal's hat. But one of them nobody dared to touch—Mencia's cousin Guiomar de Castro. Henry had chosen her for his anguished charade.

Guiomar, after the Queen, was the most beautiful of them all. Her beauties of character are less apparent. "A woman of singular presence,"⁸ she was also one of singular shrewdness. Grasping and vain and ambitious, she jumped at Henry's proposal: everything for nothing—what neater, what more convenient? And she made him pay dearly for her connivance. "Soon she was rich,"⁹ Galíndez tells us drily. Money and silks and pearls fell like a Danaë-shower in her unruffled lap. She picked up benefices, glebes, annuities. She trailed around on Henry's arm so encrusted with diamonds, *"tan enjoyada"*¹⁰—so "enjeweled"—that she was a "marvel"¹¹ to behold.

It is painful to see him thus exploited. More painful yet, perhaps, to watch so much effort expended to no result. For the mask, like the misery behind it, is entirely transparent. "Exhibitionism," Marañón diagnoses. "Pseudo-amour. . . . We doctors know how often men's sexual conquests are fakes for public consumption."¹² And few were fooled by it then. Palencia uses almost the same language: false love, this shrill crow with Guiomar, "empty" relations "intended but not achieved."[13] Even Castillo, Henry's official biographer, falls back on a curious phrase. *"Pendencia de amores,"*[14] he calls it gingerly. *Pendencia:* what does it mean? Love "pending"? It might be anything or nothing.

Juana was least fooled of all. She was infuriated, of course. But her anger did not spring from sexual jealousy; none knew better than she how little cause there was for that. What enraged Juana was the affront to her position. For Guiomar grew daily more arrogant, more presumptuous. She gave orders around the palace; she sat in a chair; she ignored the Queen and laughed at her commands. Juana was proud herself, no girl to bear such insults. And finally she exploded. One day at Madrid, in a pet, she refused to attend a bullfight and announced that none of her ladies should go to it either. Guiomar again disobeyed her; she even went up in a "tower"[15] where she could watch—and be watched—in state. Juana seethed in her chamber. But when the carnage in the plaza was ending, her wrath flowed over. She rushed to the tower and waited on the stairs. As Guiomar came down, she fell upon her. Hair flew, nails raked, Juana pulled off a shoe and beat her "on head and shoulders."[16] Henry came as fast as he could. He dragged the two apart; he held Juana back by the arm. "Madam," he shouted, unable to control even his voice, "do you find such conduct seemly?"[17] His big grip was so tight that Juana dropped in a faint. She lay on the floor, unconscious, for an hour.

After that spectacle, Guiomar had to go; there was nothing else for it. But Henry's poor gush of bravado was not yet spent. With Guiomar packed off, he sought another accomplice for his fictitious *"galanteos,"*[18] Catalina de Sandoval. Catalina was just as willing as her predecessor. She proved, however, considerably less astute. In fact, she kept a real lover on the side, a boy from Córdoba. Henry learned about him—after everybody else. It is very nearly inconceivable that he should have had the luckless youth beheaded, yet there it stands in the record: an act entirely counter to his nature, clear witness of disarrangement and of daze. Catalina he made Abbess of San Pedro de las Dueñas, outside Toledo—and thus sent matters reeling from bad to worse. The nuns would not accept her; they were devoted to their own Abbess, doña Marquesa of Guzmán. Troops, in the end, had to break down the doors of the convent and eject doña Marquesa.

So that, too, had blown up in his face. Twice burned, twice made a laughingstock: it was enough. Abruptly Henry dropped the futile disguise (and never went back to it; in all the rest of his life there is not even the mention of another woman's name). Yet the tactic with which he at once replaced it was even more reckless, more indicative of extremity. For now—almost with a shrug, a grimace of despair and defiance— he embarked upon the wholesale elevation to high office of obscure young men.

One should not, of course, ascribe this fateful new move entirely to the fibrillations of a stricken heart. Politics, too, informed it: "The King," Castillo says, "took thought that certain of his lords had schemed against him, and to forestall a like occurrence, to shield his state and live with more security, he fixed his mind on raising creatures of his own to great position."[19] Nor was there, in theory, anything wrong with an attempt to infiltrate and counteract the Grandes by bringing in fresh blood, blood which would have no ties or obligations to the ancient clans; Isabel the Catholic was to use the device triumphantly. What shows the full confusion, the caution thrown to the winds, is the very nearly crazed abandon with which Henry chose his instruments. Isabel selected wisely—*letrados*, lawyers, scholars, the best brains of school and church. But Henry simply lunged out for those he found most at hand—his daily companions. And that, in general, meant the bottom of the barrel.

We already know Miguel Lucas and the sons of Diego Arias. Yet lacking in mass and stature as these three may seem, they are titans compared to others of Henry's "creatures" whom he now began to pitch to many of the loftiest positions of the realm. Young Beltrán de la Cueva, destined to outsoar and outshine them all, will presently appear; for the moment, let him stand waiting at the door. Some of the others are too minor, or too repulsive, to detain us: Martín de Vilches, one of the pretty warblers in Henry's choir whom he made Bishop of Avila; the chronic drunk Barrasa, appointed—"with exquisite fitness"[20]—comptroller of vintners and butchers; Bartolomé del Mármol, with his lucrative trade in the foreskins of Christian lads for Moorish bounty. But two of these worthless new protégés, these "*hombres nuevos,*" might briefly hold our attention: Juan de Valenzuela, named Prior of the Order of San Juan, and Gómez de Cáceres, made Master of Alcántara. Not only will they reappear on many occasions: they offer prime examples of the shoddy crew with whom Henry is to be increasingly surrounded, of the further weapons which he almost thrust into his enemies' hands.

Valenzuela, like many of his kind, came from hot Córdoba. His father was a tinker, his mother a laundress. But pots and pans were not to the taste of the willowy boy. Somehow, while the court was in the southern metropolis, he managed to fall in with Villena's brother, Pedro Girón. "Most available of all for illicit necessities,"[21] Palencia calls him—and a little further on, with less varnish, a "whore."[22] Like Lucas, he loved the theater and the dance. Unlike Lucas, he carried his passion for costume right into the streets: he went publicly dressed as a woman, with painted lips and eyes. It cost the worst sort of trouble for Henry, at Girón's and Villena's prodding, to create him Prior of San Juan. True, the office had fallen empty. But the Chapter had their own candidate, "a noble and ancient gentleman"[23] named Juan de la Somoza. Not until Somoza was imprisoned and starved to withdrawal could Valenzuela be installed. Palencia happened to be present at Somoza's renunciation. Strong-stomached though he was, he could not stand it. He tried to leave, but the Archbishop Carrillo, in charge of the matter, required him to stay. Suddenly Valenzuela pranced in to take possession, shrieking "insults and obscenities"[24] at the broken old man.

Gómez de Cáceres, the new Master of Alcántara, was not much better. Extremadura was then as poor a province as it is today. And Gómez was one of its poorest. He began "with the state of a mule"[25] —that ultimate cut in the social vocabulary of the age. He did, however, have good looks and a tall and "arrogant"[26] build. He determined to make the most of them. He had come up to court with the Count of Oropesa. But young Gómez had larger ambitions than mere counts. And one day, at another bullfight in Madrid, he found his chance to make a mark. Henry was present; he sat watching at a window. What he saw was the sport's most perilous trance: the bull, an unusually fierce one, had the *torero* (who at the time performed on horseback) close against the wall. Suddenly there was a shout, necks craned: an *espontáneo*—Gómez—had jumped in. He pulled off his cloak as he ran and used it for a cape. With one magnificent twirl he lured the bull away. With his sword he gave it two sharp thrusts in the throat. The monster staggered down; the crowd went crazy. Impressed as he always was by athletic prowess, Henry leaned from the window and beckoned Gómez over to commend him. The boy rose fast after that; his days of scratching for subsistence in Extremadura were over. On a single occasion Henry gave him four thousand *doblas*. By the time he reached twenty he was *mayordomo mayor* to the Crown. From there it was only a step to the mastership of Alcántara. That, at least, involved no starvation of sick old men; as we have seen, it had been vacant—like the even greater one of Santiago, still held in reserve by Henry—for several years.

Drunkards, bullfighters, pimps, unlettered louts and touts from nowhere: the new official circle. Official—that, of course, was the trouble. Everyone realized, had always realized, Henry's fondness for scum. So long as his ragtag kept to the lodge at Balsaín, or their private dens, perhaps they were harmless enough, perhaps even had their element of the comic. But there was nothing remotely risible —especially to the Grandes—about seeing them "exalted,"[27] and if such rash conduct offers final proof of Henry's inward threshing after his new marital catastrophe, it served as well to drag him even deeper into public woe. The barons can hardly be expected to have stood calmly by while important charges which had always been their own rich prey vanished in baseborn hands. And their reaction was almost immediate. In 1457, still smarting from the failure of the Granadine war and now goaded by the fresh menace to their ancient prerogatives, suddenly they drew together again, suddenly they bared their teeth in another plot.

On the occasion of this second conspiracy of the magnates, if Palencia and Valera are to be believed, the father took over from the son: it was the Count of Haro himself who assumed the lead in venturing his "person and estate"[28] with a view toward what was called (euphemistically enough, for Haro, although he managed to acquire the name of "The Good Count" and ended his days in a monastery, had motives no more altruistic than anybody else) "the reformation of these realms" and "the service of God and the King."[29] But tall as Haro stood, he was perhaps not even *primus inter pares:* many of the greatest magnates of the kingdom were quick to gather beside his banner of revolt. Alba and Benavente joined him.

The Marqués of Santillana, chief of the Mendozas, was soon drawn in. So too, apparently, was the rising house of Stúñiga, under its current head the Count of Plasencia. It goes without saying that the Admiral loomed large in the plot, and one is safe, although documentally unsupported, in presuming that the Manriques were deeply involved. Familiar names all: most of them, the reader will observe, had been among the rebels at Olmedo, and some in the abortive coup of the youngsters during the campaign in the south. But one startling new figure, one added recruit who will swell and obtrude himself more and more as our story progresses, does now appear in the list of the insurgents: Alonso Carrillo, Archbishop of Toledo.

Carrillo's reasons for turning against the Crown which he had defended in the Olmedan wheatfields and joining this noble confabulation of 1457 are not so easy as some of the others to unwind. It is true that he had long ties with the Castilian aristocracy, and even with Navarre and Aragón (his nephew was Bishop of Pamplona; his illegitimate son married the daughter of the Navarrese Constable, Pierres de Peralta, Juan's right hand; Juan himself, a man not conspicuously given to gratitude, was later to say that "with all his realms"[30] his debts to Carrillo could never be paid). But perhaps, at the date, his motives come down to simple pique over Henry's interference in ecclesiastical affairs. The misuse of the vast funds raised for the Moorish wars by the Bulls of Crusade—that is, their deflection into the pockets of Henry's friends instead of those of the Church—had been bad enough. But even more closely, such matters as Henry's appointment of Valenzuela to the Priory of San Juan and his installation of Catalina de Sandoval as Abbess of San Pedro de las Dueñas were a painful burr to Carrillo's Christian pride: the Order of San Juan fell properly into his own jurisdiction, and the affair of doña Catalina, since San Pedro de las Dueñas stood just outside Toledo, gave him all kinds of embarrassments and umbrage and finally brought the whole archdiocese under ban. For it is touchiness, even more than his bluster and petulance and childish irascibility, which seems to have been the key to Carrillo's character: all through Henry's reign, and on into Isabel the Catholic's, he was destined to fly into mulish sulks at any slight, either real or imagined, to what he chose to consider the dignity of his person as well as his place. In any event, he went over to the conspirators. It was, as a matter of fact, in his towns of Yepes and Alcalá de Henares that they did much of their meeting to formulate the bill of complaints and demands which they soon sent off to Segovia.

Henry was exhorted, in that minatory reclamation, to "amend his life and castigate all evil,"[31] to govern "according to the laws and ancient statutes of these realms." He must protect and honor the Catholic faith and "the rights of the Church and all its officials" (*loquitur* Carrillo). Only honest men should handle the national finances (this at Diego Arias, busily debasing the currency and thus interfering with the nobles' own efforts in the same direction, through their private mints). Henry ought to observe more "decency" at his court and above all else "take thought for the interest of the Grandes" and have none but "notable" men in his Council (here they very nearly tipped their hand). He should get rid at once of the Moors whom he "carried around" with him, venal *regidores* and *corregidores* had better be dismissed, and it was imperative to make an immediate reorganization of the *"disciplina militar."*

Henry, one imagines, did not read the document. But Villena certainly did—and with the keenest attention, the sharpest alarm: his constant fear was a firm and united front among the barons, for that might well snatch the government from his private grasp. No doubt he smiled rather cynically as he picked his way through their collection of red herrings. But not for a moment did he underestimate the force of the threat behind it. The plot of two years before had been little else than a cabal of irresponsible boys, a *jeu d'esprit* which could easily be ignored. Now the case was much altered: the mightiest names of the kingdom were in plain ebullience, were moving toward formal league. The sudden presence of Carrillo among them, with his enormous ecclesiastical and temporal weight (he was Chancellor of Castile as well as its primate), would give anyone pause. And their demands did have a persuasive ring: for the first time the opposition had come up, if only by accident, with that viable program for the realm's governance which, since he had none of his own to offer except a quite naked lust for power, was what Villena most dreaded.

Perilous as the situation was, however, matters might still have been worse. The one immutable law of Castilian politics in the fifteenth century was that no conspiracy against the Crown could even hope to succeed without help from Aragón. It followed that the nobles, now joined, would seek to renew their alliance with Juan; the specter laid at Olmedo stalked close again. And from that it followed, in Villena's nimble mind, that the best possible thing to do, the best possible defense, was to seek such alliance himself; thus he might draw the plotters' sting, thus their rebellion might shrivel and fall apart. Henry was easy enough to persuade to the idea: he had not seen his uncle and former father-in-law for a long time, and it was never in his nature to hold hard feelings. Juan might prove more difficult, but messengers went off to him: would he consent to a meeting, aimed at exploring a treaty of peace and amity between the two Crowns? It turned out that he would, for reasons which in a moment we shall examine, and the messengers returned with that encouraging reply. The conference, with both courts to be in attendance, was set for late spring in Alfaro, upon the common boundaries of Castile and Navarre.

Much depended, clearly, on the outcome of this meeting with Juan. Both Henry and Villena were nervous, and to fill the intervening time they decided to make a tour of Vizcaya and Guipúzcoa on their road to it; they had to go north anyway. Not once had the Basque provinces seen a king—principally because none had ever cared to risk his person among that savage race. But no danger was foreseen for Henry. It was felt, on the contrary, that his own "rusticity"[32] would be an asset among those "dwellers in mountains and caves,"[33] and after arranging for the Queen to meet them in May at Alfaro they started up into the high, harsh lands. The trip, for once, turned out unqualifiedly well. Henry was a great success among the hirsute Basques, Villena took advantage of the general good will to gouge heavy new taxes out of them on their maritime trade with England, and the second week in May they came down through the melting snows and the first pale lupines to Alfaro and the banks of the Ebro. Juana had managed to arrive on time. And Juan was waiting five miles away at Corella, across the border, with his own Queen and their little son Fernando, just turned five.

The tone of the ensuing "Vistas" of Alfaro was considerably less to Henry's taste than that of his recent stay among the mountaineers. For some curious reason—perhaps to make up for the King's own failure in martial dash—Juana and her damsels came dressed as Amazons: they wore helmets, they carried swords and shields and lances. Fortunately they abandoned this foolish attire for the state encounter of the two retinues. But what they substituted for it was almost equally bizarre: "Never have I seen, my Lord, such an array of costumes,"[34] wrote Martín de Irurita to the Prince of Viana, and unleashes a whirlwind of contemporary fashions which tries one's knowledge of fifteenth-century Spanish to its uttermost: snoods, gorgets, carmagnoles, scarves of bespangled tulle, boleros, fringed little Syrian toques. The two queens took an instant dislike to each other. Valera's jibe about their "great difference in condition"[35] is all too apt—Juana of Castile a shallow girl still in her teens, Juana Enríquez a mature and intelligent woman then approaching thirty and the devoted helpmeet for a husband's political career which her Castilian homonym so obviously was not. Any public sarcasms, however, were avoided, and the ceremony in the springtime fields was a brilliant one. After it, the courts went on together to Alfaro for a night of celebration. And three days later young Juana rode over to Corella for a return visit to Juan (he was her uncle as well as Henry's, her mother's brother) and another round of gaiety and *"muy gran fiesta"*[36]—fiesta which her husband, predictably enough, did not elect to attend.

But if all this visiting and partying bored Henry, and no doubt Villena and Juan, the real purpose of the meeting—the move for an alliance—was remarkably well served. Villena found plenty of time to sit down with Juan behind closed doors, and it developed—or so the Marqués imagined—that Juan was putty in his hands. He did not even make much complaint, as it had been feared that he might, about Henry's failure to pay him the large indemnity for the Castilian holdings which he had been promised three years before. Yes, he was quite agreeable to a pact with Henry. No, it would not be necessary to approach his brother Alfonso off in Naples; he could vouch for that friendship as well. He did, however, have one concession to ask of his own, one favor in return for his cooperation. They had all been seeing, these past few days, his sturdy young son Fernando. Might he not provide, one day, a suitable husband for Henry's half-sister Isabel, who was much of an age? They could strike this agreement at once, as proof of their new concord. And while they were at it, they might as well turn the engagement into a double one: Juan had another child by his second Queen—Juana, a girl of two—who would be equally suitable for Isabel's younger brother Alfonso.

Casually as he tried to make his suggestion, it had huge importance for Juan—and for the world. It marked, in fact, his initial step in a whole new plan for the repossession of Castile. His own prospects of ever wearing the rival crown were growing thin indeed: he was edging sixty, and with failing sight and health. But perhaps, if all went well, his two new children (oh not, of course, that odious brood by his first marriage) could at last flesh out the ancient family dream. Henry had no child—and now, it might reasonably be assumed, would never have one. His young brother and sister were his lawful successors. If Alfonso married Juana, and Isabel Fernando, then one of the Aragonese offspring was bound to sit, in time, on the Castilian throne. We do not know how well the tireless old plotter succeeded in concealing his emotion as he put forward this latest project, especially when he spoke of young Fernando. But under the double weight of political expedience and helpless adoration of the bright, obedient little boy—for love, so long delayed and all the more tyrannical for that, had finally pierced Juan's flinty heart—surely his voice came very close to trembling; his usual cool mask, as he sat face to face there with Villena in the quiet and portentous room at Alfaro, very close, for once, to cracking.

But Villena leaped at the bait. He was accustomed to live by improvisation, for the needs of the moment; the psychology of someone like Juan, who could sacrifice anything, endure anything, for a distant future goal, was quite beyond his grasp. Even if he sensed Juan's drift, the betrothal of four small children probably struck him as little enough to pay for the avoidance of dangers much too present, much too real. He agreed with alacrity, and the bond of friendship was sealed. The conference then broke up; everybody prepared to go home. We glimpse Juan at the parting, his graceful hand with the meticulous nails now relaxed upon the bridle, and on his lips that rarest of expressions for him, a genuine smile: he had taken the first move, and doubly bolstered it, toward winning the Castilian crown for his own seed. We glimpse Henry beside him, tongue-tied and awkward but eager, as always, to please; it is their long adieu, they will never meet again. Villena, too, had cause for his own smile of satisfaction, mounted beside them and watching. Aragón had been neutralized. His gamble against the nobles had paid off.

Yet deep new threats hung over all three of them, gathering like the Maytime clouds, as they twitched their reins and turned away and started down their flat, far-running roads. If Villena had been right about the barons—and of course he was, as usual; of course without Juan's aid they felt themselves not strong enough for open revolt; their conspiracy collapsed, or at least sank underground again—nevertheless a further menace to his power, one fully as hard or harder to contain, was soon to confront him. Had Juan surmised what dangers lay ahead for the marriage plans he had just launched, what terrible reefs and raging whirlpools, even his dauntless spirit might have flinched. And Henry himself was going home to a whole Pandora's box of private troubles: the buzz, sting, merciless gnaw of his young new *camarilla*—and the loss of his best friend.

10.
First Farewell

How had he failed to foresee it? Henry asked himself, sitting again in the Alcázar at Madrid and listening to the quarrels and bicker in the anteroom outside. All he had meant to do when he brought on these new protégés was to find a little peace, a little human gratitude. One would think that people who had never had anything would not be too hard to please. Yet the more you gave them, apparently the more they wanted. In that they were already proving just about as bad as the nobles. He had simply made another of his mistakes; everything he touched seemed to go wrong, sooner or later. Well, he would have to face it. Fortunately he still had lots of money. Perhaps with that he could content them all: sad thought, and not very conducive to self-esteem, but no other came forward. One thing, at least, was sure: he would never expose Segovia to such squabbles and indignities. (What on earth were they doing out in the antechamber—trying to tear the whole place down?) No, Segovia he must keep inviolate, his bower, his sanctuary. Henceforth he would hold his court as much as possible right there in Madrid. The tottering old palace could be fixed up. The forest of El Pardo, only a few miles north of town, might do for another animal preserve. He would find a way to make out in this latest complication. But he did not like it. He did not like it at all.

And there was someone who liked it even less: Miguel Lucas.

We have observed the strange dualism in Lucas's nature, the worldliness and piety in troubled yoke. It would be difficult to say how much his open animus toward Henry's latest companions sprang from moral disapproval, how much from knowledge that the cash and perquisites now being showered on them meant less for him. The question is further convolved by his real, and unexampled, fondness for the King. Yet here, too, doubts assail us. Was Lucas honestly grieved to see Henry thus mulcted and imposed upon? Or did he merely smart to have his own primacy challenged, to watch the increasing scramble for a place in the royal esteem which had so long been his alone? But if the cause eludes, the result is clear. He could not, would not, get along with the new crowd.

Valenzuela, particularly, rubbed him the wrong way. Perhaps they were too much alike; perhaps in that rouged and flouncy Hebe, as in a mirror, Lucas saw what he himself had just missed being, what he had such a horror of ever becoming, or of even being thought. They glowered, they parried; they were drawn insidiously together by mutual tastes and then flung violently apart by mutual revulsion. Gómez de Cáceres, too, got on his nerves: so athletic, so relentlessly virile. They all got on his nerves. He was sure they ran to Henry with lies intended to undo him. He found more and more trouble in controlling himself among them, in behaving with Christian grace. There were sneers and sudden spats. There was endless tattle in corridors.

Henry, whose own distress at the situation was genuine enough, talked to him about it. He must not feel pushed aside. Their friendship was too old and too deep ever to be endangered. Lucas did not see it so; the proof went otherwise. But how? Henry bewilderedly asked. When had he failed him? Had he not knighted him, time gone by, in the Vega of Granada? Had he not made him *corregidor* of Baeza and given him the lieutenancy of Alcalá la Real and of the great castle at Jaén? And not just Lucas himself; he had helped the entire family. His stepfather held a pleasant and useful position down in the south. His brother Fernán was a high official of the Wardrobe.

The Wardrobe! Lucas must have been sorely tempted to laugh: that collection of moth-eaten rags. But he kept to the point. Yes, it was true, he said, and of course they all were grateful. Yet look at what Henry had done for some of the rest. Look at Gómez's brother, for instance. He had been made a count, the Count of Coria. What was Fernán's post, in comparison? The thought of young Gómez set him off again. Oh, how could Henry put up with such awful people —people who did not even go to Mass?

Henry, as always, was stung to quick defense. Perhaps, he admitted, they were a little grabby. But there was no need to be so sanctimonious, so self-righteous. This happened when one went around too much with priests. Priests? Henry himself might be a great deal better off if—but Lucas stopped. They were both going too far; they fell into hurt silence. Finally Henry ended it, and in the only way he ever knew. He had an idea, he said. He believed he would make Lucas private chancellor to the Crown. The scroll of appointment could be drawn up the next day—with handsome flourishes, perhaps even touched in gold and vermilion, the sort Lucas always liked. But come now, no more of this. They must not talk in such a manner again.

They did, however. They had to. The naming of Gómez as Master of Alcántara saw to that. The prize was a great one, greater even than coronets, and Lucas's resentment once more boiled over. Henry knew that to cool it he would have to do something really splendid. He thought about it with care (or as carefully as he ever thought of anything: his decisions were always of the heart). The realm still had no Constable. That important office had been vacant since Luna's death. During the last four years, and perhaps for just such a purpose, Henry had held it back. Now the moment for bestowal seemed to have come. Would Lucas like to have it? Would he? Lucas's own tender heart burst open. He knew better than to embrace Henry. But there were tears of joy, of gratitude, of repentance at having doubted.

So came to pass, in the Alcázar of Madrid on March 25, 1458, the famous investiture of Lucas as Constable of Castile. For once Henry allowed the full pomp and stretch of majesty to be displayed. (Even the choice of day, the Incarnation, shows a desire to please.) Henry sat, that Saturday morning, on a dais at the end of the long throne room; Lucas stood beside him. Close examination of the guest list reveals a striking fact: except for the Count of Paredes, obliged to be there in official function, not one of the old nobility attended. But Henry had done all he could to gather a brilliant company; under the *mudéjar* ceilings a tide of knights, archbishops, ambassadors, even a Papal Nuncio, glittered and heaved. When trumpets announced that everything was ready, it parted and drew back against the walls. Suddenly the doors at the end of the *sala* were thrown open; between them blazed Castilla king of arms, bearing a folded banner and decked in a tabard—lions rampant on argent, gold bars upon gules—which no one had ever seen. A gasp went up; evidently Lucas was to be ennobled as well as made Constable.

Such was indeed the case; Henry, when he decided to give, often gave with both hands. Castilla paced down the expectant hall; he knelt at the throne and tipped the banner forward. Henry cut its corners; the full flag, with the same bars and lions, cascaded out. A patent was read creating Lucas baron, and Castilla delivered his new ensign to him. But that was not all. Trumpets blew again; a second and longer parchment was produced. It granted an earldom to Lucas (*pace* Gómez's brother). To mark the further elevation, three knights approached the dais with casks of sweetmeats and a brimming golden cup. Henry sipped symbolically at the cup and passed it to Lucas; they shared the sweetmeats. And at last came the climax. Whole troops of heralds stepped forth; whole choirs of silver trumpets rang. A third parchment making Lucas the realm's Constable, this one endless, was unrolled and grandly read. His *maestresala* presented Henry with the great baton. He turned it over to Lucas, who dropped on his knees and bent to the royal hand. Henry —a final favor—let him kiss it; then he rose, stepped down from the dais, took Lucas's arm, and the bright murmurous company, to the King's Music, flowed out behind them and on to the waiting feast.

Baron and Count and Constable, three titles at a stroke. The whole country marveled. "A thing," mused Valera, "never seen before."[1] And at least one person who had stood that day amidst the banners and silver trumpets—the Marqués of Villena—was determined that such an occurrence, or any even faintly like it, must not be seen again.

We have said that Villena came back from Alfaro only to face new problems, fresh menace to his power. His burden, in truth, was always to be double. Not only, in the large world of politics, did he have to keep the nobles fractured and disassembled. He also needed to make sure, within the palace, that none of Henry's private circle rose too far, rose high enough to threaten his own sway. This second peril, with the startling ceremony in the throne room, now seemed to be upon him. For a long time he had been wary of Lucas, apprehensive about his growing influence with Henry. That he should have been made a *corregidor* and an *alcaide*, even a member of the Council, was perhaps not too bad. But to see him given the Constable's baton, to have him heir to Luna's mighty office, put Villena in full alarm. And worse was soon to come. Henry all at once began to talk of making Lucas Master of Santiago. Villena wanted Santiago for himself. It was, in fact, what he desired most on earth, and there can be no least doubt that the prospect of having it go to Lucas brought his mounting determination to wreck him, to get rid of him, to its final head.

We do doubt, however, and strongly, that the system he used could anywhere be matched, in a long lifetime of skulduggery, as an example of Villena's *"sutileza,"*[2] his almost diabolic genius for working on the worst in people's character to make them compass their own fall. He knew Lucas like his palm: the prudery, the pride, the latent sense of guilt and reservation which had beset him from the start. Might not a clever hand—the same deft hand which played with such profit on Henry's irresolutions and inertia—now bring those troubled feelings to the surface, churn them up to such a crisis that Lucas's frail balance would at last break down and he would seek, of his own volition, to leave the court? And what better way than to establish some fresh rival for Henry's affections who would serve, at the same time, both to rasp on the vanity of Lucas and to plunge him into further scandal, into a final, a fatal, bog of malodorous quarrels and moral rot?

Such was the vicious plan. It remained only to pick the instrument. And that was not so easy. Certainly the field was wide enough; already Lucas was at ragged odds with nearly everybody. But none of the chief candidates seemed quite right. Gómez had little stature, could never be made to have much. Valenzuela was hard to take seriously. Villena's mind caught for a moment on Pedro Girón. He, too, was at daggers drawn with Lucas; once, kept on Lucas's advice from being given a town he wanted, he went into such a rage that he ripped a table apart. But the Marqués skimmed on past Girón: it would scarcely do to embroil his own brother in such an affair. No, best to find someone new; that would turn the screw still tighter. He thought over the list of the other young men, the pages and supernumeraries, in the court. And finally he made his decision: Beltrán de la Cueva.

The choice was catastrophic; probably it was the most costly mistake of Villena's life. Yet at the moment, Beltrán must have struck him as being the perfect implement. He had everything that could be expected to appeal to Henry, everything that Henry lacked: he was gregarious, dashing, articulate, an extrovert, an Andaluz, a stud among women, and not, so ran the gossip, unavailable to men. Above all, he possessed that quality which Henry always found so refreshing—a lack of complication: such thoughts as did find access to his brain were chiefly of tournaments and balls. About the best thing Castillo can say of Beltrán is that he was open-handed and affable and a highly skilled horseman, and even his official modern biographer—librarian of the ducal house he founded—is unable to make him out as anything more than a gorgeous blank. We cannot be sure about his age; undoubtedly he was quite young, perhaps nineteen, at the time. His origins are even less certain. Some would have them high, and rustle up one of his ancestors with Alfonso XI at the battle of Salado, carrying the papal banner. Palencia, on the other hand, insists that he descended from swineherds. It was almost an accident that he had come to court at all; stopping at the Cueva home in Ubeda on the Moorish campaigns, Henry had taken a fancy to the oldest son in the family, but the father begged him to accept one of the younger brothers instead and Henry obligingly agreed. Since then, two years before, he had hung about in the wings.

But suddenly he was in the wings no longer. Villena, intent upon his stratagem, went back in that steamy theater and brought him, more than willing, to center stage. In rapid succession the dazed young man found one honor after another, one title after another, thrust into his hands. Eighty thousand florins from the Bulls of Crusade are reported to have gone to him: more money than in all of Ubeda. He succeeded Gómez de Cáceres as *mayordomo mayor* when Gómez moved up to the Mastership of Alcántara. Henry was delighted with the young new Adonis. Beltrán (don Beltrán, people were already calling him) was delighted. So was Villena. Everyone was delighted—except Lucas.

For Villena's scheme worked fast. It may be that the fruit was even riper than he had imagined, even readier to fall; Lucas's long tension may have been just set to snap. Or perhaps it was the success of someone like Beltrán, with his cheap and shoddy attitude toward everything from Church to sex, that finally opened his eyes to the full corruption of the court, that brought his gorge up uncontrollably at everything in it—and at himself. In any event the sparks soon began to fly, the well-laid fuse to hiss.

The first muffled explosion came in that very summer of 1458, brief months after the investiture as Constable. One morning Lucas was nowhere to be seen. In the dark, and like Henry with no word to anybody, he had taken to horse and ridden away. He rode, in fact, as far off as Jaén. There he went straight to a young woman whom he had met in the course of the southern campaigns, Teresa de Solier. Abruptly he asked her to marry him.

When Henry finally learned where he was and went after him, he found Jaén in an uproar. Teresa was well born: loftily born, even—she was a grandaughter of the Adelantado of Andalucía and her father was first cousin, *primo carnal*, of the Count of Haro. Lucas's new titles, to blood like the Velascos, meant less than nothing. His tainted reputation was roadside talk; they would have none of him. But Teresa, who seems to have loved him in spite of everything, was proving equally obstinate.

Henry had to take charge. He put Lucas under what came to house arrest, to shield him from trouble, and visited him alone. But why all this? he asked, again in honest puzzlement.

Lucas had no answer, or at least none he could conveniently give to Henry. He just wanted to get away from court; he felt he needed a new and different life. But his reasons? Henry insisted. Was it Beltrán? In part, Lucas admitted; those intrigues and sordid vendettas were less and less to his taste. Yet that was not all of it; there was more to it than that—oh, he could not explain. They backed, they filled; once more they both were painfully embarrassed. They seemed to get nowhere.

But finally a solution occurred to Henry. He would authorize, would in fact command, that the *desposorios*, the formal troth, take place. But Lucas must come home with him now. Let him give a solemn pledge that he would stay two months with the court. Henry would try to content him, to ease him over this strange new crisis—whatever it was: they would talk further about the Mastership of Santiago. If at the end of that time Lucas was still not satisfied, still not happy, then he could go away. Lucas started to refuse. But as he looked back on the familiar homely face, into the great, pleading, melancholy blue-green eyes, somehow he was not able to do it, could not add another wound, another sorrow, to the many which none knew better than he that Henry already had borne. He knelt and put his hands in Henry's and swore the oath to stay.

That was only the beginning of a year-long contest between King and Constable which left them both shattered, which plunged the court into chaos, and which probably Villena alone viewed with any gratification. They spent the first part of the autumn in Segovia, perhaps with a thought toward the healing power of boyhood places. Henry, hoping to keep him longer than the two promised months, made him a present of the town of Agreda. Soon after, while Lucas was at prayer in Corpus Christi—he is more and more in churches now—a messenger came to him to say that the King had just decided to give him Andújar as well. He got up and went out through the lacy Moorish portal and into the October sunshine. He strode past the cloister of San Martín, around the corner, under the tall square tower of the Arias mansion. Then he turned into the *casas reales* and found Henry. He did not want Andújar, he announced flatly, almost angrily. What he wanted—yes, he had now made up his mind—was "place and license"[3] to depart. That would be best for everyone. It would please Villena (he guessed what bow was loosing the arrows, what hand was pushing the rival and blocking the Mastership). It would certainly please Beltrán. It would save all of them further trouble. But it would not please the King. Henry, at the rejection of his gift, lost his own control; it is one of the few times in his life when we hear him utter a complaint. What was the matter with everybody? he cried miserably. Why could there be no peace? He did his best by them all. Why should Lucas want to abandon him? They insisted, wrangled, accused; this time it grew to a real scene. But it ended, again, in contrition and an oath: Lucas agreed to remain a little longer.

Patches, frail props. The two of them went north, for a bear hunt which distracted neither, in the first snows. Henry suggested that they hold Christmas, accompanied by the full court, at Escalona, Luna's castle; he may have felt that it would flatter and please Lucas to make his wassail in that great seat of his predecessor as Constable. But it came off badly, was anything but wassail. For there the props, the buttresses, gave way. A fight broke out between Lucas's servants and those of Beltrán (of course Villena had come along). It lasted for more than an hour; several of Beltrán's men were killed. Henry and

Juana and Lucas were in the *sala* when news of the fracas arrived. Henry ordered Beltrán arrested and brought to him. He burst into the royal presence "cursing and blaspheming,"[4] his charm forgotten. Lucas gave him his back. "Sire," he said to Henry, "how can you let your *mayordomo* behave in such fashion before you? I beg your Highness to punish all this as it deserves."[5] Henry vowed that he would. "But the movers of that trouble disappeared and were never found."[6]

It could not continue; the friction, the double disgust, was eating through. Lucas did make a final promise that he would stay until the end of April. They went up past the icy rocks of Avila and came out on the gray and desolate plains. They tried Olmedo for a while, then Medina del Campo, then León. But they were all too restless, too nervous, to linger anywhere. Toward the end of Lent they were again moving about. They had reached Sahagún by Palm Sunday. And there, on that opening day of the week of remorse and penitence, Lucas could no longer stand it. He must do something, anything, to break free.

One of his toes had a callus. He called a surgeon. Burn it, he said; burn deep. The surgeon forgot to take the tool with him when he left. Lucas looked down at the wound. It was not bad enough. He picked up the hot iron. With mingled pain and pleasure he plunged it in and in; it almost severed the toe. But even that failed to work. Henry argued that he still could ride, there was no need to leave him behind, he could be bandaged well. They got on to Tordesillas for Easter itself, Lucas "with a sling for a stirrup."[7] They got back to Segovia. The morning of April 20, Henry sat for three hours on Lucas's bed: the foot was infected by then. He had to leave that night, he explained; Juan de Luna, don Alvaro's nephew, was making trouble up along the Duero. Would Lucas promise to do nothing while he was away? Lucas numbly agreed; he was past promises now—or any but one to himself. The next day, in agony of both flesh and spirit, he rose before dawn and fled to Aragón.

First he hid in the Dominican convent at Pozondón "and there held novenas."[8] It took Henry almost a month to trace him. To the four royal letters which then came "one on the heels of another,"[9] Lucas made no reply. He only fled farther, to Celha, near Teruel; he arrived on the Vigil of Corpus with his foot, at least, healed enough for him to be able to walk in the procession. But there, too,

Henry's messengers found him. He went on; he buried himself in a hamlet called Urcas, "and so secretly did he go that more than two months passed before anyone knew where he was."[10] Who did know in the end, and came to reason with him, was old Lope Barrientos, now Bishop of Cuenca and thus close to the eastern borders. Flight was useless, Barrientos argued. Nothing could be solved by that. Would he not have one more interview with Henry?

Together they rode back to Castile. Henry met them in a field outside Pinto, not far from Madrid. The Bishop left them alone. There in the stubbled wheat, under sad September skies, they wrestled with each other, wrestled each with his own dark angel. But at last Henry saw that the fight was hopeless. Very well, he said; let him go, let him go for good. And let him have, as a parting gift, any city of the realm.

It is superb of Henry to have made this truly spectacular offer only after he knew that he had failed. Any city of the realm!— "*cualquier cibdad de todos sus reynos.*"[11] Lucas might have had castled Burgos, Imperial Toledo, the caliphs' Córdoba, even Segovia itself. But what he instantly asked for—need one say it?—was Jaén.

He did not, however, go straight on to Teresa; something deeper than a callus had still to be burned away. He moved south very slowly. He seems to have felt a need—now that he had made the break—for his own kin; he went first to Belmontejo and Montizón and stayed for a while with another of his brothers. At Bailén, only twenty miles from Jaén, he wavered and turned aside once more. He swung far west; he would seek a last pardon, and strength, from the Virgin of Guadalupe. He entered the ancient monastery "at two in the morning, with many torches aflame";[12] he remained there, "not leaving the building,"[13] long days on his knees. It was, in fact, yet many weeks before he reached Jaén. And even after the wedding, as we have earlier seen, he slept for months in the same bed with his bride before he finally felt himself able, felt cleansed enough, to take her.

Lucas's ghastly story is by no means over. But in the court, in the great world which it was his misfortune both to love and scorn, we shall not see him again. That bitter reel had been danced out. Lucas had lost a career. Henry had lost the one person on whose understanding and devotion he could count. And the irony, the rare and delectable justice, is that Villena, who planned the whole thing, lost most of all in the end. For in the course of wrecking Lucas he had summoned up a genie who was destined soon to turn upon him, to cause him vastly more trouble and peril than anyone before: Beltrán de la Cueva, the blithe *flâneur*, the sword with the double edge.

11.
Don Beltrán

"At the bottom of every scoundrel exists a fool,"[1] says Palencia, emptying upon Villena yet another measure from his inexhaustible reservoir of bile. It is hard to see how anyone could call the Marqués a fool. Yet it is equally puzzling both that he should have failed to take into account perhaps the salient feature of Henry's character —his lifelong need for some kind of reassurance and affection—and that, even given his talent for the near view rather than the far, he should have overlooked the simple fact that nature abhors a void. For it was precisely these two laws which, with Lucas gone, at once began to work. Beltrán was now free to rush in; the counterpoise out of the way, his own rise became uncontainable.

The "Coplas del Provincial," that open sewer of the day, have Henry bound to Beltrán by a sexual tie; elsewhere among memoirs and documents there are ample hints, no less venomous if more veiled, to the same effect. One cannot discount the possibility. But so scabrous an explanation for Henry's sudden attachment is really not needed. He was worn out by the long emotional struggle with Lucas. After those convolutions, those Laocoön-coils, Beltrán's insouciance and directness fell upon his weary spirit like balm, like dew. And he did not stint in his gratitude: to the honors procured for him by Villena's cold calculation, Beltrán found added a whole new clutch of others from Henry's generous heart.

The royal coffers, to be sure, by then were running a bit low; what with all of Henry's encroachments on the Crown properties to satisfy his placemen, convenient gifts lay less and less at hand. Cuéllar, now turned over to Beltrán, had to be taken from young Isabel; it was left to her in their father's will. Colmenar de Arenas, which soon followed it (and whose name the recipient modestly changed to Mombeltrán), came—not without resistance and further ill feeling—from Luna's widow. But Roa, at least, was available for immediate bestowal. Nor did it cost anything to give the young tyro, like Lucas before him, a seat on the Council. Like Lucas's, too, and with even higher distinctions, Beltrán's whole family shone in the climbing sun. Henry made his brother Gutierre, although a fellow "of low habits and little faith,"[2] not only Bishop of Palencia but Count of Pernia (a title which remains in the Palentine miter to this day). The complaisant father was created Viscount of Huelma.

In short, within mere months Beltrán was *"principal señor"*[3] of court and palace. And like any johnny-come-lately he made the most of his new state. He lounged in the royal apartments. He bragged of his intimacy with Henry—and, even worse for his future, with the Queen. He bought gaudy clothes; he remodeled the vast squatting castle at Cuéllar. Most of all, however, he entertained: anywhere, anyone, everybody. Beltrán's manners in private often left something to be desired: he had a tendency to blurt out obscenities and kick down doors and pour hot slops from darkened windows on passers-by. But all agree that in public he was a great *gastador* —a great spender—and a lavish host. Henry gave him his head in that, as in all else; nothing more clearly shows his infatuation than the brief, strange, totally uncharacteristic burst of pomp and festivity which he now permitted at court. And here, for once, he succeeded in pleasing everybody; after the long regimen of serge and stinking rushes and early bedtime, Madrid joyfully launched forth upon a sea of gaiety. Fonseca, the giddy Archbishop of Sevilla with his passion for gewgaws and flimflam, gave a famous dinner where trays of jeweled rings were passed about instead of dessert. Others staged masques, or bullfights, or midnight routs with shawms and castled pasties *a la borgoñesa*. But Beltrán eclipsed them all.

Perhaps the best example of his magnificence—and one of the best, as well, of his ruinous lack of discretion—is the famous "Paso" which he mounted just outside Madrid. Ambassadors from the Duke of Brittany were in town. As hospitality, Henry had been persuaded that a long weekend in El Pardo would be suitable, and to the lodge in those bosky environs, just completed, the court repaired. Matters began unfortunately enough: two footmen made off with a sackful of the royal gilt and silver, brought down from Segovia, which was displayed on the sideboards. (Poor devils, said

Henry to the indignant butler: they earn so little, let them have it.) But that infelicity was soon forgotten in the blaze of entertainment. First there were brilliant jousts of "ten against ten,"[4] the prizes a bolt of Venetian brocade and two of crimson velvet. The second day they played at *cañas*—a hundred of them in the course, with golden bridles. The third, they all went hunting. Beltrán's great contribution, however, was still to come. On the fourth and final dawn he disappeared. His absence was much discussed. And only as they rode home, only as they rounded a bend and drew up short and astonished, did they see what all the mystery had been about.

A whole castle of painted canvas lay across their path, towers, barbicans, and casements bright in the morning air. Savages dressed in leaves—those curious figures which held such fascination for the age—guarded its wooden gate. Beltrán himself, glittering in his showiest armor, stood by with lance at rest. No knight, he announced, could pass through until he had run six jousts. And each must select, as favor, the initial of his love; he pointed to an arch, "wondrously graven,"[5] from which gold letters hung. The delighted company dismounted. They went up on three roadside platforms—one for Henry and Juana and the ambassadors, one for the *"grandes señores,"*[6] one for the judges of the tourney—draped in silks and laid for feasting: it was clearly to be an all-day affair. Well on to dusk they banqueted and followed the smite of lances. Don Beltrán defended his painted gateway stoutly. And perhaps as much through crazy rashness as bad luck (tongues loosed by malice or envy already were wagging), the letter he picked from the golden alphabet was a "J."

Riding high on the horse, this pampered Lochinvar, and it is entirely to be expected that his bold forays into an ambiance already thick with tensions should have wrought wide havoc on everyone concerned. Of his full effect upon the susceptible Queen we cannot be sure. Tradition has long had them lovers; Palencia even goes so far as to hold that Henry urged them upon each other—a charge so savage, so counter to all one knows of Henry's character, that we can only attribute it to the chronicler's almost raving spite. (Guesses about what made Palencia so bitter and hateful range from his Jewish blood to his salary of seventeen cents a day.) But it would be an act of even greater folly than Beltrán's own plucking of

Juana's initial to assert that the hot brown girl on the royal dais that festive afternoon outside El Pardo had lustful memories and anticipations as she watched Beltrán post back and forth in the lists below: there has never been, and probably never will be, any real proof that their relations were illicit. Only one thing can we claim without the slightest risk: gay, pleasure-strung, coquettish, the young Queen took a quite open fancy to the new favorite and responded like a flower in the warm sun to all the court diversions which his advent brought about.

And who shall reproach her? Marriage to Henry must have been a constant trial. It is beyond conceiving that Juana should have guessed, or cared, what inner pressures abstracted and weighed her moody husband down. All that she saw, and suffered, was the result. To be at his side she can hardly have failed to find a daily burden, if not an outright repulsion. The times when he was away were even worse: surely she shuddered whenever she thought of the bachelor parties, for which Henry was still slipping off whenever he could find an opportunity, in the other lodge up over the mountains at Balsaín. Their private life, moreover (one hesitates to call it their sex life), was plain hell.

For the desperate efforts at conjunction—an heir! they must have an heir!—went on and on. They were, by then, even trying a crude form of artificial insemination. Münzer, the physician whom we have quoted before, describes the clumsy attempt. A tube was fashioned of solid gold, and the precious object thrust into Juana. Then someone masturbated Henry (to whom this odd office fell—or why anybody should have been needed to perform it—we are not told); it was hoped to trickle semen through the tube. But the experiment failed to work: what little they at last wrenched out of Henry proved so thin and "watery"[7] as not to be worth the bother. It does afford, however, a cruel picture of shame, discomfort, embarrassment, and frustration for a proud and finicky girl. Eight times Castillo halts his meandering chronicle to sermonize on Juana's levity, and it cannot be denied that the sag of her morals was what, in the end, gave Isabel the Catholic the crown. But only the sternest of Catos would condemn the beleaguered young wife if, after her daily boredoms and nightly struggles with Henry, she clutched at such social distractions as she could find—or even if she did, in fact, receive a handsome youth like Beltrán de la Cueva into her private chambers and perhaps into her bed. She can no more be blamed than Henry for the ultimate disaster. One finds no villains—only victims—in their unhappy story.

Nor, when it comes to blame, can we cast much upon Villena for his rage and affliction at this sudden apotheosis of don Beltrán. Few will weep over Villena's misfortunes; he was a politician, and got only what he deserved. Yet it is difficult not to feel a twinge of sympathy at his plight: labor of Sisyphus, fingers stuck in the dike. And now (so soon: just when he thought he had everything calked up) the dangerous tide, the threat to his own ascendancy over Henry, was seeping back in. Beltrán—the very creature of his making!—stood close and ever closer to the throne: *"principal señor"* of the palace, in truth—and, if he could not be stopped, perhaps soon of the realm.

But that was no more than the half of Villena's latest anxiety. Suddenly the magnates—woe added to woe—once more were on the swarm. For it can come as small surprise that the worst of Beltrán's inroads were upon the haughty nobles, that the summer rain of favors falling on him should again have brought them out from among their rocks and into fresh revolt.

One does not wish to oversimplify. It is true that the barons had further grievances against the Crown in these last years of the decade; Henry's seizure of Guadalajara from the Mendozas, brought on by Villena's obsessive fear of that potent clan, was one of the sorest. Yet it seems safe to say that the real catalyst of this third and most lethal of their conspiracies which now confronts us was their hatred for don Beltrán; at sixes and sevens though they had always been among themselves, they could at least agree on that. To have spent generations climbing the social ladder, and then to find anyone at all perched on its top ahead of them, was maddening enough. But Beltrán de la Cueva seemed made by nature to set the barons' teeth on edge: vulgar, boastful, brash. In any event their confederation, twice crushed and thwarted, formed anew. And this time they did not err. In 1457 Villena had beaten them to the draw, had outrun them to an alliance with Aragón. Now, they determined, they would turn the tables. Before even the watchful Marqués knew what was afoot, they had their envoys well across the border. And Juan sat down with them and listened carefully to the invitation which they brought.

Much had been happening to Juan in the three years since we last saw him beside the Ebro. His brother Alfonso had died in Naples, without legitimate issue, and he was now King of Aragón in fact as well as effect: he could lead from new strength. But apart from that splendid ace, a few troublesome deuces cluttered the hand. His strife with his oldest son by his first marriage, the Prince of Viana, was fast drawing to its climax, as we shall shortly see. The Crown of Aragón, if becoming enough, was poorer than ever; a letter in late September of 1458 to Pedro Vaca, Juan's ambassador at Henry's court, instructs him—with no result—now to demand the elusive indemnity for his seized Castilian possessions. Worst of all, the very concession for which he had waived such payment at the Vistas of Alfaro, the betrothal of his two new children to the Infantes of Castile, seemed about to go up in smoke. Another ambassador, back from Castile in January of 1459, brought that unwelcome announcement. Henry (read Villena: the equation is constant) no longer agreed to the marriage of Isabel and Juan's adored Fernando; all he would sanction now was Alfonso's to little Juana. Juan had immediately sought another meeting to discuss the matter, first at Daroca and then at any place in the Rioja which suited Henry. Both suggestions were stonily declined.

It was surely this menace to the match for young Fernando which Juan pondered most thoughtfully as he sat listening to the nobles' pleas. Those marriages for his children had now become the very heart of all his plans. One of them already was imperiled—in fact, for the moment at least, was plainly tumbled down. Therefore, Juan's mind proceeded, the other took on an even greater importance. It must be fortified, shored; since his Juana would still have Alfonso, it must be made quite certain that Alfonso would have the Castilian crown. The boy did, with Henry childless, stand next in line. Yet assurance might still be made, in a matter so vital, doubly sure. Alfonso was heir presumptive—only presumptive. But if he were heir apparent? If Henry swore him—and had the Cortes swear him—his sole and legal successor?

Yes, he admitted, after he had heard the nobles' list of demands and complaints against Henry, they were sound enough. But they had all been used before: the failure of the war on Granada, the misuse of papal funds, the corruption of the court, and the outrageous appointments. Why not add some new weight? He had, it so happened, a convenient thing in mind. They really should insist that the Castilian succession be made more clear. Let them hold out for the investiture of young Alfonso as Prince of Asturias, for his formal recognition as heir to the crown. If they included that in their platform—oh, it was much to ask of him, poor and in oceans of trouble as he was—but yes, then he would do it, then he would consent to the alliance.

The emissaries went home with his terms. And the nobles proved amenable. More than amenable: delighted. Why, they mused afterward, had they not thought of that themselves? Alfonso and his rights would make a fine banner to wave about in public, a convincing cover for their own designs. Juan moved toward his frontiers for the conclusive arrangements. In Tudela, on October 5, 1460, the treaty arrived. It was read to him and laid before him; he picked up the pen. Long thoughts must have haunted his mind, long memories, as his delicate hand hung poised in the air: Olmedo, that night of blood and terror with Luna hot at the gates and the entente with the nobles smashed, the fifteen years of waiting and plotting and probing to weave it back again. Well, they were over now. The pen descended. Through the thickening web of his cataracts, he scrawled his name.

So grew, so came to final flower, the dark and fateful and terrible League of Tudela between Juan of Aragón and the Castilian nobles. Henry, of course, could not have known its chilling language (the barons solemnly swore "by God and Holy Mary"[8] and touching the Cross to procure full "restitution"[9] of the lost "inheritance and dignities"[10] of Juan's family in Castile; Juan made the same awesome oath to aid them against their King, and to give them new lands and titles in Aragón if they failed and were "driven forth").[11] But the mere fact that the confederation had come about—it was far too sonorous to be kept entirely quiet—was ominous enough. We have Henry's reaction when the first word of it was brought to him, in Valladolid. To the messenger who made the announcement, in public audience, he answered "briefly and obscurely";[12] then he rose and almost hurled himself—"*se lançó*"[13]—into his bedroom.

He had much to think about, pacing that silent chamber. Just what had he accomplished in his six years on the throne? All he had succeeded in doing was to drive the nobles and Juan of Aragón back into each others' arms; that worst of all possible threats, the formal coalition of his foes within and his worst foe abroad, was at last a bitter reality. Of course he still had Villena, to advise him, to take charge. Villena would think of something; he always did. But the ring was closing around him; the horizon was darkening. Even a monarch who paid so little heed to politics could see that this report of the conjunction of his enemies looked very much like the signature of doom. It fitted in so well—as a matter of fact almost so uncannily—with another piece of news which he had only then received. That mightiest of his lions in the den of the *casas reales* at Segovia—the others had turned on him suddenly and killed him and eaten him, hide and all.

Henry, least superstitious of men, was not the sort to be much ruffled by such phenomena; usually he had some calm and rational explanation for the weird portents which so terrified his contemporaries. In the great Segovian panic of 1458, when the walls quivered and split and there were subterranean groans and crunches and people came crying the end of the world, he gave them a quiet account of the nature of earthquakes. After a whirlwind which fell on Sevilla (trees rose by their roots and spiraled up and disappeared, the towers of churches were sheared off "as with a sword,"[14] cows and statuary shot through the air), he sent someone to address the "stupefied"[15] populace and assure them that what had taken place was nothing "occult" but sprang from "causes entirely natural."[16] Yet lately, one was obliged to admit, there had been the most extraordinary number of these occurrences. Huge hail and sluicing rains had swept Castile all that past summer of 1460: floods in Saharan August! On one of the few fair days, red flames licked out through the sky; the birds burned up and fell like cinders to the ground. A three-month child, in Peñalber, had risen in its cradle and delivered sermons. And now this mayhem among his lions. Odd omens, truly, and they seemed to be coming faster and faster. It was enough to give anyone pause, to make anyone stop and wonder. Perhaps events were working up to some kind of climax. Perhaps something big and strange and startling really was about to happen.

But the wildest imaginings could not have guessed what it would be. The Queen was pregnant.

12.

Uncertain Fruit

No one has ever known who fathered Juana's first child: we might as well say so plainly, and at once. With all the writhings and jerkings and philters and golden tubes, some wandering sperm of Henry's may indeed have reached its mark: in a genesis of such obscurity, almost anything is possible. But until the day when a crinkled yellow document still unturned in city file or castle turret removes all doubt (a day which, at this altitude of time, seems increasingly remote), the wise historian will withhold commitment.

We cannot even be sure of Henry's own final thought upon the subject; later his behavior in this most critical question of his life was to be ambiguous to a degree. Yet in the beginning, at least, he seems simply to have believed—like anybody else—what he most wanted to believe, what he had to believe if he was to keep even a vestige of self-respect: that the child was his. In fact, his first reaction to the news which sped down to him from Aranda, where Juana happened to be stopping when she made her momentous discovery, was one as close to rapture as so lethargic and melancholy a nature perhaps could ever come. Certain "prelates and cavaliers"[1] had immediately suggested that he would do well, given the equivocal circumstances, to indulge in little fuss about the Queen's state of *buena esperanza*. And for once he was well counseled: few spectacles more readily lend themselves to laughter than displays of connubial bliss on the part of the abnormal. But he had lived so long by bad advice that he was incapable of recognizing the good when once he saw it. His hour had arrived. He had no intention of holding back.

In a great burst of excitement and gratitude he presented Juana with the whole town of Aranda. Soon afterward he sent a splendid escort to bring her to Madrid, where he had decided that the accouchement should take place. With infinite solicitude, in order not to jolt her precious burden, Juana was laid within a padded litter. Mile after cautious mile, and led by Henry's own bodyguard of Moors, the slow procession, powdered by the first snows of waning autumn, wound down the southern flanks of the Guadarramas. When Henry learned that she was nearing, he went out with pomp and gathered court to meet her. The two processions mingled. Juana was lifted from her litter and placed—so that all the world might see her, so that they might come in open triumph—upon a wide soft seat made on the back of a mule. Henry himself held her bridle as they entered Madrid. One seldom feels sorrier for him—proud, happy, a little stunned, fancying himself as husband and future parent, confident that the years of smirks and ridicule and snide lampoons upon his virility at last were over. For he was riding straight to a worse avalanche than even the wintry Guadarramas could have loosed: with Juana's pregnancy the new-formed coalition of Aragón and the Castilian magnates had found its initial opening, the chink through which to thrust. Henry's hopes, in short, were once again to be reduced to ashes. And once again, as well, the arsonist was his uncle Juan.

Word of the Queen's condition flew to Zaragoza almost as fast as it had flown to Madrid. Its effect on Juan can easily be surmised. Already he was faced with one deterrent to the Castilian marriages for his Fernando and little Juana—the recent change of plans about young Isabel. And here, just on its heels, was another, no less alarming for its bizarre and slightly dreamlike air. Offspring of Henry's own would replace both Isabel and Alfonso as his lawful successors. Not only was the path to those two young Infantes strewn with rocks; the very goal—their hands in marriage—now seemed about to lose all point. Of course the coming child itself, whether boy or girl, would one day reach nubility. But that would mean endless waiting, thirteen or fourteen years—a Dantesque idea to anyone, like Juan, already in his sixties.

No, something had to be done, Juan realized, and done swiftly, to blight this ripening threat. To keep the baby from being born was beyond even his capacities. But if, once in existence, it could be stigmatized, discredited—best of all, proved of doubtful source? Yet how? He could not manage such a thing unaided; he was far away, half blind and in declining health, harassed of late by mounting trouble in fractious Cataluña. Perhaps with help of the Castilian nobles? But what did they really care who was Henry's successor? Wait, though; they, too, had someone they wanted to wreck, to sink, to do between the eyes—the new *jeune premier* at court, the new favorite they so dreaded and despised. Might not destructions be combined? With clever aim, might not two birds be killed with the same stone? Speedily he dispatched a suggestion to the barons. Again they were delighted with his idea. And soon, by posting messenger or whispered talk behind locked doors, the fateful directive was going out to all their agents: pin Juana's child on don Beltrán.

We do not know when this dark rumor, this seed which was to grow into a upas tree that shadowed much of Spanish history, first broke above the ground. Not until three years later do we have a written charge of Beltrán's paternity. But documents and gossip are quite different matters: almost all contemporary sources say that even in the closing months of Juana's pregnancy, even by the Christmas which Henry had thought to keep so joyfully but which now turned gall and wormwood for him, the vicious tale was catching on.

And how could it have been otherwise? The markmanship was perfect, the target hopelessly exposed. Seldom, in the long course of smears and defamations, have victims been so vulnerable; everything Henry and Juana and don Beltrán had done, all that they were by nature, had led them to the trap. Henry had formally admitted his impotence with Blanca; his stoppage with the Queen at least was guessed; his attachment for young men, be it guilty or not, was common knowledge. Juana's own lightness and lack of moral fiber were all too evident. Beltrán, to close the ruinous situation, had long been blatantly incautious, had puffed himself upon his easy access to the Queen. In sum, if people ever dug their common grave with their own hands, it was these three. And now, the push supplied, they pitched headlong into it; the scandal, fire in ready stubble, crackled and spread.

It spread in at least one fashion which a person less ingenuous than Henry might have foreseen, might even have forestalled. The Admiral and Alonso Carrillo, Archbishop of Toledo, suddenly reappeared at court. They asked to be taken back; they had seen, they said, the error of their ways and wished henceforth to be "true

Camarauz

Henry IV
A portrait from life

Landesbibliothek, Stuttgart

Henry IV
A contemporary miniature, hitherto unreproduced

By kind permission of the Duke of Frías

Casa del Arcediano, Barcelona

Juan II of Aragón
A medallion of the day

Mas

Seal of Juan II of Aragón

Archives of the Crown of Aragón

Signature of Henry IV
(*"Yo el Rey"*)

Virgen de la Mosca

The young woman with a book is popularly
supposed a portrait of Isabel the Catholic,
at about the time of her accession. The
man may be the chronicler Alonso de Palencia,
the standing female figure Beatriz de Bobadilla.

Santa María la Mayor, Toro

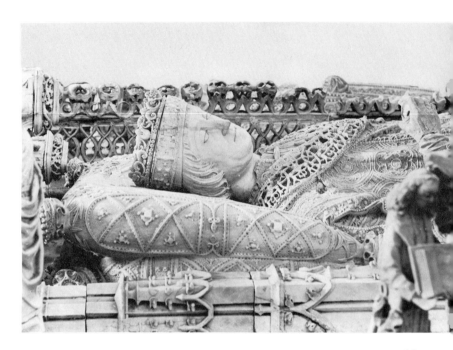

Mas

Juan II of Castile

Cartuja de Miraflores, Burgos

Isabel of Portugal

Cartuja de Miraflores, Burgos

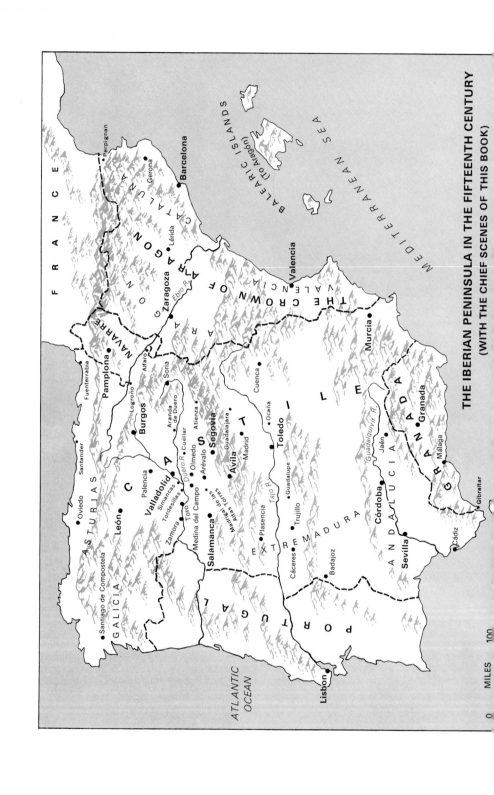

THE IBERIAN PENINSULA IN THE FIFTEENTH CENTURY
(WITH THE CHIEF SCENES OF THIS BOOK)

FRANCE

Perpignan

Gerona

Barcelona

C A T A L U N A

A R A G O N

Lérida

Zaragoza

Ebro R.

THE CROWN OF ARAGON

Valencia

V A L E N C I A

MEDITERRANEAN SEA

BALEARIC ISLANDS
(To Aragon)

NAVARRE

Fuenterrabía

Pamplona

Santander

Oviedo

A S T U R I A S

Logroño

Alfaro

Soria

Burgos

Aranda
de Duero

Duero R.

Cuéllar

Atienza

Olmedo

Arévalo

Guadalajara

Segovia

Ávila

Madrid

Ocaña

Cuenca

Toledo

C A S T I L E

Murcia

Jaén

Granada

G R A N A D A

A N D A L U C I A

Málaga

Gibraltar

Cádiz

Guadalquivir R.

Córdoba

Sevilla

Palencia

León

Valladolid

Simancas

Tordesillas

Zamora

Toro

Medina del Campo

Medina de las Torres

Salamanca

Plasencia

Cáceres

Badajoz

Guadalupe

Trujillo

E X T R E M A D U R A

Tajo R.

P O R T U G A L

Lisbon

ATLANTIC OCEAN

Santiago de Compostela

G A L I C I A

0   MILES   100

servants"² of the King. Which king they had come to serve should have been instantly apparent: both of them were hand in glove with Aragón. But Henry received them forgivingly, granted them seats on his Council—and never understood why the talk about Beltrán and the baby turned so swiftly worse.

It spread, soon, even to foreign orbits. A little after the Admiral and Carrillo, the French Count of Armagnac arrived. Ostensibly, he had come to render homage to Henry for his Asturian fiefs of Cangas and Tineo. His real mission, however, was of subtler stripe: Louis XI had just ascended the French throne, his long nose was already sniffing at Peninsular affairs, and he found it advantageous to have an observer of the explosive situation taking shape upon his southern border. Armagnac's own reputation was scarcely of purest ray: he had two children by his sister. But in a court so depraved as Henry's, a touch of incest perhaps could go unremarked. Henry, with customary kindness, gave the visitor further Castilian *mercedes*, and Carrillo, embarked even at the date on that flirtation with the French which was to bring his master so much misery, sent over the rather startling present of a thousand bushels of wheat and a like quantity of barley, a thousand casks of wine, two thousand hens, and forty turkeys.

Observers—and observed: young Isabel and Alfonso were shortly brought to court. Isabel by then was almost eleven, Alfonso eight. They had been kept in Arévalo, in Cuéllar, in Escalona—sometimes alone, sometimes in company with their mother, the unhinged Queen Dowager. But the great new turn called for their closer watch; Villena, especially, must have glimpsed the projects being spun around them by the League. Juana is supposed to have treated Isabel "with much sisterly love."³ One doubts it; what possible rapport could there have been between the pious girl and the frothy Queen? Of Alfonso, his status as heir now crumbling, we are told nothing at the moment. Anyway, they too had come; daily the old Alcázar strained and swelled like Juana's belly with even more arrivals— midwives, Jewish and Moslem surgeons, Grandes and minor outland gentry whose presence custom required for a royal birth— and in wind and snow and constant speculation, constant counting back on fingers to those visits by Beltrán ("which had been anticipated")[4] up to Aranda the preceding summer, the nervous winter wore on. But finally, at the end of February, the waiting was over: Juana felt the pangs.

It cannot be stated that she was brought to bed: the records reveal that during her delivery she was held in the arms of the Admiral's brother, the Count of Alba de Liste—a posture which would have involved some very odd gyrations had she been lying down. Apparently she had to endure her travail either crouching or standing up. And as if that were not enough, the rigors of protocol again set in. Ranged upon her right, and in that order, stood Henry, Villena, the Comendador Gonzalo de Saavedra and Henry's private secretary, Alvar Gómez. On her left were the Archbishop of Toledo, Juan Fernández Galindo, and the inevitable attorney. The one thing not quite clear about this trying occasion is the nature of the birth itself. Castillo says it was difficult. Palencia, on the other hand, claims that it all took place with little effort. But hard or easy, at last it was over, and there—on the floor or wherever she had it, and whoever had sired it—lay the baby: a squalling girl.

They called it after its mother, although soon enough this ill-fated child was to acquire the nickname which she has dragged across the centuries—La Beltraneja. And for the baptism, at least, things somehow held together; the storm still did not break. Again, and now in the private chapel of the Alcázar, Alba de Liste took a post of honor: he presented the baby at the font. Carrillo himself baptized her, assisted by the Bishop of Calahorra (Pedro González de Mendoza, still shoving up). The godparents deserve a special, and rather rueful, glance—Villena and his scheming wife, the Count of Armagnac, young Isabel. Except for Isabel, it was an unpropitious lot. And Isabel herself has been much criticized for her role: with time, the child whom she there sponsored was to be the object of her unremitting quest to supersede and thwart. But her years should be remembered; at such an age she hardly could have grasped the awesome weight of the responsibility. Anyway, no doubt she had no choice; surely she was simply ordered what to do. It is our first real picture of her, standing beside the stoup: sedate, red-gold of hair, perhaps a little owlish, uprooted now for ever from her childhood and thrown square into the banquets and jousts and bullfights—things which she never cared for—given in an attempt to dignify the event.

But if the baptism managed to come off well, it was the last of even surface calm. Henry proceeded to topple the whole quaky house of cards. During those very celebrations he created don Beltrán Count of Ledesma.

It is next to inconceivable. Everything about it was reckless, senseless, wrong. It further enraged the nobles, already in full cry after Beltrán: that blackguard in the peerage! It goaded Juan, it rasped upon the tenderest of his nerves—his family pride: Ledesma had been one of his mother's most cherished titles. And the timing itself was bad beyond belief. The needed heir had been born; Beltrán was being honored. What could it possibly signify but a pay-off, a reward? Yet heedless (or unsuspecting) of the consequence, Henry went ahead and did it: in the same crowded throne room where he had made Miguel Lucas Constable of Castile, and with equal "ceremonies and solemnities"[5] he bestowed the bright pendons of nobility on don Beltrán. Moreover the language of the proclamation added fuel to the fire. Always these royal patents bore a list of the recipient's achievements: in Council, in diplomacy or war. But the only thing adduced for don Beltrán was a vague mention of his "merits"[6] and his "willing services"[7] to the Crown.

Merits? What merits? None were, or ever had been, even faintly visible. Worse—"willing services"! With that, guffaws went up which rocked Madrid. And in their wake, inevitably, affairs swept on to the disastrous climax which had been the chief object of the propaganda from the start—rebellion, in the Cortes, against the baby's rights to be the heir.

For of course Henry had to call his Estates to acknowledge the royal infant, to swear her fealty; it was the law. He waited for two months—perhaps, vain expectation, to give the gossip a chance to subside, the seas to calm. He still may have had hope as the Cortes convened. If he did, it soon crashed down. They held their opening session on the 9th of May—and it at once became apparent that little Juana's claim to the crown was in a desperate pass.

Unfortunately, the records of these crucial Cortes of 1462 have disappeared. But information about them can be ferreted out. It is evident that the gathering was not plenary: Henry's speech from the throne refers to "those absent,"[8] and the Municipal Archives of both Murcia and Cuenca contain letters from him to their Councils —pointless, had their representatives been present—announcing that the meetings had just been held. Some of the cities, in other words, would not (nor ever did) accept the newborn Princess as legitimate heir. And the nobles fell even shorter of recognition than the *procuradores*. The chronicles have many of them giving their obeisance only through fear of reprisal or "constrained by force";⁹ Palencia asserts (and is joined by Isabel the Catholic herself in a document of almost a decade later) that several, having sworn, straightway revoked the oath. Chroniclers, admittedly, have axes to grind. But more solid witness to this balking of the magnates lies at hand. We have a letter from Henry to the Count of Benavente, written a full week after the Cortes met, insisting that he come and swear. Among the others refusing (in spite of the offer of a thousand vassals for his consent) Valera lists the Count of Medinaceli—and in this case, if in no other, Valera surely knew whereof he spoke: for years he was in the confidential employ of those De la Cerdas. As to the revocations, usually dismissed by scholars hostile to Isabel as mere figments of her imagination, two of those very papers have recently come to light.

A tempest in a teapot, the reader may exclaim; it can hardly matter. But it is far more than that, it matters a great deal: little Juana, time now makes increasingly manifest, never had full approbation as heir by Cortes and baronage, and this flaw in her claim to the succession will constitute—as Juan surely planned it—the apple of discord for the remainder of our story. Above all—here, at least, there can be no doubt, no cavil—it mattered, mattered cruelly, to Henry. The child on which he had set such store as tardy proof of his virility was publicly besmirched, attainted, branded as not his. His fragile shoot of self-esteem had been trampled down. The balm, the anodyne, had turned out to be a poison.

So shattered was he by this further calamity, so weary and—who knows?—sick with new doubts himself, that he did what his deepest instincts always craved in throng of trouble: he fled, the Cortes risen, to Segovia. Listening to music in its dim cathedral, riding the sun-baked yellow plains or buried with Gómez de Cáceres and young Valenzuela and his fawns and stags in the lodge at Balsaín, he endured—as was his manner—his latest wound in silence. There, in August, one happy piece of news did reach him: Gibraltar—that running sore in the Spanish flank, that national trauma—had finally been retaken from the Moors. But its fall was little credit, personally, to Henry: the feat had been brought off, and almost single-handed, by young Rodrigo Ponce de León, later to be the famous Marqués de Cádiz, although at the season "barely sprouted."[10] And whatever luster had been shed upon his name, Henry at once extinguished it: he arranged a match for Beltrán with Mencia de Mendoza, youngest daughter of the Marqués of Santillana.

If any capstone was needed for the months of scandal, Henry had now provided it. Again the deduction was immediate: Beltrán, having served his generative purpose, could be married off. New jibes and sneers, even nastier new rhymes, soon were going round. It is difficult to see what led the Mendozas to plunge their child into the spreading tide of filth, to accept a match which they must privately have regarded as the worst sort of misalliance. Bribes may have been used. Or perhaps they felt, since they were nothing if not flexible, that rivals who apparently cannot be beaten might as well be joined. In any case, shrewdly or by compulsion, they agreed: the new Count of Ledesma—of course now hated and envied more than ever for his conjunction with that lofty clan—could have their helpless girl.

Henry, with Juana and the whole court, went to Guadalajara for the wedding. The Mendozas—like the Velascos, like the very rich everywhere—knew how to entertain. There were bullfights, tournaments, fireworks, contests to catch golden rings on the tips of lances, parties and parties. Henry contributed a sumptuous present —if more, perhaps, to the father than to the bride: he raised Guadalajara to the rank and dignities of city. One supposes that the Bishop of Calahorra (Mencia's uncle—and now, astoundingly, Beltrán's) performed the Nuptial Mass. The great ball afterward seems to have taken place *al fresco;* the family's immense *mudéjar* palace had been substantially finished the year before but perhaps was not yet quite ready for a gathering of such proportions. It went on for ever—all afternoon, past sunset, into the early autumn darkness "with many lanterns."[11] Their varied thoughts as they danced in the high, hot, transparent night we can only guess. One would like especially to know the Queen's. But all the record says is that as soon as everything was decently concluded she departed. There is no evidence that she ever again set foot in Guadalajara.

Henry himself went off in a different direction—toward the north. A mysterious message had reached him during the festivities:

in Atienza, disguised, an agent of the Generalidad of Barcelona was waiting and seeking private audience, to tell him something that could not be entrusted to paper. Henry, too, rode almost in secret, "with very few companions."[12] And that meeting to which he galloped, all unknowing, through the dust and garnered wheat and bleeding vineyards was to prove among the most portentous of his life. It dragged him into a fresh morass of shames and failures. It internationalized his woes. In the end, and by one of those tangled skeins of quirk and coincidence which are no less common in Spanish history than in that of any other country, it took Villena—most perilous result of all for Henry's fortunes—into the enemy ranks.

But events so large require their separate chapter.

13.
Villena Defects

Villena's abandonment of Henry has its source, oddly enough, in the affairs of Carlos of Viana. That unfortunate Prince—Juan's oldest son by his first wife, brother of the divorced and even more unfortunate Blanca—has already made brief appearances in our annals. We glimpsed him, a youth of sixteen, at the betrothal of his sister to Henry on the plains beside the Ebro in 1437. During the visit of the two courts at Alfaro twenty years later, we found him figuring darkly in Juan's rancorous contemplations. But he must now be brought forward: by the year of La Beltraneja's birth his fate had grown inextricably linked with Henry's.

It is hard to work up much enthusiasm for Carlos of Viana, although historians both Navarrese and Catalan have tried. He wrote turgid essays and bad poems and worse translations of Aristotle—in one of the weakest, wobbliest hands (he had palsy, and probably consumption) to which the eyes of scholars have ever been condemned. In leg-of-mutton dressing gowns he moped about the castles of Olite and Estella, consulting his dried basilisk or fondling his lute. He was neurotic, passive, irresolute, ductile, limp. No less was Henry, it might be retorted. But where Henry was kind and modest, Carlos was pretentious and vain. For his Castilian brother-in-law's loyalty and deep sense of honor, in Carlos were substituted treachery, hypocrisy, deceit.

No basilisk will be needed to see how this guileful dilettante was exactly the sort of son to arouse both repugnance and an uneasy twinge of recognition in his father. But the antipathy was far more than personal. Although Carlos had unquestionably become the legal King of Navarre upon his mother's death, Juan—as we have observed—was set to keep him from the title and the power. Their early contention had dragged on through the final years of the reign of Henry's father and the first of Henry's own. But with the birth of young Fernando, and Juan's resolve to make that autumn child his sole successor, it gathered force. It came to a climax when the tricky Prince and Blanca—back in Navarre upon the heels of her divorce and with some natural grievances herself—put their disgruntled heads together. Juan had moved at once to grim revenge: he disinherited both of them. Then he summoned their sister Leonor, youngest of his three children by the Queen of Navarre, along with her French husband, Gaston of Foix, and made them an enticing offer: appointment as his inheritors in Navarre—if Foix would invade the realm. Gaston descended from the Pyrenees, met Carlos and his Navarrese supporters outside Estella in May of 1456, and overwhelmed them. Carlos, pell-mell, fled from the field of battle and the kingdom, never to return.

This is hardly the place to chronicle his *Wanderjahre* in search of help, fascinating (and at times even slightly comic) though they may have been. First Charles VII of France, and then the Pope, politely showed him the door. But in Naples he at last found solace with his uncle Alfonso the Magnanimous, who took him around for rides in flower-decked chariots and talked airily of sorting out his problems with his father and having him succeed not only to Navarre but to the Crown of Aragón itself. Disobligingly, however, the bejeweled wizard died, and Carlos went on to Sicily—since the thirteenth century part of Aragón. There the inhabitants found him sufficiently Italianate and gaudy to suggest his ruling in his father's place. There, too, he began negotiations with Henry—eternal champion of lost causes—for Isabel's hand. And with that he really strung his noose. Juan, who was determined that Isabel should at least remain uncommitted until he could think of some further plan to get her in his toils, lured him back to the mainland with intoxicating hints about reconciliation; he entered Barcelona to screams of joy. The Catalans, in cold reality, cared not a fig for Carlos. But they hated authority of any kind, Juan himself they had always considered a foreign tyrant out to cheat them of their precious privileges, and they found in the droopy and unexpected visitor a splendid weapon—much as the Castilian barons were finding in young Alfonso—to use against their lawful King. They pulled long faces over his trampled rights. Somewhere they dug up a wooden throne and tacked it around with crimson velvet and urged him to sit on it; it was really his. What they were unable to do was to dissuade him from being gullible enough to accept an invitation by his father for a visit to Lérida. As soon as he was in the paternal chamber, Juan clapped him into irons and locked him away in the castle's tower.

The reaction of the Catalans was instantaneous; at last they had found a good excuse for ridding themselves of Juan. Revolution broke out in the streets of Barcelona the morning of February 8, 1461. Placards went up on walls: To arms! Death for the oppressor! Free our noble Prince! The Generalidad convened in special session. Juan's governor Galcerán de Requesens, found quaking in a hollow tree, they threw into jail. Unshaven groups, muttering and clenching their fists, converged on the Town Hall and shouldered in. Red flags were waved; people leaped upon tables shouting tiresome cries about equality and democracy. By night they had worked themselves to such a fury that they decided to march at once upon Lérida. Juan fled before them: if there was one thing in the world that could strike alarm to his patrician heart, it was a mob of howling radicals. He took refuge in Zaragoza. But the vials of wrath were uncorked. The regicidal posse which had advanced on Lérida with butcher knives and staves grew to an army of thousands. Swiftly all Cataluña, from Perpignan to Tortosa, burst into flame. Valencia, long smoldering, seized the occasion to throw off allegiance. The rebellion spread overseas: Mallorca, then Sardinia and Sicily, came in. All of Juan's Crown was suddenly imperiled. With the insurgent army pouring west from Fraga, he turned his captive free.

Carlos's unhappy tale, however, was drawing to its close. Once back in Barcelona, he behaved with even greater folly than before. He dispatched to Zaragoza a list of haughty stipulations: all of Juan's officials in Barcelona must be recalled, Fernando had to be educated by Catalans, Juan himself could never again enter the Principality. On the abominated Juana Enríquez, sent at once to counter these insanities, he closed the city gates; she was left stranded and humiliated in Martorell, eaten up by bedbugs and suffering the first pangs of what she mistook for rheum. Most alarmingly of all, he pressed on with the negotiations for his marriage to Isabel. By August he had ambassadors in Castile, to sign the contracts. They brought the matter through—but were so ill advised, on their way home, as to stop for the night in Zaragoza; Juan tossed them into an oubliette and confiscated their documents.

God only knows what further retaliations the crafty old brain was planning. None of them, as matters transpired, were ever necessary. Carlos fell gravely ill. "La Enríquez! Arsenic!" the accusation arose. Pleurisy, more like. Whatever it was, he rapidly grew worse. By mid-September he was clearly done for. He made a testament; in it he willed his evanescent crown of Navarre to Blanca (a bequest which sealed her doom: Leonor of Foix, her odious sister, grabbed her and incarcerated her—and began to look through her own supplies of venom). Two days after the equinox, he died. His pale right hand, dripping with rings, was cut off and put on a silver pedestal for public adoration. The rest of him was enshrined within a tomb at the cathedral graced by his effigy crowned with a nimbus "in form of saint."[1] The Generalidad hired tramps and jailbirds, feigning blindness or lameness, to come and pray before it and leap up cured—a trick shortly uncovered by Juan's agents and literally laughed out of church.

So much for Carlos of Viana—even his dead body touched by fraud.

And what has it all to do with Henry? We have now come to that. Barcelona, too deeply committed to draw back, raged on with its revolt. Juan turned to France for aid. By the Treaty of Sauveterre in May of 1462, the French Spider and the Spanish Fox reached fateful terms: in exchange for an army to help subdue the rebels, Juan pawned to Louis his border counties of Cerdagne and Roussillon. Suddenly the Catalans looked ruin in the face: their figurehead was gone, French troops were moving south against them. Where, in their own extremity, could they hope for succor? Why, where but in Castile? There seemed to be no other refuge left. If Henry could be led to assume their cause, they might still not be lost. Once more the Generalidad met in a panicked session. They voted to hold out their wavering crown to Henry and selected a man named Juan Copones—"astute and shameless and malicious,"[2] Valera calls him —to slip through Aragón and communicate the offer.

It was this same Copones, to end our brief excursion to foreign parts, who lay hidden in Atienza while Henry rode up from Guadalajara and Beltrán's marriage. The wait had given him plenty of time to rehearse. Anyhow, even Copones's worst enemies admit that he possessed "great eloquence."[3] His speech, when Henry had finally arrived and they were face to face alone, gives proof of it. For a while he was too crushed by sorrow to start; he could only sob. Then he wiped his eyes and pulled himself together. No human tongue, he said, could relate the woes of what he had the gall to label "our Republic."[4] That evil Juan—"as surely you know, high and serenest King?"—had hounded their dear Carlos to his death. And now, the "obedient son" out of the way, he had loosed his spite upon the Catalans themselves. He was set to "dissipate their goods" and "consume their lives." Who could endure such "murders," such "unbridled rage"? Not they. When kings ceased to act "with love and mercy," vassals had every reason to fall off. Allegiance could be demanded only when deserved. On and on with sententious pronouncements of the sort. But he was working to the point. Henry himself had better claim, "both human and divine," to be their ruler. Not only theirs, in fact; by "straight descent" all Aragón— here the hook really went in—ought to belong to him (presumably through his maternal grandfather Fernando of Antequera—although why this should have given Henry more right to the realm than Juan, who was his son, could not have been very successfully explained). And when he reached his peroration, he opened every stop. "Wherefore, your Noble Excellence, we have chosen you our true and sovereign lord. On the part of the whole Principality, with all its cities and towns and villages, and by their powers, which I have brought, I now salute you as our King. In their name, I extend the fealty and obeisance of subjects—and beg, with all due reverence and humility, that you will take us for your vassals and cast around us, in protection, your imperial cloak."

"Serenest King!" "Your Noble Excellence!" "Imperial cloak!" Henry was quite as dazzled as poor Carlos had ever been. He stammered his thanks; he would do his best to be worthy of this signal honor. There was a formality, however: his advisers, too, would have to approve so large a matter. Let Copones come along with him to Segovia. There his acceptance could be made official.

But he met with difficulties in the Council. Carrillo, the Archbishop, instantly objected: his secret ties were all with Juan. Even stronger opposition came from Villena. Nothing that smiled on Henry's fortunes could please the Marqués; his power depended on keeping his master in constant straits, "reduced rather than prospered."[5] Sovereign of Cataluña—and even Aragón—in addition to Castile, Henry might well be strong enough to do without him.

That prospect threw him into such a state that for once his forky tongue spoke out with frankness. The Catalans, he said shrewdly, if none too graciously, had not the least interest in Henry himself. Their offer, like everything they did, contained a hidden purpose: all they were really after was the military aid which Copones, grilled in private, had dismounted from his oratorical high horse and proceeded to request. No, he could never approve it, would never allow it; those of his colleagues who pointed out that Juan, in similar circumstances, would hardly have hesitated to seize the Castilian crown he glared into silence. But he could not move the King. Henry, also for once, refused to listen. The Catalans had asked for him; the Catalans would have him. His mind was made up. Villena was left gnawing at his beard—and thirsting for the revenge he was so soon to find. Copones started home with Henry's acceptance—and the guarantee that Castilian troops would shortly be on their way.

Henry is often criticized for this foolish plunge into the politics of Cataluña; how, one is asked, could he have let himself be drawn so blindly into that Dismal Swamp? It was, to be sure, among his worst mistakes. But public conduct issues from private springs. These people with whom we deal are not abstractions in a textbook. They were human beings. Their feet hurt, they had headaches, they itched and belched and sneezed; their ailments and physical oddities had vastly more to do with the destiny of nations than most historians are willing to admit. Above all, they had feelings. And Henry's were perhaps especially acute. Cull, butt, pariah, fugitive from the smirk, the waggled finger—so he had lived for almost forty years. Moreover, at the time he was fresh from a humiliation worse than all the rest—the ridicule at little Juana's birth: his *amour-propre*, such as it had ever been, was very nearly at its nadir. Is it cause for comment if he fell ready prey to Copones's adulation, if he did not, or would not, realize that the Catalans had turned to him simply since they could think of no one else? Small wonder that he took the offer like a desert soil the dew: at last he was wanted, courted, needed, approved. One may, if one wishes, call it childish pride. But there are kinder, better, words for this reaction of a starved and bludgeoned heart.

A generous heart, as well: all Henry ever asked was the first crumb—he would gladly give the loaf. Of course the Catalans, he hastened to advise them, could proclaim him in Barcelona; let them raise his pennons. Certainly they could begin to issue money in his name and with his likeness. He would come himself, before long, to accept the homage of their Cortes. Meanwhile, he sent the troops which he had promised: twenty-five hundred of Castile's best cavalry, led by "distinguished captains."[6]

But this army never reached Barcelona. How they even entered Cataluña is far from clear. If they went through Aragón—the quickest way—one could ask no plainer proof of Juan's necessity, his military want. But however they came, once they had crossed the Principality they found themselves in trouble. Indeed, in a hopeless dilemma: the French army had already arrived and was laying siege to Barcelona. To get in and join their new allies they would first have to dislodge the French. But war between Castile and France was out of the question: officially they were friends, confederates, bound by ancient treaties. Both armies were at bay; after all the rush and fanfare, the only thing they could do was sheathe their weapons and sit down and peer at each other back and forth across the lines.

Hands were wrung everywhere. Now that the situation had come about, it would have seemed predictable enough. Why had no one foreseen it? (Perhaps Villena had—but kept the thought to himself, for his own purposes.) And what could be done about it? Nothing, to all appearances. The armies chafed and surged. Barcelona emitted piteous wails for help. Juan began to rattle in Zaragoza. Henry, back in Segovia, was on pins and needles: if Juan decided to move east to aid his own allies, there might be war with Aragón as well as France. Louis looked down over the Pyrenees and laughed.

It was Louis, in the end, who took some action. Had not both Juan and Henry, he suggested, lost all perspective in their long debate? Might not a foreign viewpoint be useful? Surely there was a way to solve the deadlock. He offered himself as arbiter, as judge.

Louis's motives are evident enough. It was no more to his advantage than to Villena's to see Henry "prospered," to have a united kingdom at his south. On the contrary, keeping Castile reduced and clipped by troubles—and he had a prime diminishment in mind—was his best hope of warding off its entry into the fearsome coalition of Burgundy and England and Portugal which he saw fast closing around him (an embassy from Edward IV to Henry had set out, in these very weeks, with just such aim). Why Henry accepted the proposal is something else. But Louis was new on the French throne, his reputation as a double-dealer had not yet taken wings; there was still a feeling of curiosity and even optimism about him. Moreover, he acted with consummate skill. It had been a mere captain from the French army at Barcelona (in case anything went wrong) whom he deputed to take to Henry the first hint of his availability as referee. Finding that overture accepted, or anyway not rejected out of hand, he turned to more open measures: at the Christmas season of 1462 he sent one of his "chief cavaliers"[7] in formal mission to the Castilian court.

We do not know this envoy's name. But it is obvious that he was a man both close to Louis's bosom and of considerable finesse. He wasted little time on Henry. It was with Villena and Carrillo that he closeted himself—and for some very risky talk. He need not have worried. Louis's insidious plan, which he cautiously sketched out, happened to fit exactly with the private designs of those two magnates. The price they proceeded to ask for their connivance in it, although it could not yet be officially accepted, struck him as not too high. And if his secret converse yielded the hoped-for fruit, his behavior in public won everybody's heart. A ball was held in his honor. Juana (flirtatious creature, and Beltrán, with his marriage, was somewhat less available) saw to it that he be selected as her partner. Afterward, he sighed and smiled. Having danced with so great a lady, he announced, never in all his life would he dance again. Those charming French: such a delightful race surely could plan no harm. If Henry had any doubts, Villena dispelled them: Louis's verdict on Cataluña, he perfidiously asserted, would be entirely in favor of Castile. Naturally, for so important an event as its promulgation, Louis and Henry would have to meet. A place for the encounter was agreed upon—at the river Bidasoa on their common borders. A general date was set—not long after Easter. The ambassador went home. Villena and Carrillo, Henry told him, would soon follow—in order to confer with Louis himself, to go over the French Sentence in advance and sign it in his name: they would have *carte blanche* to act on his behalf.

Carte blanche—how could he have given it so unconcernedly? Villena's opposition to the whole Catalan adventure, and his ill-concealed resentment when his advice was brushed aside, might at least have put him on his guard. Here, truly, one is left agape. But give

it he did, and the two conspirators—along with Henry's secretary
Alvar Gómez, another dog in the manger—left for France. Louis
came down to Bayonne for their arrival. Immediately the reward
for their betrayal of Henry was discussed. Carrillo's is not specified;
cash, probably, and it may have been on this occasion that he received the promise of the daughter of Pierres de Peralta, Constable
of Navarre (a kingdom where Louis, though the house of Foix, now
had much weight), for his bastard Troilo. Villena's, however, is
known: twelve thousand French crowns a year and a match of his
own second son with an illegitimate daughter of Louis. These crude
details once settled, Louis showed them his Sentence. When Villena
finally saw its staggering terms, no doubt he was sorry he had not
demanded an even higher price. But it was too late to bargain any
further; unblinkingly he stamped it with Henry's seal. Louis made
his famous aside about not having exactly lost his shirt, Villena
pocketed the first installment of his thirty pieces of silver, word
went south to Henry that everything had been profitably concluded
—an adverb which he took to apply to himself—and that he should
come along for the state ceremony.

Somehow Henry was persuaded—by Beltrán, one imagines—
that his meeting with Louis had to be brought off in the highest
style, with flourish and pomp: Trastámara must not be shaded by
Valois. Or perhaps on this occasion, devoid though Henry was of
vanity, few inducements were required. He felt less gloomy than
usual, felt almost vivacious. Soon, thanks to the generosity of Louis,
the trouble in Cataluña would be settled; he could even go straight
on from the Bidasoa to receive the plaudits of his admiring new
subjects. The Queen was pregnant again—and this time there might
not be such scandal, such outcry, as there had been over little Juana.
At least he was not going to repeat his error of parading her about.
In fact he would leave her in Aranda; there her condition could not
be so widely discussed. Anyway, he wanted no clutter of women on
this trip. He would go with only his inner circle. Of course he
would take his Moorish bodyguard, all three hundred of them;
perhaps they would make a better impression on the French than
they had ever made at home. And Beltrán and Valenzuela and
Gómez de Cáceres (too bad that Lucas could not be along, how he
would have enjoyed it) and his new *mayordomo mayor* young Andrés

de Cabrera—oh all of them. They would have a splendid time. He even decided to stop off in Segovia and pick up the crown jewels, "which he never used."[8] To that end, in February, they all rode jostling and glittering over the white roof of the Guadarramas, down through the silent pines laden with snow, into the beloved and dreaming city. There they made their final preparations. While harnesses were gilded and feathers fluffed, Henry had time to slip away to the lodge at Balsaín for a last look at his four-footed menagerie before so long an absence. But the days were pressing in. Early in March, with *"toda la sodomía,"*[9] he started north.

In Burgos they crossed with the English ambassadors, and delay or no Henry had to receive them. They put Edward's case before him. An Anglo-Castilian alliance would be of mutual advantage. They reminded him of his English ancestors, of the "perpetual amity"[10] sworn between Pedro the Cruel and England the century before. Henry listened graciously. But his Plantagenet blood (he was a great-great-grandson of Edward III) by then was running pretty thin. The reference to Pedro—murdered by the founder of Henry's line—was in questionable taste. Besides, without Villena to instruct him he never knew how to act. All he could do was procrastinate: some complications were thought up which obliged the embassy to go home for consultation. Lent almost over, through lands of the Velascos and Manriques (who shut their gates) and then the first low-running clouds in from the sea, he hastened toward the coast. At Fuenterrabía, in sight of the wide mouth of the Bidasoa and Saint-Jean-de-Luz beyond it, he rode up to the castle and took off his spurs. His retinue, like a cloud of butterflies, settled upon the slopes around it and in the village below. The historic confrontation —of which we have so many accounts, which Colmenares calls a "day of much ostentation but of even more dishonor for Castile"[11] and Commynes uses as springboard for his famous sermon on the Dangers of Princely Interviews—seemed at hand.

Yet only seemed—for at the last moment a hitch came about: just where to meet? Louis had no thought of traversing the river and leaving his own soil; the kings of France did not run abroad like housewives begging a dish of salt. But neither, by the same token, did the kings of Castile. Chancellors and Masters of Ceremonies met and haggled. Finally Henry himself, to whom such frills of etiquette meant less than nothing, cut through the knot. Why all the fuss?

One beach was much like another; what was so terrible about entering France? His advisers threw up their hands: *lèse majesté*—unthinkable! But Henry paid no mind. He was going—that was that. And he would wait no longer. Let the French be so informed, that very night.

Louis was more than ready; the next morning he gathered his nobles and took position on the river's northern bank, attired "*si mal que pis ne povoit*"[12]—and consumed by curiosity, no doubt, to see this collection of freaks and catamites which had come up from the south. Was the sun shining? We do not know; the weather is one of the few details of the occasion that nobody recorded. We can only hope so; it would have struck a fine refulgence from the Castilian cavalcade as it rode down from Fuenterrabía and debouched upon the strand—even the "*azemileros y mozos d'espuelas,*"[13] the muleteers and grooms, wore Venetian brocade. Their pennoned vessels bobbed and strained; to sound of trumpets they embarked. And once their fleet—"a veritabie armada"[14]—had put forth, once they were all fanned out and bearing down on France across the springtime water, they made an even braver show. With Henry was young Mendoza, in episcopal state. Nearby came don Beltrán, "*le conte de Lodesme, son mygnon, en grant triomphe.*"[15] Great triumph indeed. One of his slippers, thrust conspicuously forward, was studded with gems. (Why only one? It is among history's minor riddles.) The sail that wafted him along was tissue of gold—an altar cloth, reportedly, filched from a neighboring church. But some of the others were almost equally impressive. Valenzuela, the pitiful transvestite, lolled in a gaudy pinnace thronged with the officials of San Juan; one shudders to think what draperies he had chosen for the day. Another bore Gómez de Cáceres—Master of Alcántara, the beauteous ex-*torero*—ablaze among the cavaliers of his own Order. Knights, bishops, marshals, Moors, priors, and mantled counts—the river was awash with them. We cannot be surprised that Louis, as each vessel neared, twitched Carrillo's sleeve and babbled his excited question: was that the King? So dazed he seems to have been, in fact, that it must have cost him a considerable effort—when Henry finally was pointed out to him, crow among swans—to recall his royal manners and doff his greasy hat.

Henry's own condition, the great moment upon him, was even more distraught. Glimpsing from afar the salutation of his host, he still had wits remaining to return it, to uncover (for once he had not worn his heathen fez). But by the time he stepped ashore he had clearly—in spite of all his good intentions—lost his nerve. Strangers, the peerage of France, a speech, public exposure—everything that his shy, self-conscious heart most feared—loomed just before him. But this time there was no place he could flee: it was much too late—Louis was coming forward. He forced himself ahead, all teeth and elbows. They met. That Henry actually kissed Louis is matter for debate. He did take hold of his hand: whether panic had let slip his affectionate nature or he simply needed something to hang on to one would be hard put to say. Louis was totally unable to wrench it free, and locked in this hapless union they walked across the beach. No chairs had been provided; because of his hemorrhoids, Louis never cared to sit when he could stand. They came to a little ledge, a jut of limestone. There they stopped. Henry leaned back against it. Louis called to one of his greyhounds and warily maneuvered it between them. While they tweaked its ears in common apprehension, their private colloquy began.

What could they have found to talk of? These two uneasy kings beside the Bidasoa had next to nothing in common. They both liked ratty clothes and low companions, but with that their resemblance ceased. Not only does one wonder what they said; one even wonders in what tongue they could have couched it, since Louis had no Spanish and Henry little French. Latin, perhaps—although it seems a language less than ideally suited for social chat. Whatever the vehicle, Henry floundered along in it for a full quarter of an hour: surely, for him, a record. When he at last gave out, Louis responded. His own remarks were mercifully—and understandably—brief (even when he was at his best he stuttered). He broke them off with a gesture to his courtiers. They crowded in, and Henry's followed suit. The long-awaited Sentence was brought forth—a huge unwieldy parchment, with a seal of emerald wax strung on by particolored ribbons. Louis handed it to Alvar Gómez (what a choice!). Gómez elaborately unrolled it. He started to read.

Henry was lucky to have a rock behind him: otherwise his legs might have given way. For with the very opening lines he saw his ruin; the April sky fell in. Cataluña? His dreams of sovereignty there? He was ordered to get out. Get out? It could not be. But it was, it was: the horrible clauses dropped like lead, like stricken birds, like bombs. The troops which he had sent to Barcelona must be recalled. Anything they had freed already, "cities or towns or castles,"[16] had to be relinquished. He must renounce all help to Cataluña—and abrogate his claim, even his wish, to be its ruler. The ancillary dicta of the verdict—Navarre, Valencia, hostages—flowed past him, off him, in a phantasmagoric torrent, like senseless echoes in a dream. That Juan was also wrecked (no payment of the indemnity for his Castilian holdings; now he would never have money to redeem Cerdagne and Roussillon; they would remain with France) he scarcely noticed. Nothing had any meaning except one monstrous fact: he was estopped, denied, undone, in Cataluña. And all he was to have from the whole sickening mess was the *merindad*, the income, of Estella. Estella? Who cared about that?

Somehow he survived the rest of the ceremony. (His leave-taking of Louis no one chose to describe.) Somehow—while the two courts "fell togither by the eares,"[17] while Spaniards sneered at the tacky garments of the French and French sneered back about the little Negroes and "large number of handsome boys"[18] among the Spaniards—he broke away and found his boat and re-embarked. Safe on the other side, he galloped to Fuenterrabía. He flung into the castle; he dropped down upon a chair. And there he let it come; in mounting waves the full magnitude of what had happened rolled over him.

Forbidden Cataluña! But it was what he had wanted—had needed —perhaps more than anything else in his life. And now, just in his hands, it had all been snatched away. Nor was that the worst of it. Such inner blows, such private disappointments, he might endure; he was long used to them, one more—with time and patience—he might absorb. What truly galled, however, what seemed beyond all bearing, was his position in regard to the Catalans. He had pledged them assistance. He had given them his promise—one thing, at least, which he had kept inviolate, at which he had never failed. How could he bring himself to break it? And yet he had to: he had pledged his word to Louis just as well. The gaff was deep inside him. He writhed upon it. But there was no way off it, no way out. The verdict had borne his seal. Whatever it cost him, he must tell the Catalans.

He summoned Copones, who had been brought along. He made it very brief. He had changed his mind, he said. He could no longer lend his name to Cataluña, let alone his troops. The army he had sent was going to be ordered home. Please take his standards down. Do not expect his visit. He was sorry, but the whole thing had been a mistake. They would simply have to look for someone else.

Copones saw that the game was at an end. He threw away his mask. "Serenest King," he said—but how differently the phrase came out this time, how laced with irony and scorn—"giving ourselves to the Castilian House we thought to be protected—and now we are destroyed. We believed ourselves in haven—and we are cast forth. Consider, my lord . . . how foul the case will look: the very hand most obligated to sustain us has put us to the knife. Well, since you so have chosen, listen to what I tell you—and never forget it. From this day onward you shall not lack misfortunes—nor we Catalans a better hand than yours to hold us up. We care no more than that"—snapping of fingers, the cat was out at last—"for your Royal Highness. Revealed to all the world is the treachery of Castile! Come is the hour of its ruin and the dishonor of its King!"[19]

Bold language to a sovereign. But every word of it was true—and like a talon in Henry's heart. He made—could make—no answer. He looked helplessly at Copones. Copones gave him his shoulder, then contemptuously strode out. The room fell silent.

And in that silence, alone, his last poor pride a shambles, something dreadful, something not we nor he would ever have imagined, began to happen to Henry. Anger, choking and black, seems to have welled up inside him. Not at Copones: he had only done the bidding of his masters. Not even at Louis: he acted in the interest of his crown. No, anger at the one person who had worked beyond all right or decency or reason—at Villena. Villena: was it possible? Copones had phrased it well: bitter the case when the hand at greatest obligation plunged the knife. What would Villena be, ever have been, without him? He had brought him on to power—yes, almost to the scepter—from nothing, from nowhere, from the sniveling hunger of a page. Well, he had shown his sorry colors now. Worms, even such a worm as Henry felt himself beneath the lashing of Copones, could turn. Villena would find that out. Never again would Henry trust him. No more would he give his ear, his breast, to such a traitor. In shock, in helpless wrath there in the old castle by the sweep and fall of the Biscayan waters, he took that anguished resolve.

He showed it plainly in the days that followed. There were no scenes, no recriminations, none of that *"rotura,"* that open and ugly rupture, from which Henry always shrank. But in his fashion, taciturn and slow, he put the hot decision into cold effect. His seals of power he transferred to other hands: Beltrán's, Mendoza's. Villena's seat at the Council table was pointedly removed. Upon him, quietly but firmly, the door of Henry's private chambers closed.

Villena himself, at first, could not believe it. Henry was hurt, of course. But that was nothing new. Soon he could bring him round, could stroke him back into docility: had he ever failed at that before? The week went by, however, with the royal door still shut. Beltrán and young Mendoza—his worst foes—now strolled about on Henry's arm. Gradually, inexorably, he had to face the truth: Henry had set against him. And once he saw it, once he recognized the case without repair, he knew precisely what to do. No ax must fall; he could not risk a formal dismissal. Much better to withdraw, to have the final breach seem of his own choosing: *venienti occurrite morbo*— it was always his technique. The language of his note of valediction made no bones: his staying there exposed him "to great peril,"[20] the hostility against him was all too evident, he "had determined"— there it was—"to depart the court."[21] And to the words he added acts. He got his things together, collected the Archbishop of Toledo, and rode off. Safe in Carrillo's town of Alcalá he wrote at once, offering his services, to the Castilian rebels and to Juan. In short— with all his height and mass and expertise in statecraft, his lifelong knowledge of the inmost secrets both of the realm and of its sovereign—he went over to the League.

The statement needs no italics. At last the wolves were fully gathered, the ring had closed on Henry. In the coming terror, the *Dies Irae* which now bears down upon him, he will be naked to his enemies indeed.

14.

The Locks of the Storm

Did Henry realize the full significance of Villena's desertion? Probably not: at least, not then. Yet the trip to the Bidasoa left an indelible mark upon him; never again does he seem quite the same. Colmenares describes his entry into Segovia afterward—immersed in deep lassitude, spent, numb, with large "signs of sorrow."[1]

And scarcely was he home when a further grief befell him. Out of Aranda came intelligence sadly unlike what he heard from that town two years before. Juana had miscarried. One day while she was at a window (and nobody who has known Aranda in midsummer will find it strange), the sun had set her hair on fire. Attendants, hearing her screams, had run to her help; they managed to extinguish the blaze. But the shock proved too much for her. She aborted a six-month fetus, a male at that.[2]

As soon as Henry had disbanded the expedition he went to see her. Not surprisingly, he found her "thin and run-down."[3] What does surprise about this second pregnancy of Juana is the almost total silence which has surrounded it, both then and since. Why did the League not seize on it as added proof of her infidelity, as another weapon against Beltrán? Did they feel that in little Juana they already had sufficient ammunition for their defamatory campaign? Or had the Queen's condition, thanks to Henry's tardy caution, not been generally known? In any case, the melancholy event—at least outside the family circle—passed almost unnoticed. Henry himself stayed in Aranda only a few days. He did what he could for Juana's consolation and physical recovery. He pored mutely—and no doubt still quizzically—over the cradle of the other baby who had, perhaps to everybody's misfortune, survived. But his real attention seems to be elsewhere. A new idea, a new longing, was beginning to fill his mind.

He wanted to see Lucas.

It is natural enough, after all that had happened in the four cruel years since they said goodbye outside Madrid: Lucas was the one person with whom he had ever been able to unburden himself, to ease his heart. Yet it is quite as natural—and characteristic—that Henry fought down the impulse to go to him. Lucas had made his decision; the only considerate thing was to leave him to work it out in peace. Anyway, a journey to Jaén for that sole purpose would be much too obvious, would give rise to damaging comment—something which Lucas, now more than ever, needed to avoid. How nice if some other reason for a trip to Andalucía could be found; then he might visit Lucas by the way. None offered itself, however. Slowly he rode back to Segovia. No: best to forget it, to put away the wish.

But he could not forget it. Segovia made him think of Lucas even more—the scenes of their youth together, the places where they had walked and talked and sat. Wrapped in his woolen cloak, he revisited them all: the twisting streets of the *barrio* of Santa Coloma under the brooding arches of the aqueduct, the secret sedges beside the whispery Eresma, the tanneries, the Moslem forges, dark stalls in the Jewish quarter with their ancient, rancid smells that so delighted Henry but always made Lucas wrinkle up his elegant nose. And when the memories grew too sharp, the longing too intense, he plunged anew into building. His lovely plateresque retreat outside the city he had given away, to the Observant Franciscans. More reason, then, to furbish up the *casas reales:* polychromed arabesques went around the doorways, the lions' den was enlarged, new ceilings were ordered. Juana no longer desired to share his roof; he began a palace for her next to his own. He finished the Hall of the Pineapples in the Alcázar. But nothing helped; his thoughts kept turning to the south. And finally he could stand it no more. He sat down in one of his newly gessoed rooms and wrote to Lucas. Lucas replied: yes, come if Henry thought it wise (his own good heart, in spite of his misgivings, had won out). With that, Henry grew more restless than ever. But still he found no suitable excuse. The poplars turned; the year turned. It was October, November. The first snows fell—high on the topmost slopes of Monte Gobia, in the hushed forest at Balsaín.

Then suddenly, almost providentially, he had his chance: a crisis in Sevilla.

Of course Sevilla was always in an uproar of one sort or another. The feud between Guzmáns and Ponce de Leóns racked it from end to end. Its heavy concentration of Jews gave rise to special problems: false converts, relapses into heresy, "Old" Christians against "New." But in that autumn of 1463 fresh violence had gripped the city—a struggle for its miter. Fonseca, long its Archbishop, had been appointed to the see of Santiago de Compostela. Departing, he transferred Sevilla to his nephew. But Santiago, rent with disorders itself, turned out to be more than he could handle; he wanted his former crozier back. The nephew, however, was disinclined to yield it, and the clergy—still loyal (or at least resigned) to Fonseca—sent north a request for aid.

Henry leaped to grant it. Sevilla, Jaén: they were close enough together. He alerted Lucas—he would soon be on his way. So much had he thought about the trip that it took him very little time to get ready; so eager was he to depart that he decided not even to wait for his Segovian Christmas. Only Beltrán, of the young coterie, would be along; most of the others, with the jaunt to the Bidasoa, had already had enough of travel—and Henry, for the moment, of them. It tells us much, however, that he decided to take Diego Arias, his *contador mayor*, as well. The disreputable old *marrano* almost never went on these royal journeys: his health had begun to fail (he was in his seventies), he was far too busy at home trying to keep the realm's finances from total collapse. But Henry needed someone, anyone, of real experience in affairs of state. Already he was beginning to regret the break with Villena and to feel the pinch of his absence.

They reached Sevilla by mid-December. Nothing could be done about the warring magnates; they were little less than kings in Andalucía. Nor was Henry the sort of person who could have been expected to lose much sleep over heresy; he was widely considered an apostate himself. But he did at once attack the problem of the archbishopric. The turbulent young usurper was arrested and banished from the city. The leaders of that seditious element of the populace who had supported his schemes to fortify the cathedral and even seize the arsenal and the royal galleys in the river were rounded up; some were hanged, some sent in fetters back to Madrid. Harsh measures—for anyone so mild as Henry. But he was anxious to be done with it as soon as possible, to get on to Lucas. All through the tedious adjudications a flood of letters (and money, to groans of protest from Arias) went east toward Jaén—Lucas must be patient, Henry could hardly wait, "every day until he saw him was like a year."[4]

But there was yet another postponement. It seemed a pity, since they were now so close, not to see Gibraltar—something no king of Castile had been able to do for a long time. Henry intended to make the visit brief. But once he was there, he had surprising news: Alfonso of Portugal was in Ceuta, just across the Straits. Clearly the brothers-in-law should meet. Alfonso sailed across.

There is a bizarre, an unreal, quality about this reunion of Henry and Alfonso under the Rock. Beltrán served as "mediator"[5] throughout it, and we are told that Alfonso was grateful and gracious to him, that he urged Henry to uphold and even to advance the favorite's estate. Such affability in a man who unquestionably knew the gossip about his sister and Beltrán is odd enough. If he really believed in their "shameful relationship"[6]—and Palencia insists that he did—it borders on fantasy. Almost the only thing about the whole affair which can really be understood is the agreement that Alfonso should marry young Isabel, for Beltrán, whether the Queen's lover or not, still danced upon her interests, and it was entirely to Juana's advantage to see the Infanta married and shipped out of the country, to remove at least one obstacle on her daughter's path—already tenebrous—toward the Castilian crown. No matter that Alfonso was Isabel's cousin, that he was nearly thrice her age, a widower growing fat and with two children: so it was arranged.

How long it took this distressing word to reach Juan in Zaragoza (Isabel slipped through the net again, and this time to someone who could hardly be thrown into prison) we do not know. Nor can we tell the length of Henry's sojourn in Gibraltar. Some put it at ten days, some at only three. Aware of his impatience to be with Lucas, one is inclined to take the shorter figure. He sped the parting guest; he saw Alfonso—doubly his brother-in-law, if the new marriage plans should work out—on board his ship. To everybody's amazement, he conferred Gibraltar upon Beltrán. Then he hurried away.

The weather had turned miserable; it could hardly have been worse in High Castile. But Henry would no longer let anything keep him back from the one meeting for which he really yearned. Through "great waters and snow"[7] he pushed ahead. At Alcalá la

Real, nearing Jaén, he stopped: Lucas, he well knew, would want to come out and give him a state reception. A final messenger departed: he was there, and waiting. Beltrán, Lucas's old rival, unexpectedly revealed a trace of tact: he went off (or might he have been ordered?) to inspect the area's military installations. Everything at last was ready. On the day appointed, Henry came out from Alcalá and drew up with his retinue beneath its walls.

For weeks Lucas had been in a frenzy of preparation, and his welcoming parade, as it advanced on Alcalá that winter afternoon, almost stuns the eye: massed banners, glittering ranks of foot and *ballesteros*, huge copper drums slung from Arabian horses and gleaming and pounding, cymbals, enameled maces and ivory wands borne by pages in cloth of gold—on and on they came. Arias gawked in stupefaction, casting up with an expert's eye the cost of every bullioned sash and jeweled bridle. But Henry gave little heed. He was looking on, out, beyond, straining for his first glimpse of the figure he so longed to see. And finally he had it: Lucas himself at the far end of the procession—dressed head to foot amidst that splendor (wonderful man) in drab and penitential brown "to show his sufferings since he had been parted from the King."[8]

Not ten minutes more, not one, would Henry wait. Uncontrollably, *"yncontinente,"*[9] he struck rowels to his horse. Lucas, seeing him coming, himself cut free, broke away from the cavalcade. They closed; Lucas reined wildly in. He flung himself from his rearing horse. Stumbling, trying to make the three state bows of reverence as he went, he ran to Henry. He seized his hand and sought to press it to his lips. Henry tore it away. Lucas bent over and caught the hem of the royal cloak and covered that, instead, with kisses. Then he lifted his eyes. Henry was staring down at him, devouring him. They opened their mouths to speak. But neither of them—so riven were they by helpless joy, so strangled with love—could get out a single word.

They had found their voices as they cantered side by side back toward Jaén. And there was much for comment: Lucas had mounted the arrival with a master's hand. Two miles from the city they were met by the gathered clergy: copes, censers, the famous Cross of Jasper, chanting choirs. A little farther on, five hundred merry horsemen dressed *a la morisca* and with false beards and hollow silvered lances bore down on them in mock assault. At the spring of Santa María another troupe of thirty, disguised as Moslem maidens, pounced from behind the crags; they danced in and out among the procession, crouching, leaping, shaking their rattles and tambourines. Just under the city walls, four thousand children on wicker hobbyhorses and flourishing pasteboard swords marched forth in welcome; a thousand more, bearing crossbows made of straw, came on their heels.

Full night had fallen as they finally rode in to town. "Matrons and damsels"[10] on crowded balconies applauded and threw flowers: the streets were ablaze with lanterns and flambeaux. Platoons of silver trumpets preceded them to Lucas's *posada*. Supper was ready. Henry, whose usual meals were slapdash affairs, more "disorder"[11] than anything else, ate on a platform under a canopy of cloth of gold. Five butlers stood behind him. The salvers of fish (it was Lent) were brought in announced by hautboys and tambors: Lucas himself, out of his friarly habit and now in miniver and brocade, presented them to Henry, upon his knees. And even when supper was over, there was still no rest. Once the exhausted guest was upstairs and in his bedroom, eight small shy boys came tiptoeing in, wearing falsefaces and tunics embroidered with orange flames, and did a little dance. Only when they had bowed and skittered away could Henry fall on his bed.

Throughout the visit he was the soul of consideration. He accompanied Lucas to as many of the services in the cathedral (so dire a place for his host, the place where everything was to end) as he could stomach; without comment he paid his respects to the handkerchief of Saint Veronica and its Santísima Faz. Nobody had ever been able to get along with the local bishop, Alonso de Peleas, a terrible person who caused all sorts of trouble and had once pulled up his vestments and urinated on the Bishop of Coria to see how his white soutane would look "of a different hue";[12] although he had been the celebrant of the Nuptial Mass in the cathedral of Córdoba, Henry sent him out of town. Another of his official acts—if one which may not have been quite so much to the people's liking—was to order release of all Moslems held hostage by the city. To see it accomplished, he went down himself into the *mazmorras* (what were dungeons to Henry?); with his own hands, Palencia adds meanly, he removed the chains of "the young men."[13]

But the weather was still too bad for much in the way of public

acts; most of the festivities took place inside Lucas's mansion. Because of the season, there could be no balls. Every other kind of
entertainment, however, was spread on: masques, concerts, *juegos
florales* and declamation of odes, performances by acrobats and jugglers, by bearded magicians in tall peaked hats and cabalistic gowns.
We do not know whether Lucas's favorite dragon was out—that
wiggly green monster of wood and painted canvas whose maw
spewed blazing young pages, their sleeves soaked in brandy which
they ignited just before they tumbled forth. (Lucas had whole storerooms of these mechanical marvels; even as a grown man he still
delighted in anything that spun or crawled or popped.) But certainly the famous tapestries that told the story of Nebuchadnezzar
were on display; they had only recently been acquired. All the great
salas, in fact, and most of the bedrooms, were hung with precious
stuffs: cut velvet, cloth of Arras, silks from Turkey and Venice and
Persia. Against that gorgeous background, under the *sala rica's*
Moorish ceiling of vermilion and azure and emerald (it is still there),
the whole city was entertained. There were receptions for the Corporation, the clergy, the University, the guilds. The gentry themselves came nightly to a banquet: everyone ate from silver, and even
the thousands of candles were embossed with Lucas's arms.

But it was not all fiestas. In the mornings, and late at night, Henry
and Lucas found quiet time to be together. What they said (what
they did) in private is not revealed. But these hours were what
Henry had come for, the reason he had endured the assizes in Sevilla
and the yawning boredom of the state visit to Gibraltar. He began
to relax, to unwind. Lucas, who could no more stop being chic than
he could stop breathing, had him wakened every morning by a
stringed orchestra outside his door. Although her husband's youth
with Henry was something Teresa would no doubt have liked to
forget, she managed to be pleasant and even gay: the time when she
would flee to a nunnery was still far off. The weather improved;
they were able to take rides, to have *meriendas*—picnics—among the
aloes and cactus.

In sum, and rare though it may sound, Henry was happy. The
days slipped by, turned to a week, a fortnight, and still he did not
leave. Letters arrived from Juana, no less uneasy than Teresa about
the reunion: what was keeping him, why did he not come home? He
set them aside. Other letters, from what was left of his Council,

came in the wake of Juana's—letters charged with warning and alarm: strange things were afoot against him in the north, plots were hatching, the League was on the move. Those, too, he tried to ignore; "he preferred not to believe them."[14] But they kept coming; they grew more ominous, more insistent. As if to support them, disconcerting omens once more began to appear: there were eclipses of the sun and the moon, a girl was born with a penis hanging from her tongue, vast armies were seen battling in the air. Finally, reluctantly, he knew he had to go.

Hints of the parting do swim up from the discreet and laconic accounts. Henry seems to have broken down at the very end: Lucas had to come back with him, no longer could he go on alone, he would do anything for him, would even dismiss Beltrán. But almost at once he got hold of himself: this time there must be no argument, no clash of wills. Anyway, they both realized it was out of the question; the damage it would wreak on too many people, the "great scandals,"[15] would simply not be worth it. They would remember, though, would think one of the other, always. Perhaps each of them knew, in that quiet room, that a troth deeper than any Henry ever gave to Juana or Lucas to Teresa was being newly plighted.

Lucas clung close beside him to the last. He rode with him down the steep cobbled streets, through the gate, past the orchards and ancient olives, out to the edge of the *dehesa*, the open fields. There Henry made him stop. With "great tenderness"[16] they said their goodbyes. Henry promised to send him money in defrayment of the huge expense to which he had so obviously, yet so willingly, been put. After that they fell silent, holding each other's eyes, wondering if this might be their final parting. But there was no point in protracting it. Abruptly Lucas turned.

Henry sat gazing after him. Then he, as well, swung the head of his horse around. The visit was over. It had been a complete success: refuge, replenishment, reprieve, font of perdurable memory. One is as grateful as Henry—settling himself in the saddle, loosening his reins, cantering slowly across the *vega* and on toward the far Sierra Morena—that he had been able to have it. For the tempest was fast approaching. Never again (and this is why we have told it, why we too have lingered) would he know repose or peace—or even safety of his person.

The rumors about intrigues and "novelties"[17] (a word which in a land so conservative as Spain must always be read in the pejorative) were only too true: from the moment Henry left for the south Villena had been at his treasonous work. The first thing he did was to slip off for an interview with Juan—at Corella, up in Navarre. There, apart from being welcomed into the bosom of the League, he received his initial instructions from its great impresario himself. The tenor of them is not hard to guess: close ranks among the barons, get Alfonso and Isabel (or at least Alfonso) out of Henry's power, both as figureheads for the imminent revolt and to prevent their being married in unsuitable quarters—in other words, quarters unfavorable to Juan's designs. Once back in Castile, the tireless Marqués began to carry out these mandates. Two of the nobles— Alba and the Count of Plasencia, Alvaro de Stúñiga—had not yet been firmly enlisted in the League. To secure their allegiance, and again in the greatest secrecy, he rode west. Plasencia seemed only waiting to be approached: his famous philippic against Henry (what obedience did he owe to such a person—"who does not even merit the name of man"?)[18] scorches the air. Alba required more guarantees—although his own were never worth the paper on which they were written. Yet he too acceded, and Villena returned to Alcalá and Carrillo, his partner in sedition. From that vipers' nest their poison continued to ooze forth: messengers went throughout the land "moving and altering the people,"[19] the Grandes themselves were adverted to "provision their castles and equip their troops."[20] Obviously trouble of the worst sort was at hand.

Just as obviously, Henry realized the fact as soon as he was home; no wishful thinking could conceal the change which had taken place while he was away, the gathering threat. What form it would assume he had no means of knowing. Yet he as well, in a fashion, took precautions. If there was to be any violence, he certainly did not want it to occur in Segovia; he set up residence in Madrid. He kept the Alcázar shut. Alfonso and Isabel, for their greater security, he quartered high in its Torre del Homenaje. Then there was not much he could do except sit and wait and see what would happen.

It was not long in coming; early one spring morning Villena moved. He called his chief confederates—the Count of Benavente (now his son-in-law), the Count of Paredes, the Admiral's oldest son Alfonso. They wasted no time: the plan—to take possession of the

Infantes, to seize Beltrán and even Henry—was already laid. With their attendants, and with weapons hidden beneath their robes, they went to the palace; they knocked loudly at the doors. When no one opened, they began to smash them in. Porters ran in defense; they fought their way past them. Henry, hearing the tumult and "sensing treason,"[21] quickly roused Beltrán. Together—and perhaps none too admirably—they took refuge in a secret passage. The barons burst into the royal apartments and found them empty: no Infantes, no favorite, no King—in short, no prey. In a desperate shift of strategy, Villena turned on his companions. He raised his voice. What were they doing there? he shouted at them. Why this disgraceful assault? Get out, get out! They saw his winks: they departed. As Henry emerged, Villena hastened to meet him. How lucky, he smiled, that he had happened to arrive for a visit at just that moment. Henry surveyed him. "Marqués," was all he answered, "what do you think of this treatment of my doors?"[22] It is generally taken as a proof of pusillanimity. Nothing could be remoter from the fact: the symbolic nature of royal doors, their representation of majesty itself, should be remembered. Villena, at least, caught the full implication of the remark. Nor can he have been under any illusion, from its cold and level tone, that his flimsy ruse had been detected. His smile faded. He shrugged, then turned and left.

The blow had failed. Indeed it had worse than failed, as things soon turned out: it recoiled upon Villena. Henry was even more distressed by what he knew to have been a thrust against Beltrán than at the one on himself. Quick as ever to spring to the support of a friend under attack, he made up his mind, at last, about what to do with the grandmastership of Santiago. He would give it— prize among prizes, "the chiefest thing," in his own words, "not only in my realms but in all the Spains"[23]—to Beltrán.

Even Henry must have realized the storm of rage which the dazzling appointment would let loose, especially in Villena's jealous breast. Nor was the Marqués slow to do everything in his power to ward off what was, for him, a total catastrophe: Santiago, the ambition of his life, draining through his fingers—and to Beltrán! Frantically he shot off to the Vatican an emissary—"a religious gentleman of great learning"[24]—with instructions to talk down and circumvent Henry's own, dispatched to secure approval of the nomination from the Pope. He induced Fonseca, as further dissuasion, to send Palencia himself. But neither the erudition of the "religious gentleman" nor the flood of billingsgate about Beltrán which Palencia uncorked before the Sacred Toe could outweigh the fourteen thousand florins Henry had thoughtfully provided. Paul signed the bulls, and Henry proceeded at once to the formal investiture.

He decided to hold it in Segovia—and to make it, for Beltrán's sake, as splendid as the circumstances allowed (many of the *comendadores* of the Order had indignantly refused to attend). There, in the cathedral, High Mass was sung, Henry holding the banner of Santiago throughout. As it ended, a robed procession, "with great flourish of instruments,"[25] wound from behind the choir. Beltrán, flanked by the priors of San Marcos and Uclés and draped in the Order's snow-white mantle with its crimson cross, strode in its midst. He came to Henry and knelt. Formally, as "vassal and Ensign of the Holy Apostle,"[26] he requested bestowal of the banner. Henry delivered it to him: for the first time since Luna's head rolled in the Plaza of the Ochavo, the realm had a Master of Santiago. Beltrán got to his feet—a Grande of Castile. Henry, too, rose and faced him. "Master," he said, in the ringing old language which dated back for centuries, "God grant you successful campaigns against the Moors."[27]

"Successful campaigns against the Moors!"—this to Beltrán, who had never been in a battle in his life, who was the chief recipient of the immense sums raised by Calixtus's Bulls of Crusade. If any myrmidons of the Comic Spirit were floating about in the vaults of the crumbling old cathedral that summer morning, they must have rocked with laughter. But there can have been no mirth—can only have been the blackest and most vengeful fury—in Villena. It is hardly a coincidence that on the very day of the investiture he signed his last and most binding pact with the nobles. Nor can we be much surprised that a new plot against Henry and Beltrán, a second recourse to violence, came almost at once.

This one was planned more intelligently: no daylight assaults, no breaking down of doors. To bring it about, Villena put himself in "privy contact"[28] with a captain of Henry's guard, Hernán Carrillo. Carrillo was married to one of Juana's attendants, who agreed to let the assailants into the Queen's palace by dark of night; thence they could easily pass, since the two were contiguous, to Henry's own.

The team was somewhat modified, with each assigned his special task: Paredes (implacable Manrique) to take Henry, Alba and Plasencia the Infantes, Villena's brother Girón, Master of Calatrava, to go straight at Beltrán and—for if what they had intended to do with the favorite in the plot at Madrid had been rather vague, it was now made ruthlessly clear—"to slit his throat."[29] Villena himself, needed close by but determined not to be caught again with his hands in the dough, secured an audience with young Isabel for the night of the attack.

But the second attempt, for all its skillful planning, proved no more successful than the first. The League, too, had turncoats, and at the very final moment—Villena was already in the palace and closeted with Isabel—someone gave the plot away. Henry sought such help as he could hastily summon. Young Pedro Arias (generally called Pedrarias), who lived just next door and was fast taking over his ailing father's place, was vehement in his advice: arrest Villena, he insisted—or better yet, kill him, and he volunteered for the job. Such others of the Council as could be called together agreed. But Henry demurred: he had given the Marqués a safe-conduct for the talk with Isabel. All he would permit was that he be confronted with the news, "to see what he might answer."[30] What the visitor downstairs had to answer anyone could surmise. Once more he threw up his hands in pretended astonishment. God forbid, he said, that such an "ugliness"[31] be true! It was all news to him. He would be off immediately to investigate. "And with that, his face gone white, he left the palace."[32] It took him only moments to cancel the assault. Then, without even waiting to go home, he fled the city and barricaded himself in El Parral, the monastery just across the Eresma which he had founded.

His escape had been no less narrow than Henry's own. But he still would not give up. One final blow, he determined, had to be attempted—and no longer with cloaks and daggers but with troops, with full military might. Henry was invited to a parley with the barons, in the fields between San Pedro de las Dueñas and Villacastín; "eager for peace"[33] as ever, he accepted. The counts of Alba and Plasencia assembled six hundred horse and lay in wait at Villacastín. Villena, a few miles away in Lastras, took up his post with three hundred more. From the north, from Turégano, Girón and the Manriques were to descend with a large force of their own, con-

verge with the others at the place of conference, and encircle Henry
and Beltrán and cut them down.

Yet chance again intervened. Henry, who had spent the night
before the meeting at the monastery in San Pedro, rose betimes and
decided to leave early for the conclave (it had been set for afternoon). But almost at the site appointed he—with Beltrán beside him
—reined sharply in: four horsemen were bearing down on them
across the plain. They waited; the dusty riders—they proved to be
scouts of Henry's—drew up. Turn back, they cried, he was heading
straight into an ambush: patrolling out of Segovia that morning,
they had seen sunlight glinting on the army of Girón and the Manriques moving south; they had ridden over and mingled with it and
discovered the whole plot. Henry hesitated a moment: he had only
twenty companions. Then he struck spurs to his horse. He raced
away, east, toward the shelter of the Guadarramas. As he went up
into the foothills, peasants ran out of their huts to ask what had
happened, why such headlong flight? He told them; they seized
their hoes and scythes and came to join him. They spread the alarm:
all through those peaks, those valleys, shepherds and farmers and
woodsmen—the people he knew and loved, the humble *raza* with
whom he had stopped so many times to rest, to eat, to visit—
streamed to his aid. There were five thousand of them by the time
he reached Segovia. Upon a tide of "acclamation"[34]—something of
which Henry had heard very little and was to hear even less—they
saw him safe within its walls.

But there was no rejoicing back on the field near Villacastín that
September evening. The conspirators had made their rendezvous,
yet once more the victim was not at hand. In "dismay and confusion"[35] they argued about what to do. Since they were finally assembled in full array, might not it be best to pursue Henry and make
an open attack? Such was the consensus. But Villena, suddenly
veering, held out against it. He was tired of these lunges that never
came off. Three times now he had tried force—and failed; some bad
luck seemed to be dogging him. Anyway, action had never been his
forte. Negotiation always worked best with Henry. It was high time
to return to that.

No, no, he told his milling companions. He had a better plan in
mind. Let them put their indictment of Beltrán and their require-
ments *vis-à-vis* young Alfonso into a formal bill of demands (of

course they could dress it up with a general picture of the kingdom's woes). Nor would they send their ultimatum only to Henry. They could get off copies of it to the cities—and to the Pope and the Cardinals as well. That way they could throw their plaint into national, even international, forum. Moreover, such a move would take away the stigma of being traitors and murderers which they were all too rapidly beginning to acquire by their recent conduct, and present them, rather, in the flattering light of guardians of the public weal.

As usual, he talked the barons around. And just where, he asked them, throwing them a bone of choice, would it be best to produce this piece of wily composition? Why not Burgos? someone suggested. They would be safest there: since the days of Luna it had been securely in the control of the Stúñigas themselves. Besides, there was a certain appropriateness in launching an official anathema against the monarch from that place: *caput Castelae*, the ancient center of the realm. They made their plans; they took such brief repose as their smoking hearts allowed them. Early the next morning they were up and gone. Deep in the northern city's mighty fortress, they set speedily to work. In a very few days they had their bill of attainder ready.

This famous document—the barons themselves called it an "*amonestación*,"[36] a warning, but history knows it as the Representation of Burgos—makes absorbing reading: one would look far to find, although it was there only fortuitously, a clearer statement of the case of the Establishment against their stray and unconventional King. They led off with a curt reminder of their earlier petitions for the reformation of the realm. Those pleas Henry had ignored. In fact, he had let matters slide from bad to worse. Now, for the last time, and that all the world might listen, they would put his misdeeds upon record. He had made a mockery of justice: everywhere the public groaned under a great weight of tyrannies and were stopped from any redress. The national economy was disintegrating: money had been debased, prices were soaring, outrageous taxes and "extortions"[37] had been slapped upon the people. Yet what else could be expected from the sort of officials he had chosen to put in charge? Men of stature and experience had been destituted, and incompetent nobodies thrust into their place. But it was not only the ineptitude of these protégés which was bringing the kingdom into ruin; their moral baseness "polluted the very air." And was the King who sat atop the dung heap, they went on, any better? At his accession he had vowed to protect the Faith, "to die for it, if need be." Die for it? Look—out burst the old familiar wounds—what he had done instead! The Moslems, their sworn enemies, he had favored rather than beset; his war against them had been made so *"tibiamente,"* so halfheartedly, that his own realms had suffered more from it than theirs. He actually had "close and secret friendships" among them. And his infidel bodyguard, that gang of thugs and perverts who spent their time befouling the Sacrament and "raping wives and virgins and violating men and Christian boys against nature"—why, he even paid them double the official salary! In fine, he showed no characteristics whatever of a proper "Catholic prince," it was clear at last that he could never be persuaded to "reform and penitence," the realm—unless virtuous and patriotic people like themselves did something about it—was heading for complete destruction.

And with that the prolegomenon, the camouflage, was out of the way; they could get on to their real purposes. They did so at once, and in words of growing insolence. "But what for the moment," they plunged in, "most urgently needs remedy—a remedy which our hearts and those of all your subjects weep tears of blood to see brought about—is the sway held over you by the Count of Ledesma, since it seems that your Highness is not the man to do for himself what normalcy requires." Not only had Beltrán dishonored Henry's "person and household, performing functions which should be yours alone." Abetted by Henry, he had tried to force the recognition of little Juana—"falsely called Princess, since it is quite clear to both you and him that she is not your child"—as the kingdom's legal heir. But this adulterous activity in the royal bedroom was by no means the sum of the favorite's guilt. He and his paramour had maltreated and persecuted the young Infantes; the Queen had even tried to dispose of them by poison, "so that the succession of these realms might come to the said doña Johana." Beltrán's possession of the mastership of Santiago, finally, was a flagrant insult to young Alfonso, who had been left it in his father's will.

Such was the "abominable" situation which Beltrán's cupidity and Henry's bungling had brought about. And there was only one way to end it: the demands now flew thick as arrows. Beltrán had to be arrested and banished. Santiago must be taken from him and bestowed on Alfonso (from whom, of course, Villena would have far less trouble in getting it for himself). The Infantes should be "liberated" and Alfonso not only proclaimed officially as heir to the crown but turned over to the League for his greater safety. All this accomplished, Henry had to swear in Cortes that he would never marry Isabel or Alfonso without full permission of the Estates—and submit, moreover, to a complete "reordering" of his "person, household, and court" by sentence of a committee later to be named. They wound up with a plain threat. If Henry would agree to these conditions, well and good. If not, they would collect their armies, summon "all Christian princes" to their aid, and with no further ado take matters into their own hands.

Henry received the terrible missive in Valladolid, where he had gone to be closer to the focus of infection. He read it with that stony-faced effort to conceal his suffering which was so often mistaken by his contemporaries for indifference or cowardice. His Council, however, flamed out in shock. But they yielded the floor (it is his last appearance) to Lope Barrientos. Age had not mellowed the headstrong old Dominican; at eighty-two he still charged in like a bull. Wrathfully he turned on his former pupil. What was the matter with him? he demanded. Was he just going to sit there and take these disgraceful insults? What was Henry waiting for? Act, *act!* Gather the royal troops, fall on the beggars! Drive them from Burgos—from Castile—by fire and sword.

But Henry stood up to him. No longer was he a child to quail beneath a ferule; he had seen much, learned much, been down a long and bitter road. "Father Bishop," he answered quietly, in the best-known speech to which he ever gave tongue, "you are very free with the lives of others. So it always is for people who do not have to wield the arms. You would have us come at any cost to battle—and men upon both sides go down into death? Obviously the ones to be sent into such conflict are not your children, nor cost you much to raise. I tell you, no. I shall handle this matter in my own fashion—not in yours."[38]

Never have Henry's compassion, his humanitarianism, his profound conviction of the futility of war—in short, his total lack of consonance with the epoch—been more clearly expressed. And never had Barrientos been more incensed: the master lessoned—it was hardly a role to his taste. He marshaled his thunders for a final bolt. Very well, he cried furiously—if that was all the thanks he got for his advice. "But mark my words," he raged on, and his last utterance is almost identical to the first which we recorded of him; "you are going to be known as the most miserable king Spain ever had!"[39] He glared for a moment at Henry across their hopeless gulf of almost forty years of misunderstanding. Then he got up and strode out—and if the reader ever wishes to see the snorty, loyal, obtuse old Bishop again, he will have to go and stand before his marvelous effigy, one of the jewels of late-Gothic art, in Medina del Campo's ancient hospital of La Piedad.

Henry himself at once went about his "own fashion" of settling the whole affair. There can be little doubt as to the form it was to take: his deepest longing—even now, even between the rapier and the wall—was to avoid unpleasantness and trouble no matter what the price. He wrote to Villena. There was really no need for all these threats, this mobilizing of armies and sharpening of swords, he said. They did not have to arrive at that. Surely the dispute could be amicably worked out. Would Villena not come down from Burgos for a talk?

Of course it was what Villena had been counting on, awaiting. Henry went up to Cabezón, a few miles north of Valladolid on the eastern bank of the Pisuerga. Villena descended to Cigales, a little off to the west. In the fields between the two towns, on October 24, their meeting was set. Fifty men of Henry's, and fifty more of Villena's, went out to inspect the place for ambush, although one wonders what they thought to find: that gentle slope lies open and bare to the wide Castilian sky. No treason—at least of armies—was in fact discovered. Henry, with three attendants, crossed the ancient stone bridge. With a like number Villena sat horsed and waiting in the field. They met. Their companions withdrew; they were left alone.

They rode a long time talking, among the dry brown thistles and the brittle corpses of the vineyards. What labyrinthine persuasions Villena used, what feeble resistance Henry put up, only the autumn clouds above them ever knew. But the outcome was foreordained: Henry alone, at mercy, the lamb in the vulture's talons. For the sake of "peace and quiet"[40] (*paz y sosiego:* it rings like a gong, tolls like a weary bell, through everything Henry did), he agreed to all the demands. Only one stipulation of his own—spar in the shipwreck —did he make: Alfonso must be promised in marriage to little Juana. Villena provisionally accepted it. The date for a formal gathering to ratify these arrangements was fixed—the end of November, and in that same spot. Then they parted—Villena to go back to Burgos and tell the nobles of their total triumph, Henry for home and the delivery of Alfonso.

It is unlikely that Juana received him with open arms: he had just consented to disinherit her daughter. And he met with other grim faces in Segovia. The Council was aghast at the decisions about Alfonso. To grant him the succession made seed enough of trouble. But to hand him to the barons—that fell little short of madness. Since the beginning of time it had been the aim of conjurations against the Throne to get possession of the heir. They could use him to lend authority to any devilment for which they had a mind; they might even try to crown him. But the secretary Alvar Gómez—his treachery still unmasked—was close at Henry's ear. His word, his royal word, he whispered. The tactic still worked with Henry. Gómez himself, accompanied by Gonzalo de Saavedra, took the eleven-year-old boy to Sepúlveda and delivered him to the League's representatives. That ruinous office done, Henry went back to the banks of the Pisuerga. The barons were already there, established and waiting in Cigales and the neighboring villages. Henry rode once more over the river. The official ceremonies began.

They are not easy to visualize: those fields stretch desolate and lonely now, the wind cries mournfully across them, the long trains cry. But the scene must have been very different in the closing days of that faroff November: days, for the business was so large and high that it took them more than a week to get it done. The full roster of the rebellion was at hand: Villena, Girón, the Admiral, the archbishops of Toledo and Sevilla, the Bishop of Coria and the counts of Paredes and Osorno (Manriques all three), Benavente, Alba, Plasencia, the Count of Miranda, the Count of Santa Marta, the Count of Ribadeo, "and many other knights."[41] Moreover, they had come in thick array—almost in open panoply of war: their troops crowded the plain; harsh winter sunlight gleamed upon serried lances, on crossbows and steel helmets with visors down and at the ready. Hemmed in, surrounded by this might, little less than a prisoner, Henry went one by one about his bitter abnegations. The fateful *cédula* was signed: "I, Henry, by the grace of God King of Castile, León, Toledo, Galicia, Sevilla, Córdoba"—it sounds somewhat like whistling in the dark—"Murcia, Jaén, the Algarve, Algeciras, Gibraltar, Lord of Vizcaya and Molina, to the prelates, dukes, counts, marquesses, magnates, masters and priors and *comendadores* of the Orders . . . do hereby declare that the legitimate succession to these my realms belongs to my brother the Infante don Alfonso, and to no other person whatsoever."[42] The barons swore allegiance to the new Prince (for thus, as heir apparent rather than presumptive, Alfonso must now be called). They gave their oath that they would work for his marriage to young Juana. Letters patent were dictated to all the cities directing them to follow suit.

By then it had grown too cold to continue out of doors; a wooden pavilion was hastily erected. Within it the final spoliations took place. Beltrán renounced the mastership (Henry had been through hell and high water to get him to disgorge it). The decree of his exile was relentlessly drawn up—on pain of death he was not to come within sixty miles of the sovereigns or the court. To coat these pills, Henry created him a duke—the Duke of Alburquerque—and gave him Roa and Aranda and Atienza and Molina as well as an annual grant of over a million. Mendoza, greatly to his surprise, was also banished. So, too, was Henry's Moorish bodyguard; the nobles, at the last moment, had managed to ram that in.

They were coming to the end of it. Little remained except to select the Commission which would winnow and order these transactions and draw them up in final Sentence. Four members, they agreed, should constitute this body—two to represent the royal interests, two for the League's. The barons named Villena and the Count of Plasencia. Henry appointed (disastrous choice) Gonzalo de Saavedra and Pedro de Velasco, son of the Count of Haro. Fray Alonso de Oropesa, General of the Jeronymites, would serve as arbiter between them in case of dispute.

And with that there was literally nothing more to do. The assemblage began to break up, the fields to empty. Henry sat sadly on horseback and watched Beltrán ride off into the December dusk. His Moslems took their leave (poor wretches, what would become of them, cast out in a hostile land?). The barons joined their troops;

standards were raised; the battalions wheeled and slowly withdrew. Villena was almost the last of them to go. As he passed by Henry, he saw Pedrarias beside him. "So you are the one," he sneered, "who was supposed to kill me!"[43]

"Yes," Pedrarias flung back. "I am always ready"—one imagines that he underlined the pronoun—"to serve the King my lord in anything he might command me."[44]

But the King his lord was no longer in much position to command. What had Henry gained—in sour, remorseless fact—from this ocean of concessions and humiliations? The promise that Alfonso would marry Juana: nothing more. And even that pledge had been obtained at an appalling, a shameful, price—the poor girl's destitution as his heir. True, he had not denied that she was his daughter; Henry was never, in all the pressures and tribulations still before him, to be brought to that. But refusing her the crown came very close to the same thing; what reason other than bastardy could monarchs have for such a drastic course, how else could his enemies —and even future generations—view it? If her origin was adulterous, he had almost proclaimed the fact. If she indeed was his (and who knew? how could he ever know?), then his conduct had perhaps been even worse: strange father who would strip, demean, annul his only child. On either count it was not—is not—an act of any grace. He had salved his conscience about Beltrán, by the dukedom, by the towns and the million. But he must have had difficulty indeed—as he too turned away and left the field to silent hawks and trampled thistles and rode over the old stone bridge for the last time—in accommodating his thoughts to what he had just done to little Juana. "Chastened and bent of neck"[45]—so Galíndez described him.

Bent of neck: *abajada la cerviz*. The phrase can stand.

15.

A Platform at Avila

If these negotiations with the insurgent barons had been calamitous for Henry, they had, as well, brought their measure of disaster to someone else—to Juan of Aragón. For the reflective reader will perhaps have been struck with puzzlement by one of the chief clauses of the pact: Alfonso's commitment to marry Juana la Beltraneja. How did this large concession, so counter to all Juan's interests, manage to slip past the League in which he played such vital part? It had been his iron purpose, yes, to see Alfonso proclaimed the heir. But that appointment was only the preface, the bridge, to something more—the marriage of the future Castilian king and his own daughter. To have the one without the other made rubble of his plans; so far as he was concerned, what the right hand gained beside the Pisuerga the left had snatched away.

No translation of the rune presents itself. That the nobles betrayed Juan is unthinkable: they needed him too much. It seems equally out of the question that they granted Henry's proviso about the girl through pressure of time: the parleyings went on for weeks, there was more than ample chance for consultation with Zaragoza. Juan may have felt that the immediate gains were worth a lip acceptance of the match, that a great deal might happen in the many years before little Juana, then only two, would be ready to marry anyone at all. Or perhaps the most convincing explanation can be found in his sad posture, in the dark perigee of his fortunes, at just this moment.

For never, in Juan's long life of adversity, had those fortunes veered more close to shipwreck. Louis still pushed at his northern borders. The Catalans kept on with their revolt: deprived of Henry's help by the decision at the Bidasoa, they had offered their crown instead to the Portuguese Constable, this latest cat's-paw of their republican frenzy had crossed the Peninsula, and together they were beating at the citadels and towns which still remained to the detested tyrant. But not all of Juan's current woes were political. By then he was stone-blind: a young page led him fumblingly about. His wife's complaint had finally revealed its hideous nature—cancer of the breast. Belabored, nearing seventy, harassed and clipped at home, perhaps he had small time or heart to give to affairs abroad. For a while he molts, he pends; in the whirlwind which is to envelop Castile we shall see little of him.

Even some of his behavior in his own domains during the period is not entirely clear. Blanca's story comes to an end at this juncture, and Juan is often suspected of having sped that end along. We recall her mournful annals—repudiated, despised for her failure with Henry, turned over for custody to her sister Leonor—and now they, at last, must be brought to their yet more tragic close. It is possible that she had conspired, although in captivity, against her father; a letter of Juan's,[1] newly discovered, suggests the fact. At all events, during the years we have been considering, he drew her more straitly in. Leonor conveyed her, finally, to the remote and lonely castle of San Juan del Pie del Puerto. There premonition struck her: she made out her will. To Henry she bequeathed the crown of Navarre (indisputably hers, by right, since the death of Carlos of Viana)—an act, according to the sentimentality or cynicism of the historian, either of old affection for Henry or of revenge against her father. And soon enough her forebodings were borne out. On December 4, 1464, the very day the conference between Cigales and Cabezón broke up, she died, inextricably presumed a victim of her sister's poison: victim indeed, if short of that—wife, virgin, martyr, frail *neige d'antan*, closed medieval garden.

Henry himself had gone from the Pisuerga to Olmedo, there to await the decision of the arbitral Commission, sitting in nearby Medina. In that familiar place the saddening news about poor Blanca reached him. He received it, in his customary manner, silent as the moon. Surely his heart was riven by far thoughts, by flashing recollections of the displayed and waiting girl with whom he had made his terrible discovery their wedding night in Valladolid a quarter of a century before, who had shared his name, if not his bed, in shy and forgiving tenderness—brother and sister—for thirteen years. But he had scant opportunity for memories, for touching old wounds. New ones were fresh upon him. On January 16 the Commissioners at Medina del Campo appointed to formalize the decisions between Cabezón and Cigales delivered their Sentence.

Why they had taken so long is hard to see. Five persons were involved, it will be recollected—two to represent the barons, two for Henry, Fray Alonso de Oropesa to smooth out the disagreements. But there were no disagreements. Henry's supposed defenders—Gonzalo de Saavedra and the Count of Haro's son, Pedro de Velasco—skipped over to the League. Perhaps Velasco's behavior should have been no great surprise: little real loyalty can have been expected from that ringleader of the first plot directed against Henry in the fields of Andalucía a decade past, that wild-eyed adolescent who had exhorted his young companions to destroy the "execrable monster." Saavedra's action, although he was friendly with the other traitorous secretary, Alvar Gómez, might perhaps have been less easily foreseen; the royal bounty had covered him with honors—knighthood, a seat on the Council, high military posts. But Henry had still not learned (was never to learn) that favors conferred lead much more often to resentment than to gratitude, Saavedra joined the vendetta, and the Sentence which went across the snowy plains to Olmedo, instead of being the promised weighing and composition of differences, was a work of the most patent and bare-faced collusion.

Anybody who survives the reading of this document (its printed version runs past a hundred double-columned pages) comes away from it with one overwhelming impression—the nobles had been victorious all along the line; not even the earlier Sentence of Medina del Campo, imposed on Henry's father by the Infantes of Aragón when they were at their zenith, had such Draconic terms. And Henry, scanning in astonishment its coiling clauses, at once so saw it. He saw something else as well. The Commission had far exceeded their prerogative. Not only had they granted, wholesale, the League's demands. They had gone on to dictate a full reorganization of the realm—almost entirely in the nobles' favor. Henry's army, they decreed, must be reduced to a mere six hundred lances. The King's Council had to be enlarged—chiefly with nobles and prelates. Severe restrictions were put upon the royal *corregidores* and the imposition of taxes. Henceforth the deputies to Cortes were to be freely elected—another way of saying that the magnates, by then in wide control of the constituent cities, could choose them. Without permission of a committee (headed by Villena), no member of the aristocracy could be subject to royal arrest. In a word, the sovereign had to relinquish very nearly all his ancient rights and perquisites and be content with something little else than his empty title: Magna Carta itself was no more a triumph of the feudal baronage over the Crown.

Or would have been—if Henry had acquiesced. For, unlike his remote progenitor upon the Thames, he did not give in. Again in rare anger, again stung by treachery—as he had been in the castle of Fuenterrabía—out of his habitual brooding and inertia, he vetoed the Sentence and dissolved the Commission.

It is immensely to his credit that he did. The Castilian throne, as we are only too well aware, for half a century had been tottering; accession to such dictates would surely have given it the *coup de grâce*. Prostrate, dismembered, hedged and degraded by its enemies to such extent, it might well never have again arisen: not even, perhaps, the genius of Isabel the Catholic could have redeemed it from so low a state. Henry, one cannot deny, has much for which to be held accountable at the bar of history. Yet with all his mistakes and gaps and derelictions, this unlucky man whose name has borne the mud and arrows of contempt for half a thousand years did nevertheless perform—and no scholar has yet had the charity, or perhaps the eye, to grant it—one very nearly heroic act. By his rejection of the Sentence of Medina del Campo, that winter day of 1465, he saved the Crown of Spain.

We see it, now. Whether Henry sensed the full import of his move is another question. What he did realize, clearly, was that he had given the League an open *casus belli*. Four months earlier, at Burgos, they had been on the trembling point of revolution; with the new goad, there could be little doubt that they soon would deliver some stunning blow. And Henry, still in that sudden burst of energy and resolve which, alas, one senses already will be of the briefest and most illusory duration, took measures to prepare for it. He at once recalled Beltrán de la Cueva and his exiled Moors. He ordered the confiscation of Villena's properties. Letters started forth to the cities; they must close their gates against possible attack and ignore his earlier command for the recognition of Alfonso as heir. Segovia itself, always his principal concern, he had further fortified. Into

Extremadura he sent messengers to the Count of Medellín and Gómez de Cáceres, Master of Alcántara, urging them to collect what forces they could and come to his aid—and received the gratifying reply from those two of his young "creatures" that they would soon be on their way.

But the nobles, too, were acting, were closing ranks. Before Henry's orders to the cities could take effect, they moved on Arévalo, a key position, and with pretext of a visit by Alfonso to his mother the Queen Dowager (it was her residence, the place where her mind was drifting away in what contemporary sources discreetly call her "indisposition")² seized it and garrisoned it with their own men. Then they went west, in swelling and ominous array, and established themselves in Plasencia, great bastion of the Stúñigas. There, in reply to a royal letter naïvely asking them to disband and to release Alfonso, they dispatched a violent missive; they had no intention of disbanding, let Henry fulfill his agreements by the Pisuerga, they were making plans for Alfonso which he would soon enough learn. The tone of this screed shows plainly that they now considered themselves invincible, that they could take the upper hand. Even Nature seemed conspiring to bear them out: one of the customary cyclones struck Salamanca, the Crown's gibbet in the *plaza mayor* was knocked down and scattered, and the local wizards and soothsayers (it is always startling, here on the very doorstep of the modern world, to find so many of these fossils still about, but the time was replete with them; Carrillo even had a magician on his archiepiscopal staff) made dismal croaks about the imminent fall of sovereign power.

Henry shrugged off such superstitions; we know him well enough to venture that. But other portents, portents far more tangible and of sufficient chill to throw an initial blight upon his confidence, thronged in; as if unloosed by the trumpet blast from Plasencia, a whole avalanche of disasters came cascading down. He lost Toledo, rich and ancient capital: two new recruits to the League, the Count of Cifuentes and the Castilian Marshal Payo de Ribera, took it over. Then the far south, always a tinderbox, blazed up: the Count of Cabra, one of the few loyalists in that area, was driven from Córdoba, and in Sevilla the oldest son of the Count of Plasencia commandeered the strategic castle of Triana. Shaken by these losses, Henry's resolution began to drain rapidly away. And private desertions soon followed on the public. Pedro de Velasco, not content with his knavish work on the Commission, decamped to the enemy, and while it is true that his father the old Count of Haro— sick of an ugly world and retired some months before to a quiet religious community of his own contriving at Medina del Pomar— was so angry at the defection that he refused all help and the young renegade had to go about humiliatingly devoid of troops or even personal attendants, nevertheless the addition of the august Velasco name gave huge new weight to the rebellion. Nor did worse fail to come quickly on. Those peccant secretaries Alvar Gómez and Gonzalo de Saavedra, fearful that their perfidy could not much longer go undiscovered, fled the court. Small loss, the reader will exclaim, and certainly it was time and time past that Henry be relieved of the long succubus of Alvar Gómez. But their departure brought a heavy consequence. As they rode west to join the League, they met Medellín and the Master of Alcántara, coming to Henry's aid. Nimbly they persuaded them that they were advancing to a trap, that Henry had sent for them only to "destroy"[3] them, and the young men turned around and accompanied the secretaries to Plasencia: instead of propping the monarch, the thousand troops which they had assembled reinforced the foe.

Of all the misfortunes which had overtaken Henry in those early springtime weeks, it seems to have been this callous betrayal by Gómez de Cáceres—the laundress's boy from Córdoba whom he had raised to such eminence—which cut him most deeply, which served to leave his brief and new-found vigor in final shards. Nothing but total shock could have explained the ease with which he fell a victim to the League's next ploy. For boldly, at Villena's guidance and in the dark secret of their knotted hearts, they had taken a culminating counsel: let Carrillo and the Admiral go to Henry feigning repentance, offering submission—but in reality to make a last infiltration of his collapsing ranks.

The tireless old pair of mischief workers went. Henry received them. He listened to their whiffled protestations, their laments. Villena, they assured him, was impossible: he wanted everything his way; they could no longer stand him. Nor could they stand their conscience. They wanted to come back to their rightful lord. Of course they needed certain guarantees: the Marqués would be furious, they had to have strong places where they could shut themselves up against his ire—Valladolid for the Admiral and Avila for the Archbishop, in point of fact. But Valladolid and Avila, Henry objected, were among the Crown's last strongholds. Moreover, he still had bitter memories of the awful winter of little Juana's birth, three years before, when these same suppliants returned to court and the scandal had so suddenly broken forth. Then they had traduced him, he reminded them. Yes—regrettably; they had to admit it. But that was all in the past. Besides, it was the obligation of royalty not to be vindictive. He must not doubt them. Why, Carrillo served at God's altar. And the Admiral was Henry's own cousin. (That he was also the father-in-law of Juan of Aragón probably went unmentioned.) They would subscribe to anything—and did, with great "signatures and seals."[4] They vowed to walk barefoot to Jerusalem should they prove false. And in the end—being who he was, being kind and credulous, being furthermore in a pass where he had to clutch at straws—Henry allowed himself to be persuaded.

He allowed himself, in brief, to be entirely ruined. Valladolid and Avila were turned over. The Council met—to decide the first move of this new coalition. Carrillo suggested an attack on Arévalo. Capture of that important holding of the rebels might break their morale. Henry could leave at once to begin the investment. Meanwhile, the Archbishop and the Admiral would be off to gather troops. As soon as their *mesnadas* were marshaled, they assured him, they would hasten to his aid.

With his meager force, Henry departed and set up camp just north of Arévalo. Alone, he could do little more than threaten. But of course, he told himself, he would soon be joined. The days went by, however, and neither Archbishop nor Admiral appeared. He searched the far horizons for the glint of lances: there was nothing but space and silence and lonely wheatfields and grazing sheep. Nervously he wondered what could be keeping them. Was it possible—oh no, not after all the promises, and yet the evidence seemed to lead to such a quarter—that he again had blundered, again had misjudged? The sense of doom so common to his melancholy nature began to enfold him. May grew. His doubt, his anxiety, grew. His situation, there on the plain and with so little company, was badly exposed. Juan de Padilla, Adelantado Mayor of Castile and a "doughty warrior,"[5] was in charge of the rebel troops inside Arévalo; if they chose to make an attack, Henry's small numbers would be in gravest peril.

And so it soon fell out: the garrison sortied. One muffled midnight, in quick surprise, they struck the camp. The royalists, caught asleep, were able to come off with at least their lives. But they came off with little else. Before the raiders withdrew, they set the tents on fire. They seized a large cache of arms. And—perhaps worst of all—they drove away the greater part of the horses.

Henry panicked. His whole position had disintegrated, was very close to desperate. One more such attack clearly might finish him. Humiliatingly or no, he had to send a plea for immediate help. He called his new secretary, Hernando de Badajoz. Go find the Archbishop, he instructed him. Find him at any cost, and tell him what has happened, tell him to come at once.

Hernando departed. Somewhere out in the plains he did encounter—pounding along in a white cloud of dust—the tardy Archbishop. He was obviously hurrying. And he rode, indeed, in panoply of war: no fewer than fifteen hundred troops clattered behind him. But he seemed to be going the wrong way. His line of march, in fact, pointed far more to Avila than to Arévalo. Baffled, Hernando addressed him. "My lord," he began, "the King is waiting for you."[6] He started to pitch ahead, to describe the emergency. But Carrillo cut him short. "Go tell your King," he roared, "that I am sick of him and everything about him. Now we shall see who is the real sovereign of Castile!"[7]

Spurring, he galloped on. Hernando rode back to the camp. Henry listened in stupefaction. Your King! But he was Carrillo's King, as well. And "Now we shall see who is the real sovereign"! Surely they did not, could not—

But they could, they were. Even as Henry stood there staring at his secretary, two further hammer blows, in rapid succession, fell upon him. A messenger streaked down out of the north. The Admiral! he warned; the Admiral had just risen for Alfonso, at Valladolid. Nor had he finished when another, hot and breathless, rode in. The rebels had left Plasencia. In massed might, escorting the young Prince, they were moving toward a rendezvous in Avila.

And with that, Henry recovered his voice. A rendezvous? But for what purpose? he cried—although he must have known by then, must really not have needed to ask. What purpose? shot back the fatal, the inevitable, reply. For one only, now open and declared: to depose him—and then to crown Alfonso.

It had come. It had happened at last. Castillo has Henry drop

upon his knees, has him lift his hands to Heaven and utter a long
and pious commendation of his soul to God. Almost the only thing
about this scene which even remotely convinces is the throwing up
of hands. Henry had reason, more than reason, for that. He had lost
—or was about to lose—his throne. The best he now could hope for
was to save himself.

Yet where could he take refuge? Not, this time, in Segovia: the
Admiral might well strike down from the north and cut him off.
Perhaps in Portugal. It seemed his only haven. He looked around
him wildly. His horse was already saddled. He lumbered up upon
it. Sicker at heart than he had ever been before, his big arms flailing
and his bulbous eyes clogged with those crowding tears which it
will still be many months before we see him finally loose in such
uncontrollable and terrible abundance, he fled toward the west.

Dethronement: it was the word on every tongue in Avila. The
rebels indeed were ready to take the bit in their teeth, to plunge to
that desperate and irreversible remedy. But opinions as to how to
go about it were as varied, as multitudinous, as the heaving crowd
to which Carrillo now played host in his ill-gotten city. Their first
intention seems to have been to bring the sovereign to a sort of
rump assize and there formally to accuse him of all his errors. But
the speed with which this idea was set aside shows clearly the large
inconvenience to its execution which must at once have occurred to
them: there was little reason to suppose that Henry, now vanishing
westward as fast as his horse could take him, would pay the slightest
heed to such a summons. Others brought forward a different and
rather more viable thought: appeal to Rome. The move had much
to recommend it. Henry lay open, painfully open, to a charge of
heresy (it was on this occasion that Villena let fly his barb about
Henry's having sought to make him a Moslem), and if Paul, the new
Pope, could be persuaded to depose him on the all too valid charge
that he "revealed no trace whatever of the Catholic Faith,"[8] then the
onus would be lifted from the League. But here, as well, discomfi-
tures thrust in. Castile had long been exempt, or at least so held
itself, from papal influence on its temporal affairs. Besides, as those
of a more caustic turn of mind among them soon commented, all
that popes really cared about was money—and Henry outmatched
them in that. Anyway, Rome always dawdled, spun things along for

ever. Time, now, was of the essence. They were assembled, poised; the moment would never be riper. Some immediate justification had to be devised for what they planned.

They floundered; they split hairs. And ultimately they took shelter in what necessity obliged them to consider precedent. In Visigothic times the crown was elective; the nobles then raised up and put away their sovereigns. Alfonso the Wise, and for faults less grave than Henry's, had been dethroned. So, too, had Pedro the Cruel—by the first Trastámara. Nor did the outer world fail to provide example; look at England's Richard II. Thin reasoning, one observes. To reach to the sixth century was going back indeed. Pedro's removal was no more than a plain murder. The crimes of foreign nations made poor bolster for one's own. But thus went the shoddy forensics; thus they decided. They needed only the master's —Villena's—approbation.

It is, in fact, upon Villena that the mind most lingers during these turbulent days in Avila. The course there being charted was entirely at variance with his character. The last thing he ever wanted was to see Henry permanently brought down; "he sought to keep him between fear and hope, at times advancing him, at times casting him back."[9] But that we long have known. With Villena it is never the goal which puzzles, it is the complexity of conduct. What view shall we take of his subscription to the dire event? It may be that the tide of revolutionary feeling was by then too high for even him to resist. Or perhaps he had a shrewd foreknowledge that the deed might ultimately—as we shall see—redound to his own aim. We cannot say. All we can hold to is the fact itself: he gave his approval. And with that final consent, the nobles moved speedily forward to the destitution. The climax to eleven years of plotting—the shameful ceremony called at the time the Schism, and by historians the Farce, of Avila, the outrage which still made Mariana shudder more than a century later and which he predicted, rightly, would be an eternal scar in the Spanish conscience—is upon us.

The date: June 4, 1465. The place: a level field just under Avila's walls. During the night, a broad high platform had been erected. That morning adroit attendants put a throne on it—then on the throne a life-sized wooden effigy of Henry, clad in black mantle, holding the regalia—and departed. Enticed as bees to clover by these preparations, a vast crowd, with noon, had gathered: Spaniards have always dearly loved a play, and perhaps the dramaturgy of this famous occasion, the skill with which the barons both threw their case before the public and appealed to its deepest nature, has never been sufficiently remarked. On any count, it seems pure theater: the expectant audience, the furnished stage, the backdrop of rose-red turrets, the bath (for by early June the springtime clouds are gone, the copper blur of summer has not yet settled in, the Abulensian sun is at its most diamond, its most radiant) of floodlights. One even finds the orchestra—shawms, waiting drums, poised trumpets. Only the players of the fateful piece were lacking. And soon they, too, came on—the assembled troupe of nobles, in velvet robes and coronets or armor and gleaming castled casques; it all was ready.

The prologue first, of course.[10] A *pregonero*, a herald with a scroll, stepped forward. He advanced on the seated effigy; he unwound the parchment. In a great voice he read out the long list of "excesses, crimes, and sins"[11] for which Henry must lose the throne. The charges read, enactment of the sentence swiftly followed. Carrillo, as Primate of Castile, began it; solemnly (or with such solemnity as that addlepate could ever summon), and to a gasp from the enthralled beholders, he removed the dummy's crown. The realm's Chief Justice—Alvaro de Stúñiga, Count of Plasencia—came next; he wrenched the sword, token of sovereign law, from its wooden hand. To complete the degradation, either Benavente or Villena himself—the accounts grow contradictory—took away the orb.

There is even less agreement about who then strode forth to play the classic part of *comodín*, of clown—for with the helpless figure now quite stripped, all that remained was to have a little fun. One source, at least, assigns this tasteless role to Gómez de Cáceres. If it was indeed the arrogant young Master of Alcántara, we can only hope that some brief memory assailed him—some vision of the day when he had stood a hot and panting boy in a bull plaza at Madrid and looked up into a King's shy, smiling face and known that his fortunes were beginning—as he knocked the figure from its royal seat. He flung and kicked it about: pandemonium of bangs and buffets on the platform, shrieks of delight, of rustic merriment, from the crowd. Then finally, tiring of his game, he spat the awful word (Gómez? Gómez de Cáceres?)—the unpardonable word, the word whispered behind the back or scrawled on furtive walls but never, not even in one's most horrible nightmares, flung out in public: *"Puto"*[12]—queer, pederast, fag. And with that he gave the broken puppet a last boot which sent it flying from the platform, down into the dust below.

The fickle watchers burst into tears and groans. We have spoken of the general bent of the medieval mind to allegory, and in the instance, superimposed on it, one should recall as well the Spaniard's deep belief in the reality of images: the statue dismembered there upon the ground was, to that audience, no mere piece of wood —it was Henry, Henry himself, dead at their feet. But the spectacle could not end in gloom, in sorrow; to cap it and give it final satisfaction, joy, pomp, exhilaration must return. The stage sprang back to life. Young Alfonso was ushered forward—the pudgy lad of eleven with his double chin and vaguely boobish look (at least so he appears in the one likeness we have of him, at Miraflores). They placed him on the throne. The crown taken from Henry was set upon his blond, bewildered head. Music burst forth. The herald, to conclude the piece as he began it, once more strode forward. "Castile! Castile!" he cried; "Castile for the king don Alfonso!"[13] And as the sun turned west and shadow from the towering walls began to dim the lights, the nobles formed in stately ranks to file before the throne and kiss the hand of their new sovereign: procession, fanfare, curtain.

Consummatum fuit: the dreadful thing was done. It contained, of course, not an iota of legality. But the fat was in the fire. Might had met right full on, and the realm at last lay split asunder: Castile had two kings.

Part Three:
1465–1474

16.
The Double Crown

Henry was already at Salamanca in his westward flight when foam-flecked couriers with news of the dethronement overtook him. For the fact itself he had been prepared. Against the peculiar coarseness and brutality of its execution, however, his sensitive heart found no defense. "I have raised up children—and they reviled me!"[1] he broke out; then he went on in the lamentation of Job—a personage with whom he has more than a little in common: "Naked I came from my mother's belly. Naked shall I return to the dust!"[2] And scarcely were these messengers of doom unstrapping their spurs and watering their horses when others began to gallop in from every side. Toledo was now utterly lost; its Alcázar and both bridges had been confiscated and the act of Avila endorsed. Burgos, ignited by young Velasco, had acknowledged Alfonso as sovereign. So had most of the south: Jérez, Córdoba, Ecija, Carmona. In Sevilla, far and away the largest city of the realm, the reaction had been spectacular: Medina Sidonia and the Count of Arcos, their feuding swords temporarily sheathed, led the whole Corporation to the cathedral, unfurled "with immense applause"[3] the sacred banner of San Fernando, and marched in splendid celebration through the streets proclaiming the new King.

The ruin seemed complete. Henry must drive along, and with all possible speed. But even as he made his preparations, there in those desperate hours at Salamanca, the pendulum began to swing. He had still not passed the western gate when other news raced to him through the golden city and made him pull back upon the reins. In from his nearby seat beside the Tormes, and leading fifteen hundred troops, the Count of Alba was cantering across the Roman bridge. And he did not come for capture. He was riding to Henry's aid.

We do not know the springs of this sudden advent; with Alba they were always turbid. "Since he had received great sums of money,"[4]

Valera subjoins darkly. Perhaps the cynical attribution is as good as any. But be the Count's motives what they may, once he was closeted with Henry he presented a persuasive case for the abandonment of flight, even for resistance. He pointed out that Ledesma, where Beltrán de la Cueva had neatly ensconced himself during Henry's worst hour of trial, was less than thirty miles away: perhaps, if summoned, the flamboyant new Duke of Alburquerque would join them. (He did, with five hundred horse, although perhaps more from "necessity"[5] than anything else: with Henry gone, he would obviously be the first person for the jackals to rip to pieces.) And others of the nobles, Alba went on (it takes a thief to catch a thief), might be attentive to the siren song of Henry's chinking *doblas*. There was no need to give up. Let him write letters, offering rewards and inducements. Let him face about and stand.

But Henry, torn between natural disinclination to activity and these first faint chamades of reawakening hope, still hesitated. His indecision, his reluctance to set aside the plan of leaving the country, is amply witnessed by two facts. They would repair to Zamora, he announced—a city almost on the border. The Queen and Isabel, he further commanded, must leave at once for Portugal—a move which, if its official motive was to seek help, surely rose just as much from a desire to get the family into safekeeping: the Portuguese King, as Juana's brother and Isabel's intended, would hold them well in charge. Little Juana la Beltraneja was of course too young for the hot, arduous trip to Lisbon, and he dispatched his Moslem bodyguard to retrieve her from Segovia and bring her to meet him in Zamora. Close upon the child's arrival in that wondrous city of Syrian domes and Romanesque arcades followed others of far greater moment. With four hundred cavalry, the Count of Trastámara (no relation) posted down from Galicia. Out of his waving wheatlands rode the Count of Valencia de don Juan at the head of three hundred more. Invigorating letters from some of the Grandes at larger distance began to be brought in: they would soon set out. Alba's prediction, in short, seemed to be coming true: Henry's fortunes were obviously on the mend.

The reasons for this rapid turn of the fateful wheel are much argued. It might be that Henry's offers—the promises of "grants and exemptions and privileges"[6] which he now was sending broadside—had simply taken effect. Or perhaps some deeper, subtler, leaven was at work. Long years before, when Henry's Aragonese uncles laid their impious hands upon his father, we saw the kingdom, stunned and bewildered by such outrage to the crown of Pelayo, veer toward its defense—and the vile flout of majesty at Avila, even such majesty as Henry's, may well have produced a similar result. Whatever interpretation we put upon the matter, reinforcements continued to pour in. A scant six weeks after the deposition, the balance of power—that goal of all Villena's selfish plotting, that state which was so necessary for his role as fulcrum and arbiter and which he alone may well have glimpsed as the most likely consequence of the deed at Avila when he gave it his consent —was almost restored. By mid-July, in fact, the royalists felt strong enough to leave Zamora and go eastward, up the river. They quartered at Toro. There, in the old russet town perched on its cliff and with its sweeping view of the wide summer plains, they could keep nearer watch upon the enemy—whose opening move, they had every reason to believe, would be an attempt to seize the Crown's remaining strongholds in the basin of the Duero.

They were not mistaken. Breathing fire and threats, the rebels had left Avila and started north; the dogs of war were slipped. Savagely they fell on Medina del Campo—and reduced it. But they did not tarry; their chief objective was, had to be, rendezvous with the Admiral. In a broad swath they swept on. At Valladolid, the Admiral flung open his gates. They crowded through. Deep in the dank recesses of his vast Gothic mansion on the Carrera de San Pablo they all sat down to take counsel, to plan their campaign.

The sessions were almost as tumultuous as those in Avila. Their way was by no means strewn with blossoms. If the settling dust of the explosion had revealed Henry's position as less disastrous than originally imagined, certain cracks in their own had inconveniently appeared. Disquieting reports of the activity at Zamora, then at Toro, kept coming. A close look at their finances revealed an unpleasant truth: they had money for only two months' pay to their soldiers. Sour thoughts were given tongue about the "mutability"[7] and "avarice" of the public and how, if Henry continued to "open his hands," people would swarm to him "like flies toward honey." Clearly, time was on his side and their own worst enemy was "dilation"; they had to strike at once. But in the haste, the urgency, their judgment faltered: they chose to split their forces. Half of

them, they decided, would go northward under Carrillo and fall on
Peñaflor. The rest would descend the Pisuerga and attack Simancas
—a prize indeed.

Peñaflor, at least, proved easy; it was caught unprepared. Carrillo
—whose priestly vows forbade him even to carry weapons, let alone
to wield them—charged in with blade awhir like a wind from the
Sierra de Gredos. The defenders gave way; he began to scale the
walls. Faced with sack and ruin, the citizens revolted. They forced
the royal *alcaide* to surrender, Carrillo was knelt to, the town was
his. But contrarious news arrived from Simancas even while he was
happily taking off his blood-drenched armor. There everything had
gone wrong. The garrison, true, was minimal, but the royal commander turned out to be Juan Fernández Galindo, a valorous knight
"long used to trials and dangers."[8] The town itself was strongly,
almost impregnably, placed. The long and short of it was that the
besiegers had made absolutely no headway, and they needed Carrillo's troops; could he come at once? He again slung on his corselet.
Clanging and chortling, he galloped to the south. It was only fifteen
miles. He reached the camp that day.

Simancas's seven legendary virgins, who chopped off their hands
to make themselves repulsive to their lecherous pursuers, were not
in evidence. But something very little less unappetizing—at least to
the Archbishop—shortly was. A few hours after his arrival was
known in the city, its gate briefly opened. Instead of warriors to give
battle, however, all that emerged was a gaggle of pimply boys—the
mozos de espuelas, the stable hands and grooms. They were carrying
a straw figure with a miter—obviously Carrillo. Halfway between
the camp and the battlements they stopped. While besieged and
besiegers craned, they formed a circle around their burden and set
up a mock court of justice. In re-enactment of Avila, and to jeers and
whistles, a bill of indictment against Carrillo for his recent tricks
and treacheries was read out. Then they built a great bonfire,
chanted derisive quatrains comparing the Archbishop to don Opas
—that other episcopal villain, brother of Count Julian, who had
unlocked the Visigothic kingdom to the Moors—and tossed the
effigy upon the flames.

Pricked in his vanity, always his tenderest spot, Carrillo went
into a fury. *Mozos de espuelas* indeed! The destitution at Avila had at
least been done by lords. But not all his exhortations, his huffs and

puffs and incitements to action, had much effect. Even braced by his contingent, the rebels still could make no progress with their siege: the city showed no signs of giving in. Days, futile weeks, went by. The cicadas shrilled. The sun blazed molten brass. Rations ran short. Worst of all, ominous accounts now came in torrents about the growing activity of the loyalists off to the west.

They were entirely true. Henry's fortunes, in Toro, were even higher on the rise. The Mendozas had joined him; exhausted from trying to figure out which way the cat would jump, they had retired to Guadalajara, but the new scent of victory had lured them out. They brought enormous forces. Their neighbor, the Count of Medinaceli, had soon followed, with five hundred horse and a great swarm of foot. Many "gentlemen from the mountains"[9]—rural chivalry from as far away as Galicia and Asturias—thronged to his support. Henry even felt free to summon the Queen and Isabel back from Portugal—Juana with a halfhearted pledge of troops from its King (they failed to materialize), Isabel with a settled determination never to let herself be married to that paunchy cousin. But foreign help was no longer really needed. Toro itself was insufficient to contain the *mesnadas* already at hand; some bivouacked on the shimmering plain across the Duero, others in the orchards—thick at that season with their blood-black cherries—north of town.

Something, and very soon, would surely happen. With numbers so large hemmed in such narrow compass (Simancas lies less than thirty miles from Toro), the pressure was too great. Besides, the barons with Henry were quite as set on action and booty as they had been in Andalucía, a decade past. (What cared they that the foe, instead of Moslems, were now their countrymen and kin? All could be equally despoiled.) They chafed and prodded. And Henry—sick though he already was of martial din and confusion and "sighing for solitudes"[10]—finally yielded to their instigations: yes, they would move. At a rousing ceremony in the church of the Holy Sepulcher they had their banners blessed. Then they marched out and east. Edging the mighty river, they advanced through Castronuño; it took them hours to pass. That night they were in Tordesillas—with Simancas itself, from the high tower of San Antolín, in view. The next morning, as the vast pillar of dust raised by their march rolled skyward, rolled ever nearer and more menacing, the rebels suddenly struck their tents and fled. They fell back to Valladolid. Out upon the field which they had abandoned Henry's battalions flowed. The citizens of Simancas sallied forth to welcome them. They put up their own tents and settled down.

The final size of this loyalist army is by no means certain. Castillo gives it as almost a hundred thousand. Surely he errs: only in the next reign, and for the conquest of Granada, was the kingdom able to raise hosts of anything like such proportions. Valera says eight thousand horse and twenty thousand foot. Probably the truth lies somewhere between. In any case, it was huge—and clearly invincible. All that they needed was to aim a lethal blow. Should they make a frontal assault on Valladolid? Or might it be better, now that the rebel chieftains were away from their homes, to cut through the land and confiscate their towns and castles? There was almost an embarrassment of choices. But even as they debated, the inevitable happened. A letter from Villena arrived at the royal pavilion. He had an idea in mind, he said—one he thought might interest Henry. Could the two of them not meet for a discussion?

What motivated Villena is not hard to guess: the reaction initiated by the dethronement was plainly out of hand, Henry had advanced farther and faster than the Marqués had wished or foreseen, somehow he had to be "thrust back" again and equipoise restored. Nor need Henry's hearkening to the invitation to parley cause much surprise. For two years he had been without Villena's advice and guidance—that prop, that escape from responsibility on which he had so relied ever since his boyhood. He answered eagerly: he would be delighted. He set out at once. The annalists do not give the place of the reunion. All they record is the bare terms of Villena's offer. (Perhaps they were too jarred by its temerity to notice anything else.) Why not a truce? he suggested. A truce of—well—five months. That would give them time to bring the kingdom back to peace. If Henry dissolved the royal army, he, in return, was ready to make certain guarantees. The League would be broken up. He would see to it, personally, that young Alfonso relinquished all claim to the Crown. The lad, moreover, would be sent back to Henry. The realm once more would obey a single, a lawful, sovereign.

And Henry accepted.

"O mighty King!" erupts Castillo, in one of his most free-wheeling and verbose apostrophes. "Lord now of such power, raised now to so high a summit, brought to a state so prosperous that none of your forefathers ever saw the like! How did you dare confide in one who sought only to confound you? How could you give him credit who already, with such insults, had cast you down into disgrace? What perilous trust, what futile hope, what slippery outlook made you listen to his lies—made you believe his treasonous offers and fall prey to such deceptions?"[11]

But we know, we know. Everything Henry was propelled him to the terms. "Peace," "truce"—they were the loveliest words that could ever caress his ear. There needed to be no bloodshed, after all —none of those terrible battles which accomplished nothing, which only led to others. A dazzling prospect opened up before him as he sat there at the colloquy, wherever it was. In two days—with hard riding—he could be home again in the quiet of Segovia.

He galloped back to the camp. He called his leaders together and told them his startling intent. Before they could have any chance to object, he hastened on to what he knew would most concern them, would most quickly seal their lips. He had no thought, he assured them, of letting them leave empty-handed. He was ready with new grants "to augment their state."[12] Fitting the action to the word, he immediately bestowed them. The Mendozas, as usual, pulled in a juicy catch: the Marqués of Santillana had Santander, the young Bishop of Calahorra the *tercias*—the annual rents—of all the lands surrounding Guadalajara. Medinaceli received Agreda, Alba the towns of El Carpio and Buendía, which "he said"[13] had been his father's. The Count of Trastámara was made Marqués of Astorga. Juan de Acuña, Count of the Castilian Valencia, found himself a duke.

In its own turn, the tremedous army struck camp. The nobles started home "highly content"[14]—nor without reason: seldom had so much been given for so little. The rank and file were paid not only their salaries but a generous bonus; they too went off, in dusty march across the far horizons. Henry, when all the rest were gone, pointed his little horse's head straight for Segovia and spurred away. The broad fields fell empty, fell silent. Once more, along the great slow rivers, chameleons crept forth and sunned themselves upon the sandy banks.

Everything, in short, and on the very verge of a real decision, had collapsed.

Truce without respite, pause without composition—so went that troubled winter. For no one but Henry would have believed Villena's glossy promises: as soon as the royal army had been disbanded, he went back on them all. The League remained intact. Alfonso's title as King, rather than being withdrawn, was hotly reasserted. Everywhere, from the Biscayan Bay to far Sevilla, sores fed by the irreducible infection broke out. Skirmishes, sporadic raids followed by hasty retreats, were launched by either faction—each bitterly condemning the other for these "iniquitous"[15] breaches of a concord in which nobody had any faith. The cities, caught up in the general turmoil, swung wildly to and fro in their allegiance. Both the "old King" and the "young King"—matters had come to such a pass that no one even knew quite what to call them—were miserable, Henry spent and disjointed in Segovia, Alfonso complaining to Carrillo of the insufficient deference shown him by his new sponsors and of the "perverts"[16] to whom Villena kept introducing him. ("What is all this?" cried Carrillo, "harshly."[17] Oh nothing, Villena evaded; good God, he had more important things to think about than boyish kisses and mutual masturbation. Well, he had better think about them, the Archbishop flung back; they could hardly afford to let their young protégé start down the very path which had ruined Henry.)

Of all the realm, in fact, one class alone—the barons—found profit and satisfaction in the spreading chaos. Adroitly, predictably, they dipped in with open hands. Not that there had ever been, since Luna, much curb upon their voracity. But now at last, with all central authority gone, they were free to plunder to their feudal hearts' content. In Andalucía Pedro Girón—Villena's brother and the Master of Calatrava—carved out for himself what came almost to a private kingdom; only faithful Lucas stood firm against him. That other Master, Gómez de Cáceres, took Badajoz and Coria. Carrillo appropriated Huete. The Ponce de Leóns swooped down upon Cádiz. Medina Sidonia wrenched Gibraltar away from Beltrán's brother-in-law, left there in charge; incredibly, Henry invited the Moors—and "with affection,"[18] at that—to go to its aid (they arrived too late).

And if local vultures could seize with such impunity, it was inevitable that foreign ones should soon flap in. In the midwinter of 1466 that grievous case occurred. Gaston of Foix, in blizzards and snowdrifts, swept down across Navarre with a French army and across the Ebro.

How much this attack by Foix owed to Louis XI, how much to his wife's father, Juan of Aragón, we cannot say. Whatever its genesis, there he was: already Calahorra had fallen. Both Henry and Alfonso sped envoys north. Alfonso's bore only a curt demand to depart—and was as curtly dismissed. Henry's—it happened to be Castillo himself—delivered messages, if just as anxious, at least more mild: what "cause had moved him"[19] to this breach of honor, precisely what did he intend? Foix gave the youthful chronicler some vague and haughty proposals to take back to Segovia, but when Castillo once again rode north with Henry's answers he found matters gone from bad to worse: Gaston had moved upriver for an assault on Alfaro. The city was valiantly resisting; even the women were hurling rocks over the battlements. The French artillery, however, had opened a great rent in the walls, and it was evident that without assistance Alfaro would soon go the way of Calahorra. Castillo rushed off to see what aid he could muster. In a frantic fortnight of riding he managed to gather more than six thousand troops. With this large body—and no small sense of self-importance—he returned to the scene of battle. Foix, confronted by its arrival, saw the writing on what was left of Alfaro's walls. He raised the siege; he fled east along the river. In a matter of days he was gone from Calahorra itself and retreating toward France "with little honor."[20]

The threat of invasion had been laid. But it left wide marks. Navarre, embittered by the havoc wrought in the army's passage, was long afterward at loggerheads with France. The Bishop of Pamplona, who had collaborated with Foix, met an even more lasting fate: Juan's ubiquitous man Friday, Pierres de Peralta, stabbed him to death. It is upon Henry, however, that we find effects of the highest relevance to our tale. If, after the Bidasoa, he still had any lingering illusions about the aims of Louis, they now were dissipated. France could no longer be viewed as anything but hostile. Clearly the time had come for him to realign his commitments with the alien Powers.

It is idle to look for much in the way of foreign policy from a realm which often did not even know who was its sovereign, and learned articles upon the subject seem to be written chiefly out of desire to see one's name in print: the international (in the sense of extra-Peninsular) diplomacy of Henry's reign can, as a matter of plain fact, be very simply stated—friendship with France, interrupted by brief veers to England when France proved offensive or false. The second part of this equation, warned by the thrust of Foix, Henry now proceeded to put into effect: he signed the treaty with England which Edward IV so long had sought. Thus *ultramar*. But England was far away. He might also take heed for closer support against French threats. What more at hand than Portugal? And surely the best method to obtain its sovereign's help was the conclusion of his match with Isabel. Alfonso had been long on promises, but notably short on delivery. Once possessed of the prize, however, he could have no further ground for hesitation. And the moment was ripe for bestowal: hitherto the young Infanta's marriage had perforce remained in cloudland, but now, nearing fifteen, she was eminently nubile. Henry pressed the issue. Alfonso responded enthusiastically. They moved with considerable speed: Henry's allocation of the rents of Trujillo to Isabel, on February 20, 1466, can hardly have been anything else than one of the final steps in working out her dower.

But someone else was moving even faster. Formal alliance with Portugal filled Villena with fresh alarm. Strengthened by such aid, Henry might once again become more powerful than suited the Marqués's convenience. The Portuguese marriage had to be thwarted. He must cut across it; some other husband—and quickly —must be found for Isabel. Just whom could he put forward in the neighboring monarch's place? His agile mind spun round—and finally came to rest upon his brother, Pedro Girón.

Even Villena, on this occasion, did not have the crust to broach in person so shocking a plan: it was borne to Henry by the Marqués's confederate Alonso de Fonseca, Archbishop of Sevilla. And the suggestion was, in fact, given the nature of the aspirant, enough to leave almost anyone aghast. If we have said little about Pedro Girón, it is that the mind and eye shrink back. But here, however briefly, we must face him. Of his duplicity and greed we have had cruel glimpses; in those qualities he quite equaled his brother. In private morals he was infinitely worse. Once he had tried to seduce the Queen Dowager—and signally failed; so rigid was the virtue of the unfortunate relict in Arévalo that from the hour of Juan II's death she had never allowed herself to be left alone with a man. But if that prior attempt to make conjunction with the royal family came to nothing, Giron's assaults on humbler victims had yielded abundant fruit. (Spanish historians are fond of calling him "laden"[21] with bastards, although it is hard to see how his children could well have been anything else—in his capacity of Master of Calatrava, he was a Benedictine friar professed.) As to his society, nobody could stand it. He had almost as foul a mouth as Beltrán. He overdressed and strutted. He blasphemed like a mule skinner. His taste included boys. He was forty-three.

Such was the winsome bridegroom now proposed—pending dispensation from Rome—for Isabel the Catholic, and any inducements he might put forward in support of his candidacy would obviously have to be of the most persuasive sort. They were, it transpired, immense. He offered to bring his whole army of three thousand lances up from Andalucía and place it at Henry's service. To this aid in arms he appended another in cold cash—sixty thousand *doblas*. His Order would withdraw its allegiance to young Alfonso and return to Henry. So, too, of course, would Villena. The brothers would work together for the dispersion of the League. Moreover, this time they were willing to put it all in writing.

Henry listened to these impressive terms with widened eyes. The *doblas* (most of them stolen, anyway) were the least of it: he cared next to nothing for money—except as a means of helping his friends. But the Master's army formed the real backbone of the insurgents' forces; without it, the rebellion would almost certainly fall to pieces. Finally that prospect proved too strong for him: he consented to the match. We can cluck all we want about the price to Isabel—and surely Henry weighed it: he always felt kindly toward her; his only private letter to her which we have breathes courtesy and affection. But one large—and not ignoble—consideration he let override all else: here was another chance, and perhaps the last one, to reunite the realm, to bind its aching wound and end its cleavage.

In effect, he had once again mistaken for a way of terminating the confusion what Villena had projected as a means of keeping it afoot. And having made his decision, he went on immediately—not without pressure from the anxious brothers—to put it in march. He used his influence with the Pope to obtain a dispensation for Girón. The marriage contracts were hastily signed. Far to the south, the suitor gathered his might. Early in April, with an enormous host which bore not only "grand apparatus"[22] for epithalamial tourneys and fiestas but crossbows at the ready and tons of cannon balls (things still might go amiss), he started forth, hot through the swelling figs and budded oleanders for his tender bride. We know nothing of the reactions of young Alfonso—upon the point of being jettisoned— as this triumphant wave rolled up from Andalucía. Isabel's, however, are famous. No fate could have filled her with greater dread than marriage to Girón. Anybody—even the fat Portuguese Alfonso, even tuberculous Carlos of Viana—would have been better. The familiar scenes come on. Beatriz de Bobadilla, the Infanta's boon companion, sharpened her knife; she vowed to sink it in Girón's steamy heart the moment he passed the threshold. Isabel went on her knees. For twenty-four hours, beseeching deliverance, she addressed the Celestial Ear.

It heard her. Something did go very wrong with the advancing Master—although scarcely what he might have imagined. They were up past Ciudad Real, more than halfway to their destination, when his throat began to hurt. He ignored it: the dust, no doubt. But it grew rapidly worse. By the time they reached Villarrubia de los Ojos, he could hardly swallow; he was burning with fever. They pulled him from his horse and forced him to bed. He fought to get up, to press on to his triumph. He could not; wounds the age was skilled at healing, but with viral infections they were helpless, were carried off like flies. His fever soared higher and higher; he flailed about in agony, strangling, gasping for water, cursing God. But finally he knew he was done for. He distributed his gold and jewels among his pretty young squires. Then he went into delirium. On April 30, spewing obscenities and pus, he died.

With Girón's removal from the scene the last hope for reconciliation seemed to have disappeared. Villena went south to look after his dead brother's affairs; so tangled were they that he was gone five months. Henry brooded in Segovia—listening to music, feeding his animals, trying vainly to forget the sickening word thrown out at him in Avila. "And when the leaders are blind"—so sings Gómez Manrique, who saw it all—"alas for those who follow!"[23] Rudderless and abandoned, the realm now finally sank into that abyss of misery, that utter ruin, upon the brink of which it so long had trembled. Nowhere, admittedly, were the 1460s Europe's finest decade. The same civil strife, the same sort of split allegiance between its rival Roses, tore England apart. France lay panting and ravaged after the Hundred Years' War. But in the land under the Pyrenees a whole way of life, a whole epoch, was coming to an end, and these death throes of its Middle Ages are dreadful to watch.

This is the Castile so mournfully depicted in the "Coplas de Mingo Revulgo" and the "Cancionero de Baena": the royal shepherd with rent cloak and broken staff, his flocks unattended and starving, the wolf with gleaming fangs hovering round. This is the prostrate realm of Pulgar's famous jeremiad to the Bishop of Coria: Andalucía transformed into a desert, Murcia cut off and silent, robberies and rapes in Toledo, Extremadura in the grip of outlaws, all of Galicia devastated, the fields of Medina and Valladolid and Salamanca and Zamora put to the torch. People cowered in their blackened huts. No one dared cultivate the crops—marauding gangs of soldiers, unpaid and mutinous, roamed up and down—and famine swept the land: fifteen thousand died in the south alone, that tragic year. Journeys were out of the question. Such foreigners as business or politics did oblige to venture in clung terrified together. Appalled by the lawlessness and desolation, envoys of Charles the Bold so far forgot themselves as to tell Henry, to his face, that Castile was the "shame"[24] of Europe. Another embassy, one from Bohemia, wandered dazedly about for weeks amidst the dust and bugs and hostile natives before they could even find him—and when at last they did, in Olmedo, left us their incomparable picture: the royal couple sitting on the floor in a room darkened against the summer heat, Henry bored with their mission (they had come to enlist sympathy for their excommunicated King) but fascinated by the oxlike wrestler who was one of the party, Juana reaching up in wonderment to touch their rippling yellow hair, and then the observation, priceless beyond whole drawers of official documents, that she and Henry did not sleep together, that they were at odds and he had nothing to do with her, *"sie sagen, er mug nit mit ir zu thun haben."*[25]

At odds: everyone at odds, at bay, at very nearly the end of a rope which held them all in cruel knots but which never quite seemed to break. And the pressure, the tension, soon grew even worse.

When Villena came back from the south, late in September, he was
bent upon new havoc; the intervals of his fiduciary labors had given
him time to concoct a further scheme for the disruption of the
realm. He suggested a conference of both the factions, in Madrid:
he had, he announced, what well might be a means of final settlement. The contending leaders came warily in. They gathered in the
old Alcázar on the cliff above the river, and he broached his plan.
Final indeed: it turned out to be no less than a partition of Castile.
Let Henry, he proposed, reign in the north—and Alfonso in Andalucía. It would have meant, one sees, a complete disjunction, a
permanent fratricidal strife. And whether the *caudillos* in the Alcázar so saw it or not, they threw up their hands. They argued. They
dragged in other grievances, other interests. The more they
debated, the farther apart they grew. In the end, however, they
rejected the proposition: the issues by then were far too deep, too
bitter, to be resolved by any line drawn across a map.

But Villena's bag of tricks was by no means exhausted. He had
not been able to chop the kingdom in two. Yet perhaps he could at
least split open the loyalist ranks. If Henry could be lured to some
act of flagrant injustice against one of his innermost circle, then
others of it, shocked by such ingratitude and fearful of similar
consequence to themselves, might fall away.

Of course he had to select a victim. Pedrarias, now *contador mayor*
with the recent death of his rascally old father, seemed suitable; no
one—except Lucas, who was out of reach—had been more true to
the Crown. He would also need an agent; it was the plotting of
knavery, not its sordid execution, which most appealed to Villena's
taste. And why not Fonseca again? He called him in. He explained
as much of the project as he thought the Archbishop could grasp.
The chief thing, he emphasized, was so to "indignate"[26] Henry
against Pedrarias that he would clap him into jail. The method he
left up to his interlocutor's own considerable talents for mendacity,
although he did offer a few hints.

It is sad to be obliged to report—but indicative both of the state
to which the harried monarch had been reduced and the craft and
magnitude of Fonseca's lies (Pedrarias was on the point of defecting
anyway, he insisted; moreover, he was stealing things in Segovia
right and left)—that Henry lent himself to this design. Down from
Segovia he summoned Pedrarias, whom he had left—along with his

brother Juan, now risen to be its bishop—in the city's charge. Obedient and unsuspecting, the faithful servant came. He entered the courtyard of the Alcázar and started to dismount. Suddenly he heard the gate grind shut behind him. *"Sed preso!"* cried the bailiff. "You are under arrest."[27] People appeared from nowhere and surrounded him. He tried to fight his way through. But someone, from behind, gave him a huge terrible wound "that smote to the bone."[28] He fainted with it; he fell from the saddle, gushing blood, and was carried away and locked up in the Torre del Homenaje. Henry himself took horse—for Segovia: at the last minute it had been decided to make a clean sweep of the family and seize the Bishop as well. One of the Arias retainers outrode him, with a warning. Frantically the Bishop began to fortify his palace.

He need not have bothered. Somewhere, somehow, high in the snowy passes of the Guadarramas, Henry's honor, his sense of decency (much as it once had done to don Alvaro de Luna in an alley in Burgos), returned to him. He slowed, his conscience tugging at the bridle. The Ariases—his lifelong friends! What was he about, had he lost his mind? He stopped and swung around. He galloped back to Madrid. Up in the Torre del Homenaje he went. He implored Pedrarias's pardon. He called his own physicians. Remorseful, mute, attentive, he sat for days beside the sufferer's bed in the windy old tower.

But Pedrarias never forgave him. Bad though the physical wound turned out to be—it failed to heal, it plagued him the rest of his life, matter kept oozing out of it, and when the discharge did briefly slacken his whole body swelled—a deeper hurt, an implacable desire for vengeance, had been planted in his breast. It was to grow and grow; one day we shall see it yield perhaps the bitterest fruit which Henry had to taste in all his life. But even then, even with Pedrarias still not up from his furs and fever, the first dark warning of it struck. Henry had gone for a hunt. The winter dusk was gathering as he neared Madrid on his return. He decided to spend the night at Fuencarral, in a lonely farmhouse upon the hamlet's edge; it may be that he could not face again the intrigues and arguments in town. Some of Pedrarias's men had stalked him. In the silence, in the midnight, they fell upon the house, with drawn daggers and swords.

Henry managed to escape—naked, and apparently through a window—into the fields. (The soldier in his bed was not so fortunate, and the reader can easily imagine his fate at the hands of the assailants: leaving Madrid by the Alcalá gate in 1495, Münzer saw the corpses of two men taken in sodomy and hanged with their genitals strung around their necks.) But the call had been a close one. Henry's thoughts, as he limped about through the frozen fields with his bare shanks shivering and his teeth clicking like castanets, cannot have been less cold, less piercing, than the silent winter stars above him. He did succeed, at last, in finding some peasants who lent him a farmer's smock. The garment must have appealed to him. But surely it was the only thing about the awful experience—about the entire past year—which gave him any pleasure. Set on by thugs, hounded like a common criminal! Well, he deserved it—betraying Pedrarias. Were the hatred and suspicion all around beginning to poison even him? And he might sink lower yet, might be brought, in desperation, to God knew what, if matters continued to drag on like this.

But they did not, could not: a hand even more artful than Villena's was about to reach in and seek to put an end—for his own purposes—to the deadlock, the stalemate and inanition, which the Marqués worked so assiduously to maintain. Early that spring a familiar figure, a figure with a long Navarrese face and saddlebags embossed with a Constable's baton, rode out of the east. It was Pierres de Peralta. And his arrival could mean one thing and one thing only: that Juan of Aragón had come to life.

17.

Olmedo Again

Juan's reappearance as a chief actor on the Castilian stage should by no means be taken to indicate that his troubles were at an end. Quite the contrary: they had turned—if such a state of affairs can be imagined—more desperate than ever. His Queen and loyal help-meet was in the final stages of her malady. Louis gnawed increasingly larger holes upon his border. The revolt of the Catalans raged on, and under fresh command: Pedro, the Portuguese Constable who captained that unseemly spectacle when last we glanced at it ("King Pedro," he saw fit to call himself), had died, and although espousal of their cause was rapidly beginning to look like a one-way ticket to the Styx, they had now enticed René of Anjou to take his place. René, owner already of so many phantom crowns, was far too ancient and decrepit to go in person. But he sent his son—Jean, Duke of Lorraine—as surrogate, and with heavy reinforcements. Angevins, French, Catalans—great tongues of flame were licking in at Juan from every side.

It was his very extremity, in point of fact, which now brought him back into the arena of Castile; he had no other place where he could possibly turn for aid. Not, of course, from its lawful sovereign —archenemy avowed. (Juan, autocrat himself, can have been under small illusion about the validity of Alfonso's coronation.) But the League, the League. For years he had been abetting their own plans. Now the time had come when they must reciprocate; there lay his best, even his only, hope of being able to drive out the foes who were enveloping him and then recover *"les parts e terres a Nós rebelles."*[1] And he wanted no airy promises from the Castilian magnates. What he needed, and urgently, was whole squadrons of their men of arms, platoons of crossbows and pikes.

Such was the mission borne by Peralta as he cantered in through the eastern hills in the spring of 1467. Tireless as ever upon his

master's service, he went straight to the rebels in their lair at Avila;
the conference in Madrid had at last been angrily broken up. And
he met a warm welcome. His daughter was affianced to Troilo
Carrillo, the Archbishop's son. He had always got on famously with
the Admiral—now growing old, but still unflagging in his Aragonese son-in-law's support. The Maytime of accord speedily put
forth flowers. Spirited talk sprang up about declaring young Alfonso of age and pushing on toward his marriage to the Aragonese
Infanta (never, no matter what the other exigencies or crises, must
those matches—the golden key, the Ultima Thule of all Juan's desir-
ing—go unattended). Before long Juan was able to write to his
ambassador in England that the League, "*stant pacifichs e sens guerra,*"[2] had committed itself to hasten forces to his relief.

"*Stant pacifichs e sens guerra*"—yes, of course that was the rub, and
a big one too. The barons could hardly be expected to send their
troops out of the country while still faced with an enemy at home;
even Juan was unable to deny the logic of that. Obviously he could
look for no aid until there was a settlement of the conflict in Castile.
Some means of hurrying along that resolution had to be sought out.
Couriers posted between Zaragoza and Avila with anxious questions and dutiful replies. What was preventing the League, Juan
wanted to know, from bringing matters to an issue? Henry's army
had been disbanded; surely Peralta could stir up a decisive battle
while the insurgents were still in such advantageous pose. Yes,
Peralta reported, most of the rebels—especially Carrillo—were
ready, even eager, for such a turn. But someone seemed to be holding them back. Who? Villena. Ah, Villena. There must be some way
to suborn him, to draw him to their point of view. Wait, Juan had
to think a while. Instructions on the point would soon follow. They
did: suddenly Peralta was sitting down with the Marqués and dangling before him a most remarkable offer—the marriage of young
Fernando and his own daughter.

We need not be taken in by this strange move; Juan can never
have seriously entertained the thought of throwing away his dar-
ling, his prize, the most precious piece in his high gamble for the
Castilian crown, on a mere Beatriz Pacheco. Anyway, Villena
balked. Glittering though the prospect was, sorely tempted though
he must have been—especially after the recent fiasco of his brother
in the same direction—to align his family with the *sacra Majestad*

itself, he vaguely sensed some trap; at the last moment, fearful of "bringing the whole kingdom down upon him,"[3] he shied off, he refused the bait. That attempt to win him over, to circumvent him, had not worked. There he still sat—obstructive, mulish, as determined as ever to keep affairs on leash. So long as he was around, Peralta's commission to break up the military impasse in Castile could come to nothing. And there seemed to be no way to pry him loose.

But in the end Villena's own greed accomplished that. Just at the juncture he made up his mind to appropriate the mastership of Santiago. We know how insatiably he had always lusted for that dignity. He had ruined Lucas to keep it out of his hands. Three years before, beside the Pisuerga, he had moved heaven and earth to wrench it away from Beltrán de la Cueva and have it bestowed, theoretically, upon Alfonso. Theoretically, no more: the Pope, at Henry's instance, had not yet executed the bulls. The great office still hung unconferred—gorgeous, tantalizing, available. And now Villena resolved to take it, willy-nilly. In June he persuaded Alfonso to convoke the Order—for Ocaña, down over the mountains, in New Castile. Whether he had also forced the youthful puppet to renounce his own claims, or whether he trusted his private wiles and eloquence to bring the assembled Order round to his formal nomination, is not altogether clear. In any case, its *comendadores* and priors and Thirteens began to converge on Ocaña. And off to join them Villena rode.

The cat finally was away; Peralta and the rebels were free for action. Immediately they took counsel about the best means to prod the enemy. Perhaps, they figured, it would be by breaking through the line from Valladolid to Segovia and thus intercepting communications between those two bastions of Henry's power. They moved north with all their train. They seized the strategic bridge of Puente Duero; its loyalist garrison fled. Once across the river, they decided to drive on and capture Roa. But there they failed: Beltrán, to whom the town had been given three years before, sent help over from Cuéllar and they were obliged to fall back. Prosperous news, however, soon reached them from Olmedo. The royal commandant of that important city—of course for an emolument—was willing to open the postern next to his house and let them in. So rich a plum merited changing their plans. They swung back south. The palm was crossed and they took possession, took stout seat behind those familiar and formidable walls. Rebel barons in Olmedo, the arm of Aragón propulsive and alift: memories waken, ghostly armies stalk the poppies, tension begins to stretch, to sing, in the midsummer air.

There was tension in Segovia, too; Peralta's inflammatory tactics had taken their first effect. Henry was stung by the loss of Olmedo. Whether or not he still had anything "to do" with her, the place belonged to his wife. Moreover, the mean and ugly way in which it had been occupied was particularly suited to distress him. He wrote to the Mendozas. Just what did they think of a performance like that?

What the Mendozas were thinking was that it was about time for them to return to Henry. They had been much interested (those buzzard eyes missed nothing) in an event which occurred in Toledo a few days past: the *marranos* and crypto-Jews of the Imperial city rose in Henry's favor, and although Alvar Gómez, Henry's ex-secretary, who held the city for the League, had crushed the movement, it seemed symptomatic. Perhaps Henry's position was again looking up. Perhaps it behooved them to scramble once more on what might well turn out, after all, to be the winning side. The Marqués of Santillana, head of the family, not only answered Henry's letter sympathetically; he went over to Segovia for a visit.

Yes, he agreed, the business of Olmedo had really been pretty disgraceful. Henry certainly needed help if he was to ward off further misfortunes of the kind. He offered to rejoin him with his whole clan, with all their forces. More: they would do everything they could to wean their kinsman Pedro de Velasco (he had married one of the Mendoza sisters) away from the rebels and to Henry's cause. But this time they put the stiffest price ever on their support. They wanted, in return, no less than custody of little Juana la Beltraneja: tutelage of her—although of course they did not say this to Henry, they put it on the basis of a guarantee that he would have no more dealings with the League and leave them in the lurch—would make their political as well as their social position virtually unassailable. Henry, touched by their concern and generosity, agreed (apparently the mother was not consulted). Santillana's brother, Iñigo López de Mendoza, Count of Tendilla, arrived to collect the hostage. Up over the cloud-hung pass of Malagosto disappeared the puzzled child. Down through it, a few days later, came the entire armed might of the Mendozas.

But there was no need to stay in Segovia, they reasoned with Henry once they were at hand. The best thing was to get on to Cuéllar: there they could both join their son-in-law Beltrán and be closer to the enemy in Olmedo. They rode through the pines and cornflowers; the gaudy Duke took them all in. And Alba, they suggested; Henry really ought to summon Alba, too. A messenger went off to the Tormes—and returned with one of Alba's usual poor-mouth whines: he was terribly hard up, he had no cash for troops but if Henry gave him some he would see what he could scrape together; a quarter of a million ought to do it. Henry sent the money. "But I know he won't come,"[4] he said sadly. Nor did he; he was hoping to conclude—and soon did—a more lucrative arrangement with the rebels ("Alba! Alba!" snotted stableboys by then were chanting all over the realm: "What are we offered for the Count of Alba ?").[5] A different arrival, however, soon more than filled that gap. Pedro de Velasco did indeed appear. He brought two of his brothers and a cousin and six hundred horse and a swarm of infantry—so happy was his father at finding him disposed to mend his ways and return to the legitimist fold that he had given him all the Haro troops.

Very much of a family affair, one sees—Mendozas, Beltrán, Velascos. And what a family: their musters, assembled in Cuéllar, came to over four thousand—some sixteen hundred horse and twenty-five hundred infantry. It was a heady business. The League, their spies told them, had nothing like such numbers. Many of its chieftains were away—Villena of course gone to Ocaña, the Count of Plasencia home on a visit, the Master of Alcántara occupied with matters of his Order far off in Extremadura. Let them attack Olmedo at once, they insisted. But Henry demurred: no spilling of blood. He had a better idea. For days messengers had been coming over from Medina del Campo with anguished pleas for help: the town itself was for Henry, but the League held the great castle of La Mota which dominated it and kept harrying the hapless citizens. It was the sort of appeal that always moved Henry. Preferable, he countered, to go to Medina's aid; the castle, even at the sight of such a juggernaut, probably would yield.

But that fell far short of what the magnates wanted. They gath-

ered for consultation behind Henry's back. There was a way to
humor him, they decided, and still to achieve their own ends. The
path of an ostensible march to Medina would take them almost
directly past Olmedo. When they neared that town they could
wheel, turn south, and pounce upon it. They went back to Henry.
Very well, they told him: the relief of Medina. On August 18,
pennons and steel bright in the canicular sun, they all set out.

Most of the rebels were delighted by the news (not only the
royalists had spies); matters seemed to be playing right into their
hands. Henry's march, wherever it was going, plainly was headed
west. They could thrust up across it, intercept, bring to battle.
Carrillo, already breathing heavily, was prepared to challenge the
whole royal army singlehanded. Peralta alone took a more sober
view. Yes, he agreed, of course it was what he wanted—a decisive
clash. But perhaps the moment, he pointed out, was not so oppor-
tune as one might have wished. Just what sort of force did they have,
in effect, for such a confrontation? Realistically he cast it up. The
Archbishop and young Alfonso (thirteen, of no use). The Count of
Luna—but in bed with a bad leg. The Clavero of Calatrava, in
command of the Order's light cavalry, although some of those, say
fifty, would have to be sent off at once to reconnoiter the movements
of the enemy. Oh, and of course the Count of Miranda, from his
neighboring castle of Iscar; although Miranda himself was admittedly a poor sort (besides being a notorious coward, he had deserted
his youthful wife to live in flaming sin with the rancid old Dowager
Countess of Treviño), he did have available troops. A total of six
hundred horse, at best. It was not enough, Peralta concluded. They
simply could not afford the risk.

But that very day of their conference, a great stroke of good
fortune befell them. The Admiral, apprehensive himself in Valladolid, had sent one of his sons with a battalion of lances to Olmedo, and on the way they seem to have met another force coming
over from Coca led by Fernando de Fonseca, the Sevillan Archbishop's brother; at any rate, unexpectedly they all rode in—more than
three hundred strong. And only a few hours later Pedro de Hontiveros, the Stúñigas' clubfooted *mayordomo*, arrived with troops of
the Count of Plasencia and his daughter the Countess of Benalcázar.
With these providential reinforcements the rebels' whole situation
had abruptly changed. In horse (and that was all that really counted,

these are cavalry battles) they now almost equaled the royalists. Peralta's reservations vanished; he turned as jubilant as everybody else. One wonders if he started a courier down the long road to Zaragoza with an encouraging dispatch to Juan—the plan was working, battle was imminent. Perhaps he did not have time. He had taken vigorous control of preparations. Suddenly Olmedo boiled with martial activity; it resounded with the din of armorers and blacksmiths, with excited commands. Let the foe come now, if they wanted. They would be met head-on.

And coming they were. That first day out, that Tuesday, they had not made much progress: the royal host was too large to organize easily, a battalion of light cavalry under Juan Fernández Galindo was poorly trained and already giving trouble, they spent the night among the sandy gulches, very little on from Cuéllar itself. But Wednesday they were moving fast—and, Henry thought, rather too much toward the south. He did not like it, he said uneasily. There might be danger of some sort of clash if they kept on like that. No, they asserted; it was the shortest way. They held to it and in the late afternoon reached the Eresma—five miles only from Olmedo, although they still could not see it: they were behind the long bleak butte that lies to the northeast of the town. There they decided to camp. The pavilions went up. The *fardaje*, the baggage train, disposed itself: thirty great carts and a thousand burdened mules. They watered their mounts; they ate. The leaders retired to their tents to get what rest they could before the attack.

For one of them—Beltrán—there was very nearly no sleep at all; if the morrow was to produce the single act of real valor or usefulness in his life, it was certainly not his night. He was hot; he seems to have been more than customarily out of sorts. Unable to settle himself, he paced in the breathless dusk along the bank of the river. Beyond it hovered the light horse of García de Padilla, Clavero of Calatrava, sent in reconnaissance by the League; all day they had flitted on the army's flanks, but now, with the fall of night, they had edged closer. Close enough, in fact, for faces to be made out. Beltrán glimpsed a familiar one among the squires—a boyhood friend from back in Úbeda. Haughtily he called to him and summoned him across, under safe-conduct. He led him all through the camp. When they had made the whole vast circuit and were again at the tepid little stream, he stopped. Would the rebels, he asked, ever think of opposing, with such paltry forces as they had, a host like that? He rather thought so, said the squire—shrewd enough not to tip the wink, to let the enemy know that Olmedo, too, now burst with almost similar might. Beltrán was brusque. Thought? Was that all? Very well, the squire ventured; he would take an oath upon it. Beltrán threw back his head and laughed contemptuously. Oath for oath, he retorted; he promised the squire fifty thousand *maravedís* a year—he could easily afford it—if things so turned out.

Nor was that Beltrán's only visitor in the sultry, vexatious night. He did at last give up his nervous striding and seek his couch. But along after twelve he was unceremoniously aroused: a courier of the Archbishop of Sevilla, on his way from Coca to Olmedo, had slipped through the guards and found his tent. Yes, what? Beltrán demanded. Oh, the Archbishop (who tried to keep a foot inside both doors) wanted to give him a warning. He had learned from his brother, down in the rebel citadel, that forty of Alfonso's knights had taken a solemn vow, should matters arrive at battle, to seek him and slay him: be prepared, be wise, adopt some other armor than your own. Disguise! cried Beltrán. His cuirass and helmet were already laid out for the morning. He showed them to the messenger. Take a good look at them, he told him. Describe them well in Olmedo. "They will learn soon enough," he boasted, "just who the Duke of Alburquerque is!"[6] He went with his wakener to the flap of the tent. After he had gone, he still stood looking out across the drowsing camp. The full moon hung above it, a huge hot orange. Stacked weapons glinted; restless horses neighed. Well, it would soon be over. That smatter of fools off in Olmedo, behind the mesa —what sort of resistance could they put up? A quick stroke, a cleave of lighting: question of an hour or two at most. Probably, however, the rebels would not even come out. If they had their wits about them they would deliver the town at once.

But the sleepless Duke was wrong. They all were wrong. They rose betimes in the dawn which had brought no cool: they took their gritty breakfast. Perspiring already, they formed again in the column of march: Fernández Galindo with his balky and ill-armed battalion at the head, behind him the Mendozas and Beltrán, the baggage and infantry next, and the Velasco forces bringing up the rear. (Henry, with a handful of "those he loved best,"[7] rode frowning and apart.) Nothing opposed them, nothing presented itself; the Clavero's patrol had disappeared. They passed on through the shimmering fields: clank, thud on baked earth, muffled jangle. Turning south, they emerged from behind the mesa. And then suddenly, incredulously, they were jarring short at what they saw.

Drawn up on the plain athwart them—ready and waiting, in full battle order—lay the League's whole army.

Wave after crowding wave of shock rolled back through the lines and brought them all to a moiling halt. The leaders disengaged themselves. They converged upon Henry. What had gone wrong with their information, who had sowed these dragon's teeth among the enemy? Well, no matter, they clamored; let them go ahead, let them attack. But Henry, still under the frail belief that their destination was Olmedo, again objected. There might yet be a peaceable solution, he told them, a way for them to pass. He would seek parley. He sent off a Trinitarian and a trumpet to find Carrillo in the host before them. The message—mild: all they wished was to march on west, please unblock the path. Carrillo's answer—furious: there were other routes which they could have taken to Medina, they were obviously out for trouble, come on, come on. And see, added the apoplectic prelate (matching Beltrán's bravado)—to make me easier to find. He slapped a white *camisa* down over his armor and then tied around it, crosswise, a flaming scarlet stole.

There was nothing for it: battle. Henry embarked upon a halting little speech to his captains: war never solved anything, he would much have preferred that a conflict be "excused,"[8] he gave his consent to it only under "protestation."[9] But he broke off in the middle of it. A lone figure was galloping toward them across the plain—Peralta himself. He had certain business with Henry, he announced as he drew up. Together they went aside. No one has ever known what ruse the Constable had in mind. It was not needed; whatever it might have been, he abandoned it at once. For Henry, anxious to please, to be gracious, was making a suggestion of his own: perhaps Peralta would like—would be good enough—to arrange the royal ranks. He was so skillful at that.

Skillful—undoubtedly: but in whose benefit? Seldom indeed does one of the enemy have a chance to order a rival host. It was a heaven-sent opportunity, and Peralta set instantly about to take advantage of it. First he stationed the baggage, with the whole peonage to guard it, considerably to the rear. That was normal enough. But what he did next was much more telling—for his aim. The army had already turned west; Fernández Galindo's squadron, which led its march in column down from the north, had thus become its southern flank. That unit, Peralta knew through expert observation if not through his scouts and the squire from Ubeda, was the royal army's weakest. He pulled it out—and replaced it in the vital center of the line. Nor was he yet content. He persuaded Henry to take position far behind it, near the baggage. Then his damage was done; he surveyed the final disposition. And so can we. The Mendozas now formed the extreme southern flank—facing the rebel troops of the Clavero of Calatrava. To their right lay Beltrán —across from Fonseca. In the middle, Fernández Galindo—with the powerful *batalla* of the Admiral's son, two hundred bristling and close-packed men of arms, directly in front of him. On the north, on the royal host's far right, the Velascos were opposite Carrillo and the troops of the rebel counts of Luna and Miranda and the Stúñigas.

So sat they all, at the ready: lances aloft and visors closed. Between the two long lines the August plain lay silent and empty: the terrified reapers caught there that morning about their work had long since fled. Yet with neither sovereign immediately on the field (Carrillo had firmly deposited young Alfonso—along with the craven Miranda—in the portal of the Convent of Santo Domingo), there was no one officially to unleash them, to give the order to engage. And already it was midafternoon; the march, the marshaling, the parleys, had taken hours. The heat mounted, the strain mounted. Horses broke out of line and were nervously pulled back. Hawks hung in the yellow sky. Commanders fretted and swore.

What ended it, what finally loosed it, was an accident. Pedro de Velasco, up on the north, was growing increasingly concerned about his position. It had been good enough in the morning, but now—for like all the royal army, he faced west—the sun fell in his eyes. The sources say only that he made a "sudden move."[10] It can have been no other than to turn the rebels' northern flank, to force them to shift about and take the same disadvantageous stance. But Carrillo, who stood before him, guessed his aim. With equal speed he flung north an interposing squadron. The outriders tangled. Steel upon steel, their encounter split the stifling air. The whole army heard it, even glimpsed the swirl, the flash, the first rising dust. And no longer could they hold in. Pell-mell and shouting, swords drawn or lances down, the long rebel line bulged, burst, poured unevenly eastward: it had begun.

Uneven—for the Admiral's mighty battalion, in the center, out-galloped them all. It smote like lightning against the royal squadron of Fernández Galindo—placed by Peralta, with such cunning, directly in its path. At the first shock those green troops panicked; not even their brilliant leader—the hero of Simancas—could keep them in control. They broke; they fled. As they streamed away to the east, they collided with the baggage. The peonage left to guard it, infected by their terror, joined the rout. On in pursuit of them rode the Admiral's son—past the overturned wagons, the abandoned arms, the milling and rearing mules. Past Henry, too: nearby, the reader will remember, he had taken—been tricked to take—his post. It was precisely what Peralta had thrown for. He turned to Henry. Save yourself! he cried across the tumult. Defeat! And it certainly must have seemed so, with helpless hundreds of the royal cavalry flying by like torn clouds in a hurricane and young Enríquez and his triumphant myrmidons pounding after. If Henry hesitated, it was only for a moment. He struck swift spurs to his horse and veered away toward the south. Cutting wide around Olmedo, he vanished into the west.

Whether the Constable also sped off or bolted back into the town we do not know. No doubt he figured that with the monarch fled the royal army would quickly give in. It was a good medieval calculation. But in the event it failed: Peralta's scheme, begun with so high a measure of success, went suddenly astray. Henry's departure was either unnoticed or unregretted, and the whole front, with mace and sword, with indiscriminate clang and shout and billow of choking dust, had violently engaged. The two fronts, rather, for the flight of Fernández Galindo's squadron and its pursuit by young Enríquez had torn a great hole in the center of both lines, had left the encounter, there at its very start, composed of two separate salients—on the south Mendozas and Beltrán against the Clavero of Calatrava and Fonseca's brother Fernando; on the north the *batallas* of massed Velascos opposite Carrillo.

And let us take it from south to north: Mendozas first. One of the brothers, Juan, had turned his back even before the initial blows and raced away. But his squadron—its numbers are not given in the records—cannot have been large: the clan's force was still almost intact as it bore thundering down on the opposing troops of the Clavero. It struck them with fearful shock. The Calatravan contingent were only light cavalry at best. Moreover, they had been left exhausted from their two days and nights of patrol. They could not withstand the impact; the Mendozas broke through them like cannon balls, and they crumbled, reeled off, and fled in disarray. When the Mendozan hammer formed again and turned and drove back to the battle line, they found little left on which to fall; already they had smashed the League's far right.

Next to them on the boiling front, however, just to their north, Beltrán was hard beset. His opponent, Fonseca, had hit him *"con terrible empuje,"*[11] with staggering force. The forty knights sworn to bring him down rode in Fonseca's ranks, and they had no trouble descrying the vaunted armor; they drove straight to him and hemmed him round. Valiantly Beltrán fought them off. He had a noble horse, his favorite, in full plates and graven throat piece—and it served him well; "without need of spur or guidance"[12] it pirouetted, elided, nimbly glanced away. But the murderous foe pressed ever closer; one of them finally managed to sever Beltrán's reins. He began to tire, to fail. Yet just as he was about to go down, the ring around him broke: the victorious Mendozas, their own work done, had galloped to aid him. Santillana, his father-in-law, caught him up. He righted himself, he found new vigor. Glimpsing Fonseca in the melee, he catapulted against him. They met in single combat, swords clashing, great spiky balls on iron chains swinging and flailing. Beltrán knocked off Fonseca's helmet—then with a fierce thrust ripped open his head. He cut down two squires who had fought through to help their master. Fonseca himself, "with the agony of his wound"[13] (he died of it four days later), lurched from the saddle. And seeing their leader defeated, his whole squadron broke in disorder, followed the Calatravans into flight. The Mendozas and Beltrán were left free to draw their ranks together, to catch brief breath and stanch their wounds and count their casualties. They had lost perhaps a third of their number. But in front of them, the entire southern half of the rebel army had now been destroyed: fled, captured, killed.

The southern half, yes—and so much for it. But the other great sector of the army, up to the north, where Velascos were pitted against Carrillo—what of that? There the din, the confusion, and of course simultaneously, had been even worse. It, too, had opened with a savage strike; only moments after young Enríquez had aimed his initial blow, Velasco loosed a roaring squadron led by his cousin Juan against the rebel ranks. It wrought a similar havoc; it tore straight through. But once it was passed—and turned—it found itself confronted by a solid wall: Carrillo, recovering, had quickly closed the gap. Caught alone behind the enemy lines and thinking that the whole foe might face about and destroy them, they deserted, they spurred away westward.

Little they knew: Carrillo had far too much on his hands in front of him to think about his rear. For it was there on the north that the worst of it, the real fury of the battle, came. Fury, as well, with little order, little sense: very nearly from the start the captains on both sides of that salient had given up any effort at control. Only Carrillo, charging hither and yon among his rebel squadrons, managed to keep them in some semblance of rank (he and Beltrán —after the ducal horse—are such heroes as the battle had). His left arm, run through by a lance in the terrible first blow of Juan Velasco, was bleeding rivers. But he fought on like a demon— slashing, rallying, yelling. Twice he took time to streak across the plain to young Alfonso and pant out—although one has difficulty imagining what he can have told him—an account of the progress of the fray. All that blood! cried Alfonso. Just my horse's, the daffy old bonze cried back—then shot away again to the encounter. And finally he began to have the best of it; finally the Velascos began to sag and buckle before him, to yield ground toward the east. The sun was going down: their fortunes with it. And all at once they collapsed; in a wild tangle of shattered armor and wounded horses they turned and roweled frantically away.

After them! shouted Carrillo—capture them, kill them, end it all; he saw his chance. But he lost it; avarice snatched it from him. His troops, in their pursuit, had reached the abandoned royal baggage —and they reined in: the temptation for plunder proved too great. Shamelessly, while the escaping Velascos scattered off toward the safety of Cuéllar and Coca, they fell to looting. (Where is honor? What has become of knighthood? The world of Chivalry indeed is almost gone.) The Archbishop rode desperately among them, trying to beat them off, to force them loose. He had little success; unheeding, they threw down their own weapons and broke open the chests and boxes and crammed their arms with booty and sped from the field. All he was able to hold back and reassemble—and it was all that was left of the League's whole army—was some four hundred men.

With those, however, he turned. The dust had begun to settle; off to the south, through the thickening twilight, he discerned the heave and glint of the Mendozas—finished, at just that juncture, with their own endeavors, and re-formed. He fanned out in line of attack, to drive down against them; for a moment the battle threatened to blaze up anew. But he wavered; he did not advance. Neither did the Mendozas. The light was fast failing. They were both too mauled, too exhausted, for further action. He wheeled away and withdrew. The night closed down; "darkness departed them."[14]

We, at least, can see the postlude. When the royalists found the way before them clear, they moved off to the north. In the lee of the limestone mesa, beside some wells of which the diligent can still discover evidence a little east of the highway to Valladolid, they slaked their thirst. Revived, they took up what order they could— sad remnant of the proud host which had set forth from Cuéllar three days before—and marched westward under the sulfurous rising moon. Carrillo, as they went, reconnoitered the littered field by that same lurid light: the dead horses, the splintered lances and helmets, the bits and pieces of butchered squires. Once he was satisfied that the foe had gone, he lighted bonfires—probably the mows of harvested grain—all up and down it. Then he rode off through the smoke and stench for young Alfonso. The befuddled lad was still waiting where they had left him, in the portal of Santo Domingo (Miranda had run away). Carrillo gathered him up. Together they went back to Olmedo. They blew a fanfare, they trotted in. The gates—the disgraceful episode—swung shut.

Or almost shut: it remains for us, as it remained for the royalist army, to seek Henry out. We find him at Pozal de Gallinas, some eight miles west of the battle line and not far from Medina itself. There, as he rode, he had come upon a group of farmers working in the *eras*—the threshing floors—just outside the village, backs bent patient and uncomplaining to their bitter lot: his kind. He had stayed his horse and dismounted; he walked among them, shyly visiting—but casting, meanwhile, anxious glances toward the east. He must have known almost at once that he had been duped again, that the battle was not over: the white clouds of dust towering ever higher on the horizon would have told him that. But he had no way of unriddling them; he could only wait and wonder. He lingered all afternoon. Evening drew in. The hot sky paled to citron, to lilac; the first calm stars appeared. It was almost full night, and he and the toiling peasants fallen silent (threshers thresh late in High Castile with an August moon), when the outriders of his weary army came upon him and told him he had won.

But had he? "No other battle can be found where it is harder to distinguish than in this"—says Palencia, during his narration of its chaotic course—"which faction had the advantage."[15] The same statement can be made with equal veracity about its result. Medieval practice conceded victory to the side which remained in possession of the field; Alfonso's undoubtedly did that. Yet no army able, like Henry's, to form again in any kind of order and resume its march unopposed and unpursued could possibly be considered vanquished. Another criterion of the day—loss of the royal standard—gets us no farther: Alfonso's was taken, to be sure—but so was Henry's, found by the looters in one of the chests, since he had refused to let it be displayed, and carried off. The totals of rival banners captured, too, cancel each other out. The rebels seized seven—among them Beltrán's, two of the Mendozas', two more of the Velascos' (with their appropriate big black crows). But five fell to the royalists—the Admiral's, the Fonsecas', those of Calatrava and the troops of the Count of Plasencia and the Countess of Benalcázar. Lists of the casualties, once one has untangled them, only contradict. Nor do foreign accounts, on this occasion, give much help. Historians in general take on unquestioning faith the announcement sent home by the Milanese ambassador Panicharolla—that Henry had been the victor. But Panicharolla, on August 20, 1467, was reposing in Paris. Anyway, it has not been observed that shortly afterward news of quite different sort, news claiming a full triumph for Alfonso, reached Milan; young Sforza must have been left as puzzled as everybody else.

Uncertainty, confusion—then and today. A single thing can be said with any finality about the upshot of this second battle of Olmedo. That one fact, however, we know as surely as Juan himself must have known it, sitting in the Aljafería of Zaragoza and raising his quenched old milky eyes to whoever read him the dispatch. His move had failed. Nothing had been really decided, after all, by the encounter; the conflict in Castile was not settled. There would be no reinforcements for him from the League. He—and of course his boy, now come fifteen—would have to go on alone.

Settled—far from it: the deadlock turned yet worse. Late that same night of the battle Henry and his troops entered Medina, and the next morning they set about the business for which Henry had imagined they left Cuéllar in the first place—reduction of the castle. They got nowhere with it. La Mota was too strong a citadel to be taken by assault, and negotiations with its rebel garrison produced only the temporizing promise that it would yield if not relieved in fifteen days. About all the royalists could do was wait and hope that during the period enough reinforcements of their own would come in to frighten off any movement against them from Olmedo. And their numbers were, in effect, upon the rise. Entire squadrons which had deserted during the battle sheepishly returned. New recruits—from Salamanca and Zamora, from Huete—appeared. The arrival of Pedro Manrique, Count of Treviño, brought the total of Henry's fresh forces to some two thousand. (It may seem odd to find a Manrique offering his services to the Crown, but Guiomar de Castro, forcibly retired to Guadalupe after her fist fight with Juana on the stairs at Madrid, had finally lured Treviño into matrimony and then persuaded him—perhaps there was, after all, some spark of decency and loyalty in that diamond-encrusted breast— to join the legitimist ranks.)

But if the power in Medina was mounting, Alfonso's grew even faster. Villena came back from his fruitful trip to Ocaña, now elected—although still not invested—Master of Santiago, and with many hundreds of the Order's heavy cavalry. (Unsurprisingly, he "chided"[16] the confederates for having given battle.) Soon afterward a flood of levies, sent for long before, poured in from the rebel south: sixty-four hundred, to be exact. Gómez de Cáceres and the Count of Plasencia returned from the distant places where they had been engaged upon their private business. With this and that, Alfonso's own new recruits in Olmedo came to very nearly nine thousand. A scant twelve miles apart, both armies, now grown to more than twice the size they had been a fortnight earlier, glowered and fingered their swords.

For a few days—but only that, only briefly and illusorily, like everything else—there did seem to be some possibility of bringing the whole issue to an end: the Pope had finally decided to intervene. He sent a Nuncio—the titular Bishop of León, Antonio de Veneriis—armed with a sentence of excommunication against the rebels if they did not renounce Alfonso's cause. Early in September this person, an unattractive combination of pomposity and cowardice, showed up at Medina's gate. Henry, who was acquainted with him, had him escorted to the *casas reales* with all the ceremony which he knew he thought correspondent to his rank. He revealed his mission and then launched forth upon a windy and condescending lecture about Henry's own obligation, once the insurgents had capitulated, to forget their errors and receive them with his "royal bowels inclined to mercy."[17] Yes, Henry said politely when it ran down, he had always been more than ready to take the sinners back. He sighed. But he doubted, he went on, that the Nuncio would have much luck, "so hardened were they in their damnable project of revolt."[18]

Veneriis did not share the opinion. He dispatched to Olmedo a summons for the barons to present themselves and hear Paul's ultimatum. Villena replied that they had not the slightest intention of presenting themselves, that the Pope had better mind his own business. Atrabiliar messages went back and forth. Finally Villena agreed to a meeting, but only in the fields between Olmedo and the nearby Convent of La Mejorada. Veneriis decided to spend the night before it at the convent. He was inconsiderate enough to arrive almost at midnight, and then had the nerve to order the Prior turned out of bed (it was Saturday, the one night of the week when Jeronymites did not sing twelve o'clock matins) and complained bitterly to him about the lack of a suitable reception. The Prior of La Mejorada was not, himself, one of the Church's more lustrous ornaments: he had the reputation of baptizing his by-blows with his own semen. The two men of God, in the torchlit corridor, flung insults at each other like fishwives. But that was nothing compared to the scene of the next day.

Midmorning: the autumn sun. Veneriis sat mounted and resplendent in the open fields, sentence of anathema clutched in his hand. A cloud of horsemen—three hundred—drew on from Olmedo. But they did not look like negotiators. *Jesumaría!*—they were men of arms, and with lances down, at that. Panic-stricken, he turned and tried to flee. But they overtook him and surrounded him. No, no, he babbled; they did not understand, he was a papal emissary. He unrolled the sentence and attempted to read it. They tore it away from him. "Die! Die!"[19] they shouted. He was being pulled down. Only the sudden appearance of Villena and Carrillo saved him. A mistake, Villena soothed: a confusion in orders. They talked. We do not know what they said. At the end of it, however, Veneriis rode amicably back with them into Olmedo. Anyone who cares to examine Paul's bull *Redemptoris et domini nostri* will discover that it gave the Nuncio full power to act as he thought best. But whether its *"quomodocumque et qualemcumque"*[20] had envisioned the possibility of his skipping over to the enemy is something else. That, nonetheless, is precisely what Veneriis did: either bribed or fearful of new violence to his person, he settled in at Olmedo with the rebels.

And then, mysteriously, they all vanished.

So strange a thing: so baffling, so ominous. At first the watchers in Medina thought they were about to be besieged: *maestres de campo* had materialized from Olmedo and dotted the plain with tents and what looked, at a distance, like mounds of provisions. But nothing happened. After a while royal scouts crept forth for a closer look. The tents were unfurnished, the supplies a fake: obviously a blind for some other movement, some different thrust. The scouts and spies rode farther. They found Olmedo itself deserted; the League's whole army had decamped. There was evidence of march toward both Arévalo and Portillo, but the foe was in neither of those towns. It grew more perplexing than ever. Where had they gone? What mischief were they planning? Nobody knew.

Nobody knew, that is, until the late afternoon of September 20, when a hot messenger came galloping from the east. He went straight to the *casas reales;* he found Henry, he fell on his knees. *Albricias,* Spaniards call the reward to those who bring glad tidings; fortunes have been made like that. But death, too, can come to the harbingers of disaster, and the news borne by that kneeling messenger was terrible indeed. He must have been sweating with more than his long ride, with visions of ax or gibbet, as he sought for words and found none and tried again—the rebels, the rebels—and at last did manage to get it out: they had captured Segovia.

18.
A Supper of Trout

It was true—horribly, stunningly true: Pedrarias had finally taken his full revenge. By secret emissary to Carrillo and Villena he had offered to betray the city; next to the episcopal palace of his brother there was a postern, he would open it, through it they could slip in. Behind their screen of false preparations, and in a prodigious night march of forty-two miles, the entire rebel army went east. They arrived just before dawn; under cover of a fog which had conveniently come up, they swarmed inside. Perucho de Monjáraz, commander of the Alcázar, was evidently part of the plot: he made only token resistance. The populace itself—so trusted and beloved by Henry—afforded little more opposition. Alfonso had confiscated the *casas reales;* a thousand men of arms occupied the central plaza of San Miguel. When he left, the messenger ended, only the fortified gates of San Juan and San Martín were still holding out.

Henry behaved like a madman. "My Segovia!"—his lions, his Flemish altarpieces, his tiled patios, his precious guitars! He jumped up, sat down, jumped up again, and ran raving back and forth. But suddenly one gleam of light, in all that black avalanche of woe, did pierce through to him. The gates of San Juan and San Martín—if they had not yet fallen, there might still be hope. He broke off his "insensate"[1] gyrations. They must go, he cried. They must be on their way at once to the relief. Impossible, his companions told him. Against an army of the size of the League's, and a city so strong, they would have no chance. Yes, they would! Henry retorted hysterically. At least they had to try. He would fight himself; he was ready to be hacked apart under the walls. Bring him a sword— assemble the army. They tried to calm him, to restrain him. They could not; he dashed out in search of his captains. He gave them chaotic instructions: get your weapons, hurry, they were marching immediately.

It can hardly have been in much order that they set forth. Almost by his own frantic will, Henry pushed the host along. They crossed the battlefield, still stinking and heaped with debris. They were approaching Iscar. And there the Count of Treviño rode over to Henry: high on that frowning crag perched the love-nest of his mother and craven Miranda. It had to be destroyed; no longer could he stand the "infamy"[2] to his name. They were so close, and in such numbers (perhaps his joining the royal ranks had been less disinterested, less "spontaneous,"[3] that at first appeared). Let them attack.

Galling through any loss of time must have been to Henry, it was difficult to deny so natural a request. He commanded a halt. While he chewed his nails below, the army started up the rocky slope. They stormed the heights. By scaling ladders they entered the castle; it surrendered. The lustful old Countess was torn from the arms of her lover and delivered to Treviño. He straightway dispatched her to the family hearth, under heavy guard. The delay was over. They could go on.

Only suddenly there was no reason to go on. New messengers from Segovia had ridden in, just as the army was regrouping, and hurried to Henry. The gates of San Martín and San Juan, they told him, had capitulated; the rebels were now in complete control of the city. And—they, as well, hesitated—there was something else. Alfonso had gone up to Balsaín and wrought vicious havoc among his animals. How many of them had been killed was not yet known. But the boy, with his own hand, had slaughtered forty of the deer.

Even Henry's worst enemies take pity on him in this dreadful moment."Not all the other catastrophes which had befallen him . . . affected him so much."[4] "*Golpe mortal,*"[5] says Palencia, "a mortal wound." And indeed it was. Under the force of it all the fight, and as swiftly and utterly as it had filled him the afternoon before, drained out of him. His animals—that, too. Then everything was hopeless. He turned brokenly from the messengers. He issued orders to stop, to give over, to abandon the Segovia road.

They moved on, instead, to Cuéllar. There, numbly, Henry addressed his chieftains. Thank you, he said; he had no further need for them, he was disbanding the army. They started to go home— Mendozas to Guadalajara, Treviño to Nájera, Velascos for the north. Going home: *felices ellos,* lucky they. That was all he wanted now, himself, the one sick need left in his heart. Even though the dear city was no longer his, he knew he could never rest until he had been back to it at least once again and seen with his own eyes just what had happened to his belongings, how extensive the carnage at Balsaín had really been. But how—with the whole place in enemy hands?

And then, out of the depths of his misery, he bethought himself of a chance—the Archbishop of Sevilla. Fonseca had been even more skillful than most of the magnates in maintaining relations with both camps. Through his agency Beltrán had been warned of danger the night before the battle. Perhaps he would intercede with the barons. Coca, the Fonseca family seat, was only a few miles away. Henry climbed on his horse. He reached the huge castle of rosy brick; he knocked at its gate. Fonseca received him "with small honor and less ceremony."[6] But at least he did receive him. Help me, help me, Henry begged; "he had to be where his heart was,"[7] no matter what the cost. Please ride down to Segovia and try to persuade the barons to grant him entry. He would do anything in return.

These fiends, these swine. Fonseca's eyes lighted up. Anything! The Mendozas—hateful people, he had always despised them—had just managed to acquire control of the little Beltraneja. Well, here was a way to go them one better. But it was fearfully risky, he protested. To come to Henry's aid, to shift sides like that, might expose him to all sorts of dangers, of reprisals. He needed to make his own position very secure. In fact, he would have to be given full custody—and permission to hold her under surveillance in any place he wanted—of the Queen herself, as hostage and guarantee.

Juana was the least of Henry's concerns in that afflicted state. Hastily he agreed. The Archbishop adorned himself and bustled off. When he finally returned, Henry rushed to him in a torment of suspense. The traveler sighed: oh, what trouble, what an ordeal. But he had been successful. Villena and Carrillo were willing to let Henry make a visit. They had, however, put down conditions. He could bring only four attendants. And he must come on a mule.

A mule? Henry would gladly have ridden an orangutan or a hyena. Accompanied by Fonseca, he started away as fast as he could go. Just outside Segovia's walls—insult on injury—he was met by Alba and Gómez de Cáceres. Surrounded by their pikemen, on his humble little mount, he rode up through the twisting streets and

across the drawbridge of the Alcázar and—stranger in Paradise—
into its familiar columned court. Perucho, too, the traitorous *alcaide*,
received him sourly—*"de mala gana.*"[8] And once in, they would not
—maddeningly—let him out to go to Balsaín. Nothing, they announced, could be done until after a formal meeting with the
League. Well then, cried Henry in despair, they must have it immediately. Ah no, they told him, everybody was much too busy for
that: Villena's investiture as Master of Santiago was being prepared
for the next day.

Henry did not attend—may not have been asked to attend—this
famous ceremony in the church of San Miguel. While the ancient
banner of Santiago was delivered to Villena and the great mantle
settled about his shoulders and the *comendadores* and priors of the
Order knelt one by one to do homage, he strode near breaking (oh
his animals, his animals, what had become of them, what was left
of them, poor defenseless things?) through the deserted halls of the
Alcázar. Nor was the investiture his only frustration, the only
delay: on the following morning, September 30, the exigencies of
Fonseca interposed. The Queen had to be turned over to him at
once, he insisted. That, too, took time. But by nightfall her leathern
arcas were finally packed and she started off with the Archbishop
for his castle fortress at Alaejos. The barons appointed their conclave with Henry for the next day.

He was still managing to hold together as he sat on whatever they
let him use for a throne and made his supplicating initial speech: he
was ready, he assured them, to do anything to end "the abominable
pestilence"[9] of this "disorder,"[10] he put his "person and honor and
fortune"[11] entirely in their charge; he "implored"[12] them to arrive
as speedily as possible at some honest "composition" which would
leave him free to be about his affairs. The Count of Paredes, Rodrigo
Manrique, was entrusted—because of his "charm" and "eloquence"
—with the League's reply. "Charm" is not much in evidence in it.
All very nice, he said. But from the beginning the whole trouble had
been Henry's fault. Everybody with any brains knew that Alfonso
was the rightful King. When Henry himself came around to that
admission they would be glad to treat him in such manner as "the
memory of his former rank"[13] deserved. This insolent exordium out
of the way, they at once got down to their ruthless business. Vague
offers of restitution within six months were made. There was noth-

ing in the least vague, however, about the concessions which they demanded in return. The Alcázar—and with it, of course, domain of the entire city—had to be officially given to Villena. The Treasure was to be broken up. A great clutch of its most priceless objects must go to the Count of Plasencia; Fonseca, when he went off with the Queen, had left a list as long as one's arm of the royal jewelry which he wanted for the further bedizenment of his person. What remained of it would then be transferred to the Alcázar of Madrid —and Perucho, to compound the piracy, put in command of that tramontane citadel.

"Outrageous enslavement! Ignominy!"[14] cries Palencia himself, usually so ready to gloat at any fresh debasement of his master. But Henry gave no heed: *"ningún caso hizo."*[15] He did not care (probably, in his condition, did not even realize) what he was throwing away. By then he was beyond thought for much of anything except his longing, mingled though it was with gathering dread, to be done with the whole chafesome business and get up to the lodge. Almost eagerly he signed whatever they laid before him.

Only then did they let him go. He found a horse and had it saddled for the fateful journey, the bitter accounting at Balsaín. But fast as he went, news of his abysmal surrender to the barons had preceded him. He was scarcely out beyond the aqueduct and leaving the *barrio* of Santa Eulalia when someone caught at his bridle. He looked down into a familiar face. It was a farmer from the environs in whose hut he had often spent the night. Henry may have started to greet him, but the old man cut him short. "You wretched King!" he flung out. "How you seek your own perdition—and ours, as well! You know how much we all have loved you. Yet now you abandon us and reject us—as you seem to reject even yourself. You act like a man who takes himself for vile, who thinks he merits no better than insults and disgrace. What has become of your sense of honor? Have you no pride, no dignity, at all?"[16]

His voice went "hoarse";[17] he stopped. But it had been enough, more than enough. Scorn from his barons—even from princes and kings—Henry had long since schooled himself to endure, perhaps had never really meant a great deal to him. But this rebuke by one of the simple *raza* was beyond all bearing, was the drop which finally made his cup of suffering overflow. We have never yet, more marvel, seen Henry weep. Now, though, and all at once, they come

—the wild salt tears. They broke from him in a cataract; they burned, they poured. Strangled with them, blinded, he wrenched his reins away. *"Se alejó llorando"*:[18] sobbing, he fled.

Still through that scrim of tears he roweled on up into the mountains. Still with coursing eyes he drew on to the lodge. The gate was open. The guardians—the faithful dwarfs and Ethiopians—had disappeared. An ominous silence hung over everything. He dismounted and stumbled in.

It was terrible. It was even worse than his darkest fears could have imagined. True, there did stand disconsolate—and Henry ran to it —his huge prized mountain goat; "knowing how much he loved it,"[19] Villena (and the act is his only decent one of which there is record) had ordered young Alfonso to spare it, to stay his reeking hand. But that was the sole survivor. Strewn everywhere around— blood-caked, their throats ripped open, their wide glazed eyes reproachful and uncomprehending—lay the stiff corpses of his ocelots, his does, his lovely sleek leopards, his gazelles, his baby bears: dead, dead, all dead.

There are few moments more harrowing in Henry's story. The brutality with which he was treated by his enemies can never have particularly surprised us: although this book is laid in a far time and a far country, nevertheless the tragic tale it tells—of man's predation on man, of how the herd drives out the maverick and the crafty and powerful destroy the innocent of spirit—is as ageless and universal as life itself. But that they should have killed his animals really does seem a little too much. One turns away, one does not care to watch it: gentle Henry in the murderous glade at Balsaín, with his arms around the neck of his *cabrón montesino* and the tears, the tears so long contained, the tears—at last—of helpless and total heartbreak, streaming down his ugly face.

The Segovian holocaust had a humbler victim—Castillo. Apparently the young chronicler made a brief trip to the city, of which he was a native, after the battle. On his departure to take his place again with Henry in Medina, and for reasons best known to himself, he left a traveling chest of his personal effects not at his family home just off the *plaza mayor* but in the whorehouse where his mistress plied her unhappy trade. (Castillo—a priest—is generally considered so much nobler and more high-minded than the rest of Henry's chroniclers, but when it comes to morality there appears, in frankness, to be little choice.) With the city's fall, he was naturally disturbed about his possessions. He asked for, and obtained, a safe-conduct from the League, with a view toward securing them. But something happened while he was on his way. Two throbbing soldiers of the army of occupation chose to visit that particular den of joy. After their easement, and probably quite drunk, they fell to tearing the place apart. They came upon Castillo's chest; they hurled it around for a while and then smashed it open to rifle it. Disappointingly, its chief cargo was only a great bundle of papers which meant no more to this pair of gap-toothed illiterates than the scratching of hens. But they thought it might interest their betters, and when they were finally through with their rampage and went off and left the exhausted ladies in peace they carried it away.

Interesting indeed: it turned out to be the manuscript, which he wrote day by day, of Castillo's history of the reign. Carrillo flipped idly through it. But soon his eyes began to pop from his head. By the time he reached the account of Olmedo—"riddled with falsehoods"[20] about the overwhelming "victory"[21] of the royalists and the "annihilation"[22] of the army of the League—he was having forty fits. He called in his associates; banging on the table, he read them assorted passages. Their first reaction was incredulous laughter. But at the description of the battle they, too, flew into a rage. When Castillo presented himself at the gate of San Andrés, his safe-conduct was derisively crumpled up and thrown out of the window and he found himself slapped under arrest and hauled off to face the assembled barons.

Records of the interview vary. In Castillo's own version, he stood up manfully against their onslaught—and even delivered a sermon on loyalty which left his accusers dissolved in remorse. Other sources sing a different tune: they have him cowering throughout in abject silence. And one feels inclined to believe them. Pert though Castillo was, he can hardly have been expected to lecture the Primate of Castile. Furthermore, the horrifying announcement that his manuscript had just been turned over for "correction"[23] to his bitterest competitor—Palencia—would have been in itself enough to leave any author dumb with shock. Cringing or defiant, however, the result of the interview was that Alfonso ordered him put to death.

The sentence was not carried out; probably even scatterbrained Carrillo realized, when they all calmed down, that they had too many other concerns for the long canonical process necessary to bring a member of the clergy to the scaffold. Nor do we know what became of the filched chronicle. Palencia claims he returned it to the Archbishop, but no trace of it has ever been found. At all events Castillo, since he had no copy of his manuscript, was confronted with the sickening task of sitting down and rewriting it from memory—the reason, of course, for those abundant errors in fact and chronology which so betoil the historian in its entire first half.

But if the youthful chaplain was kept bent over his desk with flying fingers all through the ensuing winter, for our characters of greater bulk it was a time of stasis, of pause—and for one of them, at least, the calm before the final storm. Isabel and Alfonso, reunited in Segovia after their separate durances, soon went on to Arévalo, where they had passed their childhood and their mother continued to maintain her residence. The Dowager Queen (one inevitably thinks of her as old, although she had not yet reached forty) was by then quite mad; legend has her fleeing up and down the dark stairs of the castle pursued by ghostly voices cawing Luna's name. Alfonso himself, in reality, was still not very much more than a prisoner, for the chieftains of the League had settled watchfully down around him. But he tried to strut, to play the little King. He took Isabel off for a visit to Medina del Campo and its great fair. They rode together on the wide wintry plains, under the marble clouds. Records have been left of a rather repulsive pageant mounted to celebrate the lad's fourteenth birthday. Eight damsels of his court did themselves up "with feathers"[24] to represent the Muses and chant *fados* welcoming him to the age of virility, coyly referred to as the springs of Helicon. Isabel herself, swathed in furlongs of white gauze, read the final one—some pitiful doggerel by Gómez Manrique in which the proud young auditor, hailed as "Alfonso XII," was congratulated on his past "triumphs and successes" and assured—alas, how meretriciously—of even greater "glories" to come.

For Henry, however, there were no pageants and odes, no auguries of future "triumph." Truly homeless now, "more like a poor pilgrim than a monarch,"[25] he roamed about on the silent *meseta*—bleaker than ever after the ravages of civil war—with almost literally no place to lay his head. Not only Segovia was gone. All the other great cities which had served as capital seats for Castilian kings—Toledo, Valladolid, Burgos—were also held by the League. Nor could even Madrid, emerging at last from its long insignificance, thanks to Henry's patronage, be considered safe: Perucho had assumed his command of its Alcázar, and that individual no longer merited the slightest confidence, as recent events so bitterly proved. Towns, and even the most modest villages, shut their gates against the wanderer. Into such discredit had he fallen that his very servants were ashamed to admit in public "whose they were."[26] So weary was he that when at last the Count and Countess of Plasencia, long pillars of the League, offered him refuge, he instantly, almost humbly, seized the chance for a place to stay and set forth for Extremadura.

The reader will not imagine that this turnabout in allegiance on the part of the Stúñigas was any more altruistic than Fonseca's or Treviño's. Its obvious origin was pique: they had offered their young daughter as a bride for Alfonso—who proceeded to laugh in their faces. Nor was their household, as Henry discovered immediately upon his arrival, the world's most restful or serene. The Countess, a huge and "virile"[27] woman, ruled both her husband (he happened also to be her uncle) and the vast family estates with a rod of iron. She, in turn, was dominated—if nothing more—by the loud and snobbish wife of the lame family *mayordomo* Pedro de Hontiveros, whom we met at Olmedo. To be sure, Henry was spared at least part of the bicker of this untidy quadrangle: don Alvaro and doña Leonor lodged him ("for greater honor"[28]—but more probably to keep him under stricter watch) in the stout castle rather than their residence in town. But he was endlessly harassed and worked upon by his hosts. Having failed in the ambitious gambit for their daughter, they tried to gouge something handsome out of the hapless guest for their infant son. Henry had nothing left which was quite commensurate with their exalted ideas, and they shifted to further honors for themselves. The Count wanted Trujillo, that *ignis fatuus* of so many baronial dreams. Henry offered it to him for Christmas; they marched down to take possession, but its *alcaide* refused to deliver it—and they all dragged themselves back to Plasencia.

Tempers mounted with the Christmas disappointment—as well

as with the naming of Pedro González de Mendoza to the miter of Sigüenza and that fresh distinction for a family whom the Stúñigas knew to be already so much their social superiors. The weather grew colder and colder. Before long Hontiveros was murdered by one of his innumerable enemies. Villena came west on a visit, and briefly it looked as if Henry's exile might soon be over: the period of six months set for the resolution of his affairs was almost at its close. But the Master's purpose proved "more to lie than to fulfill his promises, more to delay than to act";[29] once in control of Segovia, he had no thought—as anyone except Henry would have realized long before—of letting it loose. That last wan hope flickered out. And in its embers, news arrived from Aragón of a far larger death than Hontiveros's—Juana Enríquez had at last been carried off by her cancer. Henry, however, was not the sort to take any pleasure in this culminative misfortune to his uncle. It only made him sadder. By then he probably wished he were dead himself.

In fact, the one really nice thing that happened during the whole dismal winter was the receipt of letters from Jaén. Good, generous Lucas: he was never much of a correspondent, but he knew even better than most people what the loss of Segovia must have meant to Henry, and finally he sat down and sent off a batch of missives toward Extremadura with the aim of ameliorating what he also knew must be a pretty cheerless sojourn in the windswept city on the granite plain. He wrote to the Count: as a great "mercy"[30] he begged him so to arrange matters that his guest, "our true sovereign and lord," be "well served" and provided with "repose," and meanwhile to work diligently for "the restoration of his estate and honor." He wrote to doña Leonor, politely urging, since he knew how "important a role"[31] she played in the family, that she surround the King with every "delight."[32] He went so far as to swallow his pride and send a note to Gómez de Cáceres, his old rival, who lay then at nearby Béjar: after reminding the aging Adonis as discreetly as possible of the "nurture and advancement"[33] which he owed to Henry, he went on to suggest that he ride over to Plasencia and do what he could for the comfort of their mutual master. But of course there was no need for circumlocutions or formalities in what he wrote to Henry. Take care, he pleaded. Please let him know how he was getting along. Think of him always, surely better times were coming, he himself—the truth shines through, as it always does with Lucas—was none too happy.

It is a beautiful letter; it brims with affection and solicitude. Henry stood in an embrasure of his drafty tower to catch the pallid winter light and reread it many times. He gazed out across the ancient city muffled in snow, across the gray roofs and shut casements and misty belfries topped with their huge, hushed nests of storks, and a familiar longing began to fill him. Lucas, Lucas: Andalucía, the early spring, innocent children in a roundelay, the silly old green dragon and everybody laughing. Laughter. He was sick of the Stúñigas. Late in February he left.

There is no documentary proof that he set out for Jaén. We have only his heart—and the fact that he was trending south. Whatever his intention, he did not get very far. In Guadalupe, only fifty miles along, he stopped. Perhaps the weather was too inclement for him to continue. Perhaps he was more exhausted than he realized. In any case, once having stopped, he stayed. The convent, a year before, had been under fruitless siege from the rebels—and turned topsy-turvy by the swarms of neighboring peasants who took refuge inside it with their cows and pigs. But already the friars had cleaned it up and restored it to its customary peace. Again the corridors dreamed; again slow tides of plainsong swelled and ebbed in the shadowy choir and birds lifted their own melodious anthems in the *mudéjar* cloister. Henry's mother was buried in the quiet Gothic chapel. (He sleeps there too, now that it all is finished, and the stone saints stand guard and the long Extremaduran sun goes over.) March came, and April; the rockroses spread their pink carpet across the fields, the air hung warm and fragrant. And still he tarried, he sat on—playing his lute, content to drift, sunk deeper than ever in languor and passivity, in that neurotic paralysis of the will which had always been his bane and which now was chronic and incurable. He seemed unable to move, to throw off the leaden weight in his legs, his arms, his breast.

He might never have gone had it not been for the sharp turn of events in Toledo. The city, little less volatile and unruly than Juan's Barcelona, suddenly renounced the League and declared again for Henry—"like a dog" (the graceful phrase is Palencia's) "eating his vomit"[34]—and this time the rising had been a success. Poor substitute though Toledo made, in Henry's opinion, for Segovia, the prize was a great one; he had to take formal possession. But as he rode off toward the Tajo in early June of 1468, he can have felt little satisfaction, little real hope: three awful years had passed since the Schism of Avila, and it looked as if the civil war might be flaring up into new violence, as if the long nightmare of a disputed scepter and a cloven kingdom might go on for ever. He could not know that, even as he went, the dark Eumenides of the House of Trastámara, up on the summer fields beyond the Guadarramas, were rattling their dice for a dire roll which would bring the situation to an abrupt and unimaginable end.

The setback at Toledo had caused deep consternation in Arévalo. Villena immediately saw a threat to his new possessions of the *maestrazgo* south of the mountains. He was all for quick departure with a view toward recapturing the lost city; it seems to have been the one occasion in his life when he felt disposed to definite military action. Carrillo, too, was anxious to leave Arévalo, if for reasons somewhat more humane: pestilence raged in the area, with the utter lack of sanitation and the mounting heat of summer it was bound to get worse, and he wanted to shield from danger the young ward who he knew played so critical a part in the matrimonial plans of his master in Zaragoza. (On the very day when Henry issued a rather naïve general amnesty to the citizens of Toledo, Juan's daughter had reached the officially marriageable age of thirteen.) But obstacles loomed up. The Imperial city, high on its mighty rock and circled by the Tajo, was substantially impregnable; never in recorded history, not even by Alfonso VI when he won it back from the Moslems, had it been taken by direct assault. And the rebel army, anyway, after a winter and spring of inactivity, was not at its best.

There were arguments; there were vacillations and painful questions. But in the midst of them, messengers arrived from Toledo with news which turned matters quite around. The sublevation in Henry's favor, they reported, had by no means been unanimous. The city still churned with discontent. "Old" Christians and the aristocracy, in particular, continued to favor the League. If the rebels marched down, they would meet with powerful help from within. And at that their hesitations vanished. The army was hastily assembled. Led by Villena and Carrillo and the Bishop of Coria, and with both Isabel and Alfonso snatched from their mother and securely in tow, they set forth on the 30th of June.

Like the royalists out of Cuéllar, they made little progress in the first *jornada;* apparently they started late. The next day, however, they were determined to do better: Avila lies only thirty miles south of Arévalo, and in that stronghold of the Archbishop they thought to spend the night. But it was hot. There was far less shade along the route than it now affords: most of the stands of broad umbrella pines which today so refresh the traveler in those dusty plains were planted by Isabel—and perhaps from memory of that stifling march. They grew wearier and thirstier; the way, as they started up into the foothills, became rocky and slow. They reached a village called Cardeñosa. The sun was declining; ten arduous miles still stretched to Avila. They decided to stop, to sleep, to go on in the cool of dawn.

Cardeñosa: nowhere. All anybody could recollect about it was Santa Barbada—one of the local maidens, beset by a lustful neighbor, who had sought help from Heaven and been rewarded with a bushy black beard. But its insignificance in history, that summer evening, was fast drawing to a close. The army put up their tents in the surrounding fields. Houses, of sorts, were requisitioned for nobles and royalty. Alfonso refreshed himself in his, while cooks went to work in its kitchen and a table for his supper was arranged. Hungry from the long day's journey, he hurried into the *sala.* He sat down at the table and waited impatiently. At last the platter was brought and placed before him. Fish, of course: it was Friday. Someone removed the silver cover. Ah, a mountain trout. Alfonso was said to have a special fondness—as who would not?—for that plump, white, succulent catch from the icy streams of the Sierra de Avila. He fell upon it. He ate it all.

And then—strange turn—a sudden drowsiness overtook him. Even while they were dismantling the table his head began to nod. He fought it off: he almost always stayed up late. But it was too much for him—he could scarcely prop open his eyes. He stumbled to his room. So thick, so heavy: he was too tired to undress. No matter—people slept either naked or fully clothed. He pitched on the bed. Like a stone, he sank in the engulfing dark.

They waited for him the next morning; they had all risen early, eager to be on the move. But he failed to appear. They sent a messenger to his *posada*. He came back shrugging: one of the valets had looked in, a while before, and seen the boy still drowned in slumber. They shrugged, themselves. Well—youth; let him sleep a little longer. But it grew too much longer: prime passed, then tierce. The army was formed and waiting; horses pawed; already the sun rode high. Again they sent their messenger, this time under command—get the sluggard up. And this time he returned with face gone white. The boy was awake—yet not awake. He seemed to be in stupor. He had lost the power of speech. They had better come at once.

They ran—Villena, the Bishop of Coria, Carrillo, Isabel. They rushed into the bedroom. They shook him—to no avail: he fell back limp. They plied him with questions; he could not answer. In panic they called the court physician. He stripped the pubescent body and bent to examine it. He found no fever. He found no swelling. A single place, the left armpit, proved sensitive to touch—a fact which the sufferer, in his voiceless condition, must have indicated only by a wince of pain.

In short, there were none of the symptoms—by then all too familiar—of the current pestilence. But obviously something was wrong, most fearfully wrong. Bleed him, said the physician—that last recourse of baffled medieval medicine. He unwrapped his leeches; he applied them. But nothing came out—the blood had already coagulated. And then suddenly he bent closer; he had noticed something else. The boy's tongue was beginning to turn black. He straightened up. He swung around to the watchers and spread his hands: too late, no hope.

Gratian lists among the wonders of the world a royal death not attributed to poison. Nor is Alfonso's any exception; from the hour itself there has been rumor that he was thus done in. But the case for foul play at Cardeñosa leaves much to be desired. Villena is the person most often suspected; Palencia accuses him, point-blank, of venom in the trout. Yet one is hard put to find a motive: Alfonso was Villena's chief means of keeping discord afoot. An anonymous baron had indeed once made the mysterious announcement that if they could not dominate their young charge by the methods already at their command they might be driven to resort to "another remedy";[35] this sounds, however, as much like passing irritation as anything else. The Pope's curious remark of the preceding autumn

—"God will soon summon him"³⁶—was probably no more than a lucky guess. Least weight of all can be given to Castillo's "great wonder"³⁷ that word of Alfonso's "speedy"³⁸ and "dolorous"³⁹ transit spread through the kingdom before it actually occurred; from the first morning, as we have just witnessed, he was doomed. Almost certainly Galindez's verdict is correct: disease, if of some strange sort *"que no fue conoscida,"*⁴⁰ which was not understood. There were plenty of those.

The end, at that, came not so "speedily" as the chronicler would have it—or as one might even wish. Through Saturday, Sunday, Monday he still clung to life, while the magnates raised desperate prayers—perhaps of a source less crystalline than Santa Barbada's —and offered vows to Santiago, to the Virgin of Guadalupe, to the bearded damsel herself. It was only on Tuesday, soon after nightfall, that he expired.

Tender boys throughout the provinces of Avila and Segovia, so tradition tells us, at the same moment yielded their spirits to God; reluctant to let the *"ynocente rey"*⁴¹ go unaccompanied into *"la Gloria,"*⁴² they gently smiled—and died. It makes a pretty picture —those legions of pure young Spanish souls gathering above the moonlit fields of Cardeñosa and then streaming upward, like one winged and candent flame, into the purple vault of heaven. Yet a different scene holds the historian. As the boy breathed his last, surely every eye in that crowded chamber turned, tense and conjectural, to lock on the pale figure in disarray of auburn hair and sister's heart beside the bed. And ours turns with them: Isabel the Catholic now takes her enormous place upon the stage.

19.
What the Bulls Saw

Alfonso had died on the 5th of July; Juan's powers and instructions to Peralta (in Navarre, unfortunately) are dated the 21st. They were issued amidst the most pressing peril: the Duke of Lorraine and the Catalans had captured almost the entire coast line from Barcelona to the border, Gerona itself was under investment, there were rumors of a French invasion down across the Pyrenees on the west to encircle him from the rear. Yet critical though Juan's military situation had become, the plight of his scheme to have the Castilian throne through marriage was even worse. One of his two great counters in the game—Alfonso—had vanished from the board; his Juana would never share the neighboring crown.[1] Only Isabel remained. And perhaps she was, even so, the better chance. Fernando as King of Castile made a far more auspicious prospect than Juana as its Queen; women were not thought capable of much in the way of rule. Yes, everything now depended on Isabel. First she must be assured of inheriting Henry's realm. Then, once she was formally designated his successor, her marriage to Fernando had somehow to be brought off. The path stretched plain before him as if he were not blind. How he would pierce through to the end of it, in such a wilderness of obstacles, he did not know. But he must. It was his last chance—absolutely his last. If he failed now, his whole life had been a failure.

Just when Peralta reached Castile on this second and yet weightier mission is not entirely clear. But there is plenty of evidence for the chaotic events which took place among the rebels while he was hastening in. Alfonso's corpse, the night of his death, was sent back to Arévalo. With that sad disposition, they hurried on to the safety of Avila's thick walls. And of safety they all at once had urgent need. Their figurehead, the façade behind which they had hidden their private ambitions, was suddenly gone: *"desamparados"*[2]—unprotected, exposed—is the word which most frequently crops up among accounts of their situation in those perilous hours. They seemed, in fact, to have only two possible courses. They could surrender and disband. Or they could crown Isabel, there in the same city where they had crowned her brother, and under that new banner carry on their revolt.

Unquestionably their immediate choice was for the second; they were far too deeply committed, too involved, for the first. It is unquestionable, also, that in the initial shock and confusion Isabel acquiesced to the plan: the day before Alfonso's death, and again three days afterward, she wrote letters to the city Councils of the kingdom[3] in which she assumed what cannot be construed as anything less than sovereign rights. But they changed their minds. By the time Henry's envoys arrived in Avila with anxious questions and somewhat tentative commands, they had settled on a third alternative. Not rendition, not the naming of Isabel as Queen, they told the messengers. Take back to Henry a completely different proposal: they would make peace with him if he acknowledged Isabel his heir.

The *fons et origo* of this surprising decision cannot be easily established. Peralta certainly was not yet at hand—although it is quite within the realm of possibility that Juan had already managed to get advisory letters through to his faithful Carrillo. Villena's role of course was paramount in anything done by the League: no move could be charted without his consent—or usually without his inspiration. Perhaps, after four years as leader of what had been after all a fairly discreditable opposition, the Marqués was eager to take up again his official post as Premier: he well knew, as Pulgar shrewdly comments, that Henry, in addition to pardoning him, would gladly give him once more the full *"governación"*[4] of the realm. He may have felt, too, that the young Infanta would provide an even more docile instrument than her dead brother for maintaining dissension. Yet one cannot, in the end, escape a very strong conviction that this wise choice at Avila—to *"callar el nombre de Reyna,"*[5] to abstain from the regal title and hold out instead for that of heir, of Princess—was made, although perhaps not without subsidiary counsel from Aragón, by Isabel herself.

Wise: so Isabel seems to have become, and almost overnight. Not that she had ever been anything but thoughtful, perceptive, grave.

Now, however, at seventeen and under both the impact of Alfonso's death and the blaze of attention to which she was so unpredictably subjected, those qualities had been brought to rapid flower. Upon their arrival in Avila she had drawn apart to the Convent of Santa Ana for prayer and reflection, and with the ebb of her first tumult and bereavement that balance, that farsightedness which were to constitute the hallmark of her splendid career began to emerge. It would be short of human for her to have failed to want the crown. But she did not want it (nor did Juan want it for her) on the only terms with which the barons were able to offer it: usurpation, illegality, force. Least of all did she have any thought of letting herself become the same dependent puppet of the nobles which her poor brother had been. It would perhaps be a little ingenuous to ascribe to Isabel, at this early stage, the fully developed purpose of her later life—the forging of a united and puissant nation with the nobles subjected and the Crown supreme. But she knew already, at the very minimum, that if she was ever to wear that crown she must wear it without impediment, without dubiety of claim. Patience, patience. Let Henry, incontrovertibly its lawful owner, keep it so long as he lived. But let him, just as incontrovertibly, give her the clear and unblemished right to possess it once he was gone.

In any case, such was the condition for peace—official pronouncement of Isabel as heir, as Princess of Asturias—borne back to Madrid. For to Madrid Henry had, in fact, repaired—after finally summoning up his courage to strip Perucho of command of the Alcázar and bestow it instead upon his latest young *mayordomo* Andrés de Cabrera. There, also, he received the word of Alfonso's death. According to Palencia, it plunged him into "a chasm of new melancholy."[6] Well might it have: in addition to sorrow for his brother —Henry never disliked anybody, except perhaps himself—no doubt there instantly rose before him the specter of fresh bloodshed, fresh strife. It is only in the light of those gloomy forebodings that one can fully appreciate his exhilaration when he heard the offer of the League. Hostilities would end. Villena would come back to him —and accommodation with the Marqués meant not only that once more would he have somebody to take charge of his clotted affairs but that Segovia (no one has ever sufficiently recognized the point) would again be his. Yet brief indeed that exhilaration was. Suddenly, thrusting up across it and demolishing it, casting him anew

into his crater of depression, came the knowledge of the fee for
bringing all those wonderful things about. To name Isabel his heir
required sacrificing little Juana. And that he simply did not see how
he could do. Once before, in the fields between Cigales and Cabezón, he had let himself be persuaded to dispossess and discredit the
child. Memory of the unlovely act had haunted and grieved him
ever since; he could hardly have been Henry, could hardly have
been the instant prey to tenderness for all things helpless and rejected, had it not. Was peace, was even Segovia, worth such a price?

"*Muy molesta cosa,*"[7] Castillo calls it—a deeply troubling thing.
Decisions, as we abundantly know, had always come hard for
Henry, and now he was faced with one of the most painful of his
life. He procrastinated, he faltered; he sent contradictory messages.
Pressures were put upon him by both sides. Villena went to visit
and counsel him—foretaste of what could be—on the part of the
apprehensive nobles. Fonseca, *faute de mieux* now his chief confi-
dant, rode to Avila. The Mendozas rushed down from Buitrago,
afraid that he would choose Isabel and thus work the "perdition"[8]
of their precious charge. But still he wavered, trapped in his fatal
tendency to brood over an issue until he was paralyzed for taking
any stand at all. He would; he would not. Agreements were reached
—and immediately abrogated. Finally, in mid-August, the nobles
called for a conclave in Castronuño which they hoped would settle
everything. They marshaled all their most persuasive arguments—
and failed again: he did indeed, they were told, feel a powerful
disposition to accept their offer, but he could not find it in him to
repudiate the little girl. They wrung their hands. Their cause—
Isabel's, Juan's—seemed about to go up in smoke. Apparently there
was no answer, no way to win him round.

But there was. And, ironically, it came from the one person who
had even more reason than Henry to defend the interests of the
child. At Alaejos, only a few miles away from Castronuño and their
deadlocked discussions, the Queen did something which unsnarled
the knot.

Her confinement as Fonseca's hostage had never been at all to
Juana's taste: relegation to a rustic castle among peasants and chick-
ens, smoking hearths, no dances, no new clothes. She yawned with
boredom. But soon she was yawning with something else—with

lack of sleep. Fonseca's sister Beatriz was married to the castle's warden—a grandson, if on the wrong side of the blanket, of Pedro the Cruel. Their boy, also named Pedro, served as one of the captains of the guard. Juana laid hungry glances upon him; he returned them. The fire and tow were assembled. Before long—in the snowy winter nights, in the snug curtained bed in the tall tower—the blaze was roaring lustily away. It is not surprising: a handsome, available lad—after smelly old Henry with his bugging eyes and his great horse teeth and his mushroom of a penis. What did surprise Juana, and unpleasantly, was that one morning in March she awoke beneath her naked young lover and found herself pregnant.

Two months, three months: that was easy enough. But by summer she was growing large. Well, no matter—in so secluded a place. Only suddenly it mattered very much; with Alfonso's death the reasons for Henry's bargain about her with Fonseca had evaporated, and he called her back to court. She was terrified: looking like that? Her mind, at best not agile, threshed about. And finally she had what seemed like a brilliant idea. She and Pedro persuaded the local farrier to run up some huge iron rings. Her women sewed material around them—to make wide dresses which would conceal her state. (Such was the sordid origin of the hoopskirt.) But the device proved none too satisfactory; it was heavy, it hurt. Moreover, in the middle of these guilty dodges and postponements, new messengers arrived from Henry: why the delay, unless she came at once he would have to send troops. Full panic—by then she had entered her seventh month—took hold of her. She decided on flight. If she reached Buitrago and the Mendozas, she could have the baby there —and perhaps, with luck, no scandal would ever get abroad.

Luck, however, was not granted her. They made fevered preparations for her to escape that very night. They found a big basket; they tied it to a good strong rope. Along in the small hours, after the whole castle was asleep, they hung it from her dizzy window. She crept forth and crouched inside it. Her maids, peering vainly through the darkness, lowered her bit by bit. The rope ran out. Presuming that she was safely on the ground, they let it go. But she was not on the ground at all: the rope had only been too short. Down the basket crashed.

She survived. So did the baby, despite her injuries. But all hope of secrecy was gone. Lacerated and crumpled among the rocks, she knew that at once. She could never get to far Buitrago now. She had to have attention. And where might she find it, who would give her haven and cure? A wild thought struck her—Cuéllar. Cuéllar lay much closer; perhaps she could make it there. Surely she was wrenched by a sharper pang than that of her fractured ankle: to go to Beltrán, bearing someone else's child. It was a bitter choice for a proud woman. But there seemed, in the extremity, to be no other. She forced herself up. She lurched away. Hours, days—one does not know how long it took her. But finally, collapsing, she drew in sight of Cuéllar. She stumbled to the castle and beat at its gate.

Beltrán sat merry in his hall. The page came to the door with saucered eyes. Beltrán arose and went to hear his message. The Queen, the boy stammered: she was seeking entry—and all covered with blood and obviously well along to giving birth. Beltrán stared back. The Queen? That relic of the past? Oh, let her take her troubles—and her little bastard—somewhere else. He shrugged. He rejoined his companions to tell them—and made his famous sneer: "He had never cared much, anyway, for her skinny legs."[9] All of them laughed.

Juana—wounded and fainting before the shut gate at Cuéllar. We shall see little more of her; her pit is prepared. From the day we first glimpsed her—riding in along the Guadalquivir, a giddy girl of sixteen, to her difficult fate—we have sought to be fair to her. Too fair, some might say: too bland on her follies. But it would take a stony heart indeed not to ache for this desperate and utterly ruined woman—the sister of a Holy Roman Empress and the aunt of a saint —as she faced away at last and struggled on with her broken limbs and sinful burden across the searing August desert toward Buitrago, now truly her one refuge.

Of course it was all over Castile in a few days; the revelers talked. And of course it turned the trick. Henry was stunned and shaken as seldom before, not even beside the Bidasoa. Juana's former lapses had at least been perpetrated at court. But now she had put horns on him in public. What further loyalty did he owe to her—or, by extension, to her other child? In addition, Fonseca—humiliated and made a laughingstock himself, furious with her for having escaped while in his keeping—was close to his ear. The portentous message sped to Avila. He had made up his mind; he would accept Isabel—

provided some means could be hit upon of doing it, some way to invalidate little Juana, without open injury to his name.

The nobles, for all their exultation, were swept by dismay. Without harm to Henry's name. In short, as they immediately realized he meant, without a plain charge—and a plain admission—of lack of virility. That was, indeed, a sizable order. Clearly their troubles had not yet reached an end. They were being asked to come up with some piece of casuistry, some legal sleight of hand, whereby a child could be proved illegitimate without declaring her the fruit of other loins.

And how they did it is a marvel to behold.

Well—so their deliberations began—let them set aside the question of Henry's paternity. They might as well face the hopelessness of that; he would never admit himself unable to sire a child. Anyway, the matter was, as it still is, impervious to proof. For little Juana to be definitely eliminated, some better basis than gossip and innuendo, given new substance though they were by the Queen's current infidelity, had to be found. But what other outlet? Of only one obstacle did they have no need for fear: the legal argument that any child born during the course of a valid marriage was legitimate. Not even La Beltraneja's most ardent defenders, with another baby coming, would have recourse to that. Everywhere else, however, they seemed completely blocked.

They writhed in the toils of this latest of their dilemmas. They despaired; they made fresh—and useless—starts. Only after days of fumbling and frustration did necessity, as it had done with Juana's hoopskirt, prove the mother of invention. "A valid marriage"—the phrase had lingered in someone's mind. And suddenly it slipped forth. If the marriage, in itself, were found illegal? That way they could outvault the whole question of young Juana's origin. Had there been some defect in the union of Juana and Henry that far-off day in Córdoba, then *ipso facto*, no matter who had fathered her, the child was adulterous. Was it not worth trying, worth investigating? It certainly was. They set assiduously to work.

Palencia, as we saw on the occasion, said that the wedding took place without papal dispensation—essential to make it lawful—of the couple's kinship. Unhappily for his reputation as a teller of truths (never robust), a dispensation exists. But it exists—as Isabel's new advocates at once discovered when they either unearthed it or dredged it up from memory—in a curious form. Nicholas V, the reigning Pope in 1454, had been much concerned about the circumstances of Henry's divorce. The terms on which it was granted— that Henry could do nothing with Blanca but was potent with other women—seemed to him, as they have seemed to everybody else, exceedingly odd. He could not, by canon law, permit the second marriage of a man who might turn out after all to be entirely incapable of the generative act. But he had no method of plumbing the matter, so far away. Therefore he wrote his bull of dispensation not in final but in provisional form. He named three Spanish prelates to act on his behalf. Only if they were convinced that the assertion made by Henry in the bill of divorcement was true—*"si est ita,"*[10] "if so it be," if he indeed had sexual powers with other women—were they to implement, to execute, the dispensation. And just who were the three commissionary prelates? Alfonso Sánchez, Bishop of Ciudad Rodrigo, Fonseca (then Bishop of Avila)—and Carrillo himself.

It seemed almost too good, too lucky, to be true. Sánchez was long since dead. Only Fonseca and Carrillo—both of them now determined to liquidate the Queen and her daughter—remained. The nobles stared at each other in open-mouthed delight. The key was in their hands. Let the two prelates come forth with an announcement: they had never executed the dispensation. *Ergo*, the marriage fell—and, in consequence, the child.

Probably there was nothing whatsoever to it. Although Castillo's statement that Fonseca himself had officiated at the wedding cannot be taken as too large an obstruction to the plan (he is the only chronicler who thus identifies the celebrant, and his unreliability for the early events of the reign we have latterly observed), considerations of common sense do immediately arise. Few will imagine that princes, ambassadors, even (and especially) a long series of popes, would have treated on friendly and equal terms with a monarch living in open concubinage, open sin. Furthermore, why no reference to the charge during all the past six years of bitter debate? The whole thing has an inescapable air of the contrived, of the *voulu*. But it served the need. It afforded Henry an opening, a peg on which he could hang the repudiation of little Juana without unpleasant probings into sex. And he accepted it at once. Yes, he would willingly admit that his marriage with Juana was not, nor ever had been, legal—*"que non fué nin está legítimamente casado con ella."*[11] The hurdle was past.

There were, inevitably, many details to be worked out. But now that the road was finally clear before them, they could all move forward to the great reconciliation with confidence and dispatch. A steady stream of emissaries and agents—Fonseca, Villena, Henry's attorneys, the Nuncio Veneriis, Luna's faithful retainer and chronicler Gonzalo Chacón, now firmly attached to Isabel's *camarilla*—flowed between Madrid and Avila. Short shrift was given the Queen amidst the budding terms of the Concordance; in view of the lack of "cleanliness" with which she had "used her person," Henry was to make "divorce and apartment" from her and send her home to Portugal within four months. Lest she attempt to take La Beltraneja with her and thus plant seeds of further trouble, the ill-starred child must be returned at once to Henry's tutelage. (How this feat was to be managed is far from clear; apparently it was vaguely hoped that the mother would use her influence with the Mendozas in Buitrago—where she had finally staggered in.) But the definition of Isabel's new posture took considerably more time and thought. Once she had bowed to Henry's authority and been, in return, created Princess, arrangements had to be made for the proper sustenance of her "person and table and royal estate." The title itself brought suzerainty of Asturias. It was felt by her sponsors, however, that apart from this extensive northern region she should have possessions in the Castilian heartland—and here, certainly, Isabel's own keen talent for organization and analysis is already on display. The other towns and *plazas fuertes* to be given her were proposed and accepted—Medina del Campo, Ubeda, Huete, Escalona, Avila, Alcaraz, and Molina: a skilled geographical distribution. Then the matter of her marriage was taken up. The best they could do with that was a double commitment. Henry insisted that she promise never to marry without his consent. Isabel agreed. But she too (again one senses the hand of Aragón at work) required an equal guarantee: he would force no suitor upon her. Thus the fateful question was left.

By mid-September all this intricate bargaining was far advanced. To shorten distances and speed communications in its critical last stages, Isabel and her staff moved southeast out of Avila and settled in Cebreros. Soon Henry, for the same purpose, went west to

Cadalso. The two retinues were only a dozen miles apart—and even closer to full accord: excitement began to mount. At that, a few loose strands remained. Carrillo, all along, had been plagued by reservations: beside strong distaste to see his rival Villena once more assume the realm's command, he put little faith in Henry. Suddenly he decided that the usual pledge, already inserted, of pilgrimage to Jerusalem in case of default (Henry in Jerusalem?) was not sufficient; they had to have something surer. A new messenger posted to Cadalso. He returned with a counter offer good enough for anybody: the Treasure—or what was left of it—in escrow. Then a last-minute doubt about Escalona assailed them: Luna's family might try to interfere. Henry, frantic by then to get on with it, amended that clause as well—if Escalona proved unavailable, he would give Isabel either Tordesillas or Ciudad Real or Olmedo. On Sunday, September 18, they combed through it all again, point by laborious point. Everything—at last—seemed to be in order. A scribe made out two copies of the final text. One was taken to Cadalso; Henry signed it and ordered his "royal arms" affixed. Isabel set hand and seal to hers.

There was, of course, the formal meeting and public swearing of loyalties still to be held; the long negotiations must be closed with what Spaniards are fond of calling a *broche de oro*, a clasp of gold. They decided to have it on the following day. Captains went out from both towns to reconnoiter the intervening terrain and select a suitable place. At Toros de Guisando, halfway between, they found a spot they fancied: the mountains there ease off in a rocky glade, and apparently the site had been used before, in the mists of antiquity, for ceremonial purposes—rough-hewn stone bulls stood by. They returned to their separate headquarters. The sharp September night descended.

Henry may have slept at the neighboring monastery of his favorite Jeronymites; the records do not say. All of them dwell, rather, on the activity in Cebreros. Carrillo continued to give cause for anxiety: skittish and truculent even at the eleventh hour, he showed signs of a bolt which would have wrecked everything. To ward it off, Villena thought up one of his usual ruses. Secretly he sent soldiers to light bonfires in the hills. Look, they told the Archbishops—they were surrounded by the royal armies, they had no chance of getting away. And even with the patching of that emergency, there was much to do. Isabel's tastes in private were always simple, but she well knew the value of magnificence on state occasions, and the event which lay ahead of her on the morrow was obviously to be the first real milestone of her life; one can imagine the care with which she readied her attire. The whole village, indeed, was astir with preparations—the polishing of armor, the sudden bursts of practice on trumpets, the grooming and caparisoning of horses. No doubt there was little rest for anybody. By the light of the circumambient bonfires, in a rising tide of expectation and suspense, the cold night wore on.

But finally it ended; finally the great saffron sun leaned over the bare mountains. The procession assembled. They moved out, moved on with ruffle of drums and glitter of banners across the stony fields. They reached Guisando, reached the watchful bulls. Henry sat mounted and waiting, flanked by his turbaned Moslems and with more than a thousand troops, lances aloft and pennons fluttering, drawn up behind. Isabel advanced. He advanced to meet her. The two companies joined, and a vast throng of "many and diverse people"[12] who had gathered "to witness that solemnity"[13] closed around.

The chroniclers' descriptions of this historic encounter at Toros de Guisando have long been suspect—especially their statement that Henry "freely and spontaneously"[14] admitted little Juana not to be his but the "fruit of illicit relations"[15] by his "adulterous"[16] Queen. No longer, however, can there be the slightest doubt as to what actually took place: a notarized account of the proceedings has recently been found. Veneriis, the Nuncio, began them. He exhorted the confederates to "reduce themselves"[17] to obedience to Henry as their "king and natural lord" and by pontifical authority "dissolved and untied" whatever oaths of allegiance they had made to anyone else, either as sovereign or as heir. Led by Isabel, they all swore him loyalty. Garcí López de Madrid, a member of the Council, granted them on Henry's part full forgiveness for any "offenses, spites, or injuries" which they had done to him and received them back into the royal fold. With Henry's recognition accomplished, Isabel's at once came on. Henry made it in person; eager for "true peace and tranquility" and in order that the kingdom should not remain "without legitimate successors of his high and exalted line" (it is the closest he ever came to confession that little Juana was not his child), he proclaimed his "very dear sister" heir and Princess of Asturias—and commanded everyone present to follow suit. They complied. Then all of them seem to have dismounted: a Missal with a crucifix laid across it had been provided, for the oaths must be both temporal and divine. One by one they touched the *"santos evangelios"* and swore that they would perpetually guard their pledges; next they turned to each other and made the same binding oath "once, twice and thrice," according to the ancient feudal custom—Henry between the hands of Villena, the others among themselves. Veneriis again came forward and gave their acts the apostolic blessing. Suddenly it all was over. The crowd let out its breath, began to break up.

Isabel did not even go back to Cebreros; she had brought her belongings with her, for she was now, as heir, an official member of Henry's court. Side by side they cantered away toward Cadalso, "no little inspirited, and trading congratulations."[18] They were there in time for dinner. Even before it, probably, the courier for Zaragoza set out with his heady message: half of Juan's last great gamble was achieved—Isabel would have the crown. As to the new Princess, it would be strange if she did not bring to table her best appetite since the catastrophic night in Cardeñosa more than two months before: she had a promise—signed, sealed, and papally authenticated—of which she was never to let loose. And Henry himself, when the trestles were taken up, sat down at once to business beside Villena for the first time in four miserable years. It was short enough; with a sigh of relief which surely could be heard in the Azores, he turned everything over to the familiar hands. The hatchet was buried. Villena rose and went out, first minister again.

Then, finally, Henry was free to do what mattered most. He summoned Andrés de Cabrera. Leave immediately for Segovia, he told him. Take possession of it in his name.

20.

"Flowers of Aragón"

Yet it was not, after all, in Segovia that they settled. Henry did find time early in October for a rapid journey to the recovered city; no description of the visit has been left—and perhaps none is needed. But Villena, again at the helm, decreed that the court take up its residence in Ocaña, south of the Tajo. That town was the center both of the lands of Santiago and of his private dominions, and he wanted a place where he could keep everything in unquestioned control. Not of his grip on Henry did he have any cause for doubt; he had seen at once that the frayed and depleted sovereign would be more manageable than ever. What really concerned him was Isabel.

It is obvious that in the weeks just subsequent to Guisando Villena had experienced a rude awakening about the Princess whom he had helped to pitch so high. Of course he did not have access to the gathered documents which now give such ample witness to Isabel's remarkable maturing, the annealing of her character, in the crucible of those momentous days. But he had eyes. Above all, his nose was quick as any fox's to catch the scent of danger to himself. And there it had come, keen on the autumn air—the new successor clearly was not the pliant girl he might have imagined but a vigorous adult with a mind and determination of her own. In short, he faced the same unpleasant truth which had confronted him when he raised Beltrán de la Cueva as counterpoise to Lucas—that he had created a rival instead of a tool.

And this time, the apprehensive Marqués immediately realized, his blunder would be far more difficult to repair: Isabel was anything but the lone and friendless figure which Beltrán had been. Strong forces seemed already to be massing behind her. Carrillo had stalked the court to Ocaña and established headquarters only seven miles away at his own town of Yepes. The Count of Paredes, another prime conspirator of the League, had joined him there with a heavy detachment of lances. Peralta and the Nuncio Veneriis went about with mysterious expressions; midnight messengers slipped in and out of Isabel's lodgings. The Aragonese propulsion behind these movements was only too evident—and an alliance of Isabel with Aragón would give her a more formidable stance than Villena cared to contemplate. That eventuality had to be warded off. Aragón, unhappily, lay quite beyond his reach. But Isabel was at hand. Villena had scant illusion about the course which he now must take. It constitutes, in reality, the mainspring of all his future actions: to thwart and impede this spirited young woman whom he had made the mistake of bringing forward, lest she achieve a power sufficient to challenge, or even overturn, his own.

So much for the sudden eclipse of that sun of concord and affability which had shone with such warmth upon the field of Guisando. So much for the strange reluctance which Henry, at Villena's instigation, now began to demonstrate about putting the terms of the agreement with his sister into effect; no single one of the commitments which he there had pledged did he show any signs of fulfilling. He could scarcely be blamed for not repossessing himself of La Beltraneja: the Mendozas harbored as little thought of giving up their hostage as Juana of returning to Portugal and falling into the clutches of her angry brother (by then she had given birth to her baby—a boy—and was busy assembling another with young Pedro, who had followed her to Buitrago).[1] But there was no valid reason why he should not have delivered the towns and rents assigned to Isabel in their pact. And when he and Villena revived the project of her marriage to Alfonso of Portugal—the surest way to get her out of the country and be entirely rid of her—she sought instant audience with Henry and emphatically reminded him of the promise that she would never be married against her wish. Her objections were brushed aside. Alfonso, forthwith approached, as speedily sent emissaries headed by the Archbishop of Lisbon to conclude the match. When Isabel refused to see them, Henry deputed Pedro de Velasco to talk with her and try to bend her to the royal will. Velasco got nowhere—and finally was driven to such harsh and threatening language that Isabel burst into sobs.

They are the last thing one expects of Isabel the Catholic. But at the juncture she had motive, more than motive, for them, for her obdurate rejection of Alfonso. Those midnight messengers had been coming and going on truly large affairs: already she was deeply involved in negotiations with Zaragoza for a marriage to Fernando.

Juan had, indeed, lost little time; the galvanic effect produced upon him by the news about Guisando will occasion the reader no surprise. Now that Isabel was heir to Castile, only one obstacle—to make her Fernando's bride—stood between him and the attainment of his dream. Of course that was no mean obstacle, was in fact immense—and to complicate matters he labored just then in even more than his usual state of harassment on all sides. But with Isabel's acknowledgment as Princess of Asturias the hour had struck, the full challenge had come, his goal was almost within reach. One last great effort might carry him across, and to prepare for that *summum bonum*, to strip for the final dash, he had fallen during those autumn weeks into perhaps the most febrile activity of all his active life.

First, he decided, he must strip his eyes: he could not go blind into this most critical endeavor of his career; he needed his sight as well as his brain. His Jewish and Moslem physicians had long been telling him that an operation on his cataracts held considerable chance of success. Juana Enríquez, oak-hearted though she was, had opposed recourse to that "experience";[2] aside from the uncertainty of the outcome, given the crude instruments and the lack of asepsis and anesthesia of the time, she was afraid he might run mad with the pain and terror of the "knives."[3] But the Queen was now dead, and on October 12, only a fortnight after the report of Guisando reached him, the intrepid old man—he was then past seventy—submitted to the agonizing test. It worked: the curtains of decades rolled back, once more Spain's gold and blue and scarlet blazed forth upon his ken. More—or at least for him—he again could see to read and write. He sat down with no further ado to letters and dispatches which would oil the wheels of his climactic design. He wrote to Rome: he must have a dispensation of Fernando's kinship with Isabel. The Pope was uninterested; he happened to be preparing just such a dispensation for Alfonso of Portugal—and anyway his whole Mediterranean policy was anti-Aragonese. Juan wrote again—and again. Who was Alfonso? Fernando, too, was a king (to raise his value in the matrimonial sweepstakes, he had just conferred the crown of Sicily upon the lad). Paul, however, remained adamant; in a fine Venetian rage, he even broke off the negotiations completely when Juan forged a letter (or such was the pontifical claim) purporting to be from Henry himself in favor of the marriage.

But if Juan's maneuvers in Rome were unsuccessful, those he propounded for the ensnarement of Isabel in a steady stream of letters to Yepes and Ocaña struck far more fertile soil. Carrillo and Peralta, in Yepes, of course were unconditional lieutenants; the Nuncio Veneriis, at court again after Guisando yet leaning to the cause of Aragón, must now be won to an advocacy as firm. But there were grave impediments to the intercourse of these three dignitaries: Peralta had been excommunicated for the murder of the Bishop of Pamplona, and nobody, least of all archbishops and nuncios, was supposed even to speak to a person under ban. To bridge that gulf, to serve as liaison, Juan sent another of his most trusted agents, Juan Ferrer; soon, through his mediation, Veneriis was being offered a sumptuous bribe if he would throw his weight behind Fernando's suit—an annual eight hundred ounces of gold, the miter of Tortosa, and the income of the Aragonese city of Orihuela. Aid, also, had to be sought among people even closer to Isabel, among members of her private circle. Gonzalo Chacón was Treasurer of the Princess's small court; the prize held out to him (although Juan cannily attached a string to all these gifts—they would be delivered only upon celebration of the marriage) was Escalona and Valdeiglesias, possessions of Chacón's former master don Alvaro de Luna, on top of a cool million and a *contaduría mayor* of Castile. And where Chacón, there his nephew Gutierre de Cárdenas, Isabel's *maestresala* and a young man with a sharp instinct for the main chance. To him went the glittering promise—foundation of the vast Cárdenas fortune— of Maqueda, a pension of two thousand gold florins, and future custody of the royal seal. The fact that for the moment Juan had very few of these opulent donations in his bestowal made little hindrance to their ready acceptance: if the marriage could ever be maneuvered and Fernando thus guaranteed the Castilian crown, then Aragón's financial troubles would be ended for all time. Through December of 1468 and the Christmas holidays—holidays which Henry spent restlessly and "little content"[4] and the Portuguese embassy in ill-borne frustration—insinuating voices spoke louder and louder at Isabel's ear: with no father and a mother of small comfort and a brother set on marrying her "according to his tastes and not to her own"[5] she should have an energetic young husband to protect her, the new King of Sicily was both "of equal years"[6] and "of wide discretion,"[7] on all counts a match with him was the "most honorable and advantageous and most conducive to her true happiness,"[8] and she must continue unyielding in her opposition to Alfonso.

Probably these persuasions were never really needed; had Juan only known it, his surest ally was the Princess herself. Much gilding, admittedly, has been daubed upon the great "romance" of Isabel and Fernando. But it is just as false to hold that her strong inclination toward her Aragonese cousin sprang from nothing more than crass "political convenience."[9] If she was not the sport of girlish vapors, neither was she inhuman, neither was she blind; certainly, approaching eighteen, she wanted a husband—and certainly, after the fat or sickly mates twice and three times her age already proposed for her, the thought of a youth so near to hers and known to be brave and personable and hardy can scarcely have failed to arouse some natural stirrings in her breast. At all events, she listened; she even helped. By the end of January Peralta was writing to Zaragoza (in code, so hazardous were the dealings) that Veneriis was entirely secured and that "the thing which we go secretly about"[10] might well be concluded within the week; a few days later Ferrer gave substance to that prediction in another letter announcing that the Portuguese mission had despaired and gone home, that Isabel had given her formal and irrevocable troth to Fernando ("he it shall be nor ever any other"),[11] and winding up with the injunction that now, of all times, Juan must not "flag."[12] Little chance of that: at once he sent a request for Isabel's final terms, and in February Peralta surreptitiously set out for Zaragoza conveying them. They proved startlingly stiff, for even then, even at that early stage of her dedicated career, Isabel was resolved to uphold Castilian interests; furthermore, the multitudinous clauses required among her dower from Aragón a hundred thousand florins and, as proof of good faith to sustain her in the wildly dangerous course on which she had embarked, the quickest possible delivery of twenty thousand more, in addition to the fabled gold necklace left to Fernando by his mother, worth forty thousand ducats and hung with fifteen enormous rubies and gray pearls. Juan, nevertheless, signed—in mid-March of 1469—these costly and disadvantageous "Capitulations." But he added a shrewd proviso. Auspiciously though matters were progressing, there was still an incalculable · hitch. A girl promised fell far short of a girl obtained and wedded; Isabel was very much the *princesse lointaine*—and in the power of his mortal enemies. Not, he edged into the contract, until she found herself a free agent, until she was in a position to act independently and without dictate or coercion, could he engage to carry out its terms.

His precautions were well advised: the *novia*, in point of fact, was far more seriously menaced, under far stricter vigilance and in direr peril, than even Juan could have guessed. No amount of subterfuge had been able to conceal these moves of Aragón from anyone himself so skilled as Villena[13] in that dubious art. Perhaps he did not know that the actual marriage lines with Fernando were being drawn. But surely he realized that they were in the offing, that Peralta's ominous disappearance involved events of the highest moment, and that he, as well, should gird for drastic action—in sum, that his duel with Juan, an adversary whose awesome measure none knew better, must now be fully joined.

His initial thrust in the fast-developing contest was wontedly astute. The representatives to Cortes were arriving in Ocaña. Shortly after Guisando, and before the veer in attitude about Isabel, Henry had convoked them—of course to give her their official stamp as heir. It was too late to rescind the summons. But it was by no means too late, Villena figured, to block the purpose for which they had been called. Somehow they must be kept from granting Isabel the oath. If her claim to the succession were thus jeopardized, even nullified, then her value would be greatly diminished, her chief appeal as a bride for Fernando would be swept away.

He seems, at the outset, to have tried to prevent the *procuradores* from ever sitting. And he had a certain ground: only a little more than half of the cities had dispatched their deputies; Extremadura and Murcia and the whole of Andalucía lacked voice. Those present, however, turned out to be determined to convene: they had come a long way; they had not met for almost four years and wanted to reassert their statutory rights. But once they were in session—and displaying an unmistakable predilection for Isabel and an obstinate desire to get on to her acknowledgment—Villena threw himself with all his customary wiles, and unimpeded, into subverting that intent: Henry, sick of intrigue, had gone off to Madrid and the animal preserve at El Pardo, and the Marqués, abetted by his tinseled adjutant Fonseca, was in total charge. His opening tactic was to swamp these restive Cortes with accumulated business. Inconveniently for his purpose, they swiftly disposed of it—and swung back to the question of Isabel. Next he tried bribery; it did not work. Finally he locked them in their houses under arrest—only to have them get out and reconvene. With that, he saw no other expedient than to call Henry from Madrid for their prorogation. But it seems that before the sovereign could arrive they had managed to give Isabel the oath: although there is endless argument among historians on the issue, Henry himself, in time, was to state flatly that she had been sworn.[14] True, sworn by less than the full complement of the Estates; the situation was much the same as it had been with the newborn Beltraneja, seven years before. But Villena's first stroke against the marriage with Aragón had failed: fractionally or not, the Princess still was Princess.

So shut her up, he was reduced to reasoning. Put her in some safe place where Juan and his young cub could never get at her. The Alcázar of Madrid would offer stout security, and devices were set in train for her sequestration and removal thither. But Isabel's alertness outran them. When soldiers began to infiltrate her attendants, she flashed a warning to Yepes. The Count of Paredes sent couriers to rouse the whole Manrique clan and bring them to her defense. Carrillo was even nimbler: he hurried two of his priests over to Ocaña on what looked like innocuous ecclesiastical errands, they entered into hidden parley with the town's "chief persons,"[15] and the municipal Council, forewarned (and partial, anyway, to Isabel), closed and manned the gates. The plot had to be abandoned.

But not the incarceratory purpose. The more Villena wrestled with the problem, the more it struck him that the one sure way to prevent a conjunction of Isabel with Fernando was to place her, physically, quite out of reach. But a bald seizure, as he had just had evidence, obviously would not do: what legal countenance, after all, could be put upon it? It would smack too much of tyranny, of brutality; it might arouse too much sympathy for her, might stir too many people to her aid. On the other hand—ah, he had it; his mind righted, steadied, fell back into its most familiar groove. If Isabel could be trapped, of her own choice and *motu proprio*, into giving lawful cause for her detention? At Guisando she had contracted, as Henry's sister and subject, to obey him. Perhaps she could be lured to flout his royal authority; should they go away and leave her less encumbered, she might feel tempted to some step of direct revolt. Henry, in such a case, would have full right to apprehend her, to close her in actual prison. Then see if Juan could ever snatch her for his youngster's bed!

He talked to Henry. Andalucía's latest affront was disgraceful, he told him—not answering his summons to Cortes! They really should make an expedition against Córdoba and Sevilla, always the centers of any southern disaffection. Whether he revealed his subtler design just then one cannot say. Nor do we know how much of his own motive for agreement Henry unbosomed to the Master: probably, from the outcome, very little. But our knowledge of that troubled heart by now is even less occluded than Villena's. Andalucía always meant only one thing to Henry—Miguel Lucas. And not since the Schism of Avila had he found good excuse for a trip to Jaén. Yes, by all means, he eagerly replied. Hasty preparations for departure were made. Villena attended to some pressing private correspondence (the result of which will soon become manifest) with Louis of France. Foresightedly—and vitally for his purpose— he prevailed on Henry to exact a promise from Isabel: that she would do "nothing new"[16] about her marriage while they were gone. Then, in awakening May, leaving affairs at Ocaña in deliberate suspension and Isabel under minimal guard, the court rode off.

Upon their excursion to Andalucía we cannot dwell; events—the great events toward which so large a part of our own journey has been heading—now spin far too fast to permit of much extension or delay. The travelers themselves seem to have been infected by a sense of importunity: in Ciudad Real, when Fonseca came down with tonsilitis, they decided not to wait, to leave him and push on. But they went in an odd direction. Although at Ciudad Real the normal route to Córdoba and Sevilla turned southwest, Henry decreed that they march southeast. Not until they reached Baeza did he finally communicate his purpose: before anything else, he said, he intended to visit Jaén. His messenger to Lucas took horse; a joyful response sped back. But please, Lucas added, do not bring Villena: he could never receive a person who had worked Henry such harm. The Marqués, to whom any meeting of Henry and Lucas was cause for nightmares, reluctantly left for Porcuna, near Córdoba, and the raising of levies for intimidation of that city. Henry started, at gallop, across the last twenty-five miles to the familiar haven on its tawny hill.

Yet even this new sojourn in Jaén, so long desired, is brief, sparse, brushed and ensombered by the wings of all the disasters which had intervened; gone now are the maced and liveried processions, the canopied feasts. Lucas did come forth (in moss-green damask) to give official welcome. "Oh my good Constable!"[17] Henry choked when they met, his eyes suddenly and irrepressibly "full of water";[18] the tears uncorked at Balsaín flow often now. Lucas, too, was weeping—no doubt at the changes, the ravages, in his friend—as they entered the gate. And by the time they dismounted, his unfailing intuition had told him that all Henry wanted was privacy and repose. Whatever entertainments he did have planned he immediately canceled; everything was kept simple and *en famille.* Henry played awkwardly with the child his hosts had succeeded in producing during his absence—a little boy who went insane. On Sunday the two of them climbed for a quiet picnic at the ancient Moorish castle above the town; they leaned over the battlements and looked down on the still cypresses and drifting hawks and dusty olives and talked of we know not what. When they came back in the twilight Henry bound up one of his usual shy nosegays of compliment: not for five years, he announced, had he been able to go to bed with any sense of peace or safety—the interval, almost to a month, since his earlier visit. On Monday bulls were run, with Henry apart in a sheltered *mirador.* But Tuesday the iron hand thrust in; Villena, on coals at their reunion, wrote from Porcuna that the army to threaten Córdoba had been gathered, that it was imperative for Henry to join him. Henry and Lucas discussed it: only four days, it seemed cruelly short. But Lucas did not plead; he had discovered that Henry's bondage to Villena was now beyond contradiction or repair. Last-minute promises, nonetheless, were exchanged: he would get back as soon as ever he could, Henry apologetically vowed. This time no record of their parting has been left, of

whether there again were tears. They would have poured in torrents had not fate, perhaps mercifully, held shut the curtain on what
lay ahead.

Henry rode away with an added sense of his weakness, of self-
reproach. And fresh harassments awaited him. Córdoba did cede at
the show of royal force. But once they were in, the submission
proved more apparent than real; the local magnates reneged on
their guarantees, made irate claims both against the Crown and
against one another. In the midst of these frets and annoyances,
moreover, came distressing news from Cuenca: old Lope Barrientos, on the cusp of ninety, was dead. Much of Henry's past died with
Barrientos, and surely his sadness and nostalgia were deepened by
recollection of their painful parting in the Council chamber at
Valladolid. Nor was that the end of the worn sovereign's trials.
Soon he had to endure what he always dreaded most—the facing of
strangers: a French embassy arrived.

For now the fruit of Villena's recent correspondence with Paris
appears. Louis had grown increasingly alarmed at the entente
which was closing in on him: latterly Juan had signed treaties with
Burgundy and England. Castile was his best hope of breaking
through the bellicose ring; Henry must be induced to cut his ties
with England and return to the arms of France. He had written
privately to Villena in Ocaña: could that be effected? The Marqués,
"enteramente del Rey de Francia"[19] and long, as we have seen, on his
actual payroll, replied: he was confident he could handle it; send a
mission. There, suddenly, it was, in the summer sun at Córdoba's
gate—led by the Cardinal of Albi, Jean Jouffroy.

Palencia's pen drips vitriol on this Cardinal of Albi, and he does
seem to have been somewhat less than a model of either modesty or
tact: haughtily, during an hour-long discourse in Latin, he informed
Henry that he had never had any right to alienate himself from
Louis, that his ancestors had possessed wits enough to "guard and
uphold"[20] the Franco-Castilian confederation, and that he would do
well to follow their example. Henry listened patiently to the ha-
rangue; afterward, though, he closeted himself with Villena for
enlightenment. It had to be, Villena told him; they must renounce
the English pact. But his word to Edward! Henry cried. No matter,
Villena said callously. Then, leaving Henry to start an embarrassed
and shamefaced letter to Windsor, he scuttled over to the Cardinal's

lodging for some further, some private, talk on a subject perhaps yet closer to his interests. His plot against Isabel—to trap her into disobedience—seemed to have failed: there had been complete silence from Ocaña, apparently she had not risen to the bait. But here, it occurred to him, was another chance to be rid of her, to get her out of the country by a distant foreign marriage. Tit for tat, he reminded Jouffroy. In return for the alliance which he had just arranged, why not a match of Isabel with Louis's brother (and heir, since Louis had no son) the Duke of Guyenne? The Cardinal vouchsafed to smile on the idea, and Villena went back to the palace full of his new scheme. That too? sighed Henry, putting down his finished letter. Well, if Villena wished. But was it not time to be getting on to Sevilla?

It was time past: July already pulsed and burned. Yet their advance on the metropolis was clogged by all sorts of mishaps and delays. At Ecija, which they had thought to reduce *en route*, the populace was so sullen that they felt it unwise to tarry. Antequera denied them entry. And when they reached Alcalá de Guadaira, only ten miles from Sevilla, they found the whole private army of the young new Duke of Medina Sidonia—a family implacably hostile to Villena—assembled on the hot plain directly across their path. They swung around to Cantillana, hoping to approach the city by way of the Guadalquivir. There, however, an ultimatum was brought to them: Sevilla, like Jaén, would open to Henry—but only if he came without the Marqués. There was nothing for it except that Henry go on and attempt the pacification of the city alone and unadvised.

He made his entry, "weary of spirit,"[21] on August 19. After one of those Solemn Masses which never did anything to comfort or elevate him, he took part "against his will"[22] in a state procession. Then he steeled himself to business with the truculent Sevillan Council. He stood it just two days. Abruptly he broke off; he crossed the boiling river and buried himself in the Monastery of Santa María de las Cuevas. But hardly had he begun to relax amidst its cool corridors and jasmines when Villena's urgent message from Cantillana arrived. Come at once, the Master ordered. Nothing else was now of any importance, they must hasten back to the north, their plan—after all—was working out: Isabel had fled Ocaña.

And fled she had; the tremendous race is on. Discovery that the marriage to Fernando was contingent upon her being free from restraint, made at one knows not how long an interval after Henry's departure, had much the same electric effect on Isabel which news of her proclamation as heir had worked on Juan. That freedom, she straightway recognized, must now be bought at any price. Of its consequences—direct defiance of Henry, the laying herself open to the direst sort of reprisals—she cannot have labored under any doubt. But the reward, should she succeed, was worth whatever risk: once Fernando's wife, Henry would never dare to put hands upon her, for that would mean war with Aragón. Furthermore, her conscience in the matter was clear: Henry had broken his every promise to her, had left her no choice, and while she was not unmindful of her pledge to do "nothing new" in regard to her marriage during his absence, that also could be justified—strictly the decision was not "new," it had been taken months past. All that was left was one immense *incógnita:* would she have time—and skill and luck enough—to bring the wedding about before Henry and Villena could get back from the south and head her off? She did not know. But she was determined to try. Before the summer was far along, and with her characteristic courage and resolve, she seized the bit in her teeth.

Of how she managed her *"salto"*—her famous "leap"—from Ocaña there are no details. All the rest of her hairbreadth adventure, however, is minutely documented. Her original plan was to take refuge in Arévalo; although young Alfonso had pawned that town to the Count of Plasencia, she reached secret understanding with its *alcalde* to sublevate it on her behalf. But it is a long way from Ocaña to Arévalo. During the course of her Valkyrie gallop across mountains and plains a serious *contretemps*—first in the onrushing juggernaut of catastrophes—took place: the intention of the *alcalde* came to light and he was thrown into jail. Apprised of this misfortune when she was already at the Adaja, she drew up short. Carrillo, who was escorting her, decided to turn his course, instead, for Alcalá de Henares, there to screen off any move against her on the part of the hostile Mendozas. She herself veered away west to Madrigal, her birthplace. Providentially, it received her. In the first pause since her escape she sent off to Zaragoza, through the chronicler Palencia, her prodigious announcement: she was at liberty, she had done her part, now let the dower be sent and Fernando come to claim and save her. But hurry, hurry, there might be very little time.

There was even less than she thought. The Cardinal of Albi, passing through Madrigal on his way home and finding her there, put nerve-racking pressure on her to give formal assent to the French marriage. Somehow she parried his demands. But scarcely had he departed, emitting flames, when an immeasurably worse threat befell her: one of her staff intercepted a letter from Henry to Madrigal's Council, announcing that he and Villena had learned of her flight and whereabouts, and instructing the local authorities to place her under arrest. She took immediate sanctuary in a convent outside the walls. There she wrote to Carrillo, with a plea that he rush back to her aid. But there, too, a further thunderbolt struck. Scouts brought word that Fonseca, the Sevillan Archbishop, had also received a retaliatory order from the south—to march down from Coca with heavy troops and make absolutely sure of her capture and imprisonment. He would be there in three days.

Three days: it was about the time needed, with steady spurring, for Carrillo to arrive. Isabel's faith must have been tested to the uttermost as she peered out from the wooden windows of the convent across the silent summer plain and wondered to which of the two archbishops the first troops to break the shimmering horizon would belong. To her indescribable relief, they were Carrillo's— augmented by two hundred lances which Fernando's grandfather the Admiral had started down to her assistance from Ríoseco and which chanced to meet Carrillo as he hurtled past Pozáldez. They brought, moreover, her dower—the florins and the ruby necklace; Palencia, returning with it from Aragón, had reached Alcalá just as the Archbishop was leaving. But her joy was shattered when she read Juan's accompanying letter. He could not spare Fernando; Gerona had fallen, his situation was critical. Isabel and Carrillo stared at each other. Critical? Not half so much as hers. She had burned her bridges, had staked everything on Fernando's coming and the consummation of their marriage. Without him, she was utterly destroyed.

Yet they could not linger in Madrigal; at any hour Fonseca's army might appear. In haste, but with a brave show of "many trumpets and drums,"[23] they headed for nearby Fontiveros. False hope—its gates, on Villena's orders, had already been shut and barred: the long tentacles of vengeance were now spreading up inexorably from the south, all Castile was fast closing against her. They galloped on toward Avila but were met by warning messengers: the city had been stricken by plague. They stopped; they took harried counsel. Valladolid, perhaps? Carrillo's niece was married to one of its chief citizens, Juan de Vivero. There they might find haven. Doubling back to the north, and finally running for very life, they made for the ancient city. The Viveros did take them in. They passed along, in addition, one frail shred of encouraging news: Villena and Henry were indeed marching north against her with their whole army, but they had paused to lay siege to Trujillo, which the Count of Plasencia had required as his price for adding his own forces to the punitive expedition, and Trujillo's stubborn *alcaide*, that Gracián de Sesé whom we have met before and shall see again, was holding out. How long would his obstinacy tie down the avenging host? A fortnight, even a few days, would be priceless. While trenches were dug around the Viveros' house, while provisions were brought in and frantic preparations made for investment, for assault, for anything, Isabel dashed off a last desperate appeal to Fernando. Miraculously, she announced, they had been given a little more time. But the reprieve, at best, would be brief; her sands were rapidly running out. This would obviously be the final hope for their marriage. Come, come—for the love of God.

Once again it was the peripatetic Palencia—only this time accompanied by Gutierre de Cárdenas—who streaked toward Zaragoza with the message. But on his way he learned a horrifying truth. The Count of Medinaceli, lord of all the eastern Castilian lands which Fernando would have to penetrate and presumed friendly to the match and ready to give transit, had been suborned from Trujillo and gone over—as his uncle had done at the crucial point of the first battle of Olmedo—to the enemy: he had closed his towns and deployed his bristling *mesnadas*, a great shield to block Fernando now covered the entire frontier. Palencia sped on, though badly shaken. Worse, when he reached Zaragoza he found Juan away—at Guisona, on his battlefront. But Fernando was there, and the two of them held secluded converse in a chapel of the Monastery of San Francisco. Isabel's letter set the lad on fire. The new danger which Palencia revealed only roused him further, challenged him. Why not get past in disguise? he excitedly suggested. He could take three of his friends; he knew just whom. They might pose as—well, traveling merchants. He could be their muleteer. Yes, yes, he would go, would do it—provided, of course, that his father gave permission. They hastened out; they found a secretary. Off went the message to Guisona.

Juan read it. He laid it down, and if the old man's fine white hands ever trembled, they did so then. Not conceivably could the moment have been worse. In the war, his back was literally to the wall: his entire front against the Angevins was collapsing, Segorbe had fallen, the powerful clan of Margarit which had been his chief support among the Aragonese nobility had just deserted him. There was still no dispensation for the marriage; his latest request for it in Rome, three weeks before, had failed. Above all, the enormous danger of his adored Fernando's passage was enough to give him mortal chills. A handful of youths, in precarious masquerade, braving the gathered might of the Mendozas and the Count of Medinaceli? The whole harebrained plan—so like a lad of seventeen —appalled his cautious mind. And yet, and yet—what remedy, what other choice? He was up against it—and knew it; everything he had done, had been, placed this merciless lance-tip square upon his breast. How long he flinched away from it, how long he hesitated, there is no means of ascertaining. But finally, unalterably, there in the tent at Guisona, he made the decision of a lifetime. He reached for his inkwell; he began his reply.

One wishes there were space to print it all. Each word of it is a tear; at last the rigid, long-practiced mask drops off and only the face of love, the naked face of a suffering father, remains. He opened with the words of Santa Susana—and the famous phrase has never been more tellingly quoted—*"Undique michi sunt angustie,"* "I have trials on every side."²⁴ "No other son" to inherit his realms or be a "prop for his old age" was left to him except Fernando. Even to think of the risks of the long journey to Valladolid filled him with fear "so deep and cruel that it passes description." Furthermore, he was half beside himself already with the distractions of the war. Nor did he have one single member of his Council to turn to for advice; he was entirely alone. Yet he could see that the matter was "so far advanced," the posture of Isabel so "peremptory," as to brook no more delay. If they faltered now, *"todo lo trabajado,"* all they had hitherto accomplished, would be lost. Therefore—he summoned his last courage—let him go. He sent his benediction and asked that Christ take mercy on them and guide and protect the young traveler and one day bring him back to stand again "before these eyes" unharmed and prospered, as his "decrepitude had need."

He signed and sanded the heroic missive. He gave it to the waiting courier. Then there was nothing more he could do but to set out for Zaragoza to be closer to the scene of action—and brace himself for the suspense, the agonizing wait.

By the time he reached the capital Fernando was long gone. The great tale of derring-do requires no telling here; it has entered, whole and imperishable, into the world's history—the slipping through by dark and by hidden paths, the midnight arrival in Valladolid and the unlatched postern, the torchlit meeting of the future Catholic Monarchs, the forged dispensation,[25] the hasty wedding, the young couple hand in hand up the stone stairway to the bedroom. Our gaze would focus, rather, upon Juan. Days on end he paced the halls of the Aljafería, locked in a vise of torment and doubt. He went up in a tower and looked to the west, straining to see a messenger. Finally one came. He knelt; he held out the letter which the dutiful son had risen from Isabel's arms in the cold October dawn and sat down to write. Juan took it and tore it open.

Surely his first reaction was sheer relief—a fountain, a cataract, an ocean, of simple human relief. Safe, safe, the boy was safe. Not dead in some foreign ditch, or lost or hurt or captured, but blessedly safe. Yet, just as surely, when his initial wave of joy subsided a swift new tide swept in across it and mounted and swelled and filled the farthest reaches of his being—a spreading awareness of the wider meaning, the deeper impact, of the event. Not much is known of Juan's religious nature; like everything else about him, he kept that under lid. But it would be strange indeed had not a hymn of thanksgiving to God for long labor accomplished have arisen in his heart. Stranger yet, one imagines, if his thoughts did not go winging to all his departed family: his father and mother and six brothers and sisters who had given their lives and treasure to the re-establishment of their House in its native kingdom. They could dream easy now—in the dim funerary chapel at Poblet, in Toledo, in Guadalupe, amidst the Indian splendors of the Portuguese Abbey. And he too, he realized with a huge dropping off of weight, folding the letter and turning away and starting down the corridor, at last was able to take his tired old bones to bed and sleep, sleep, sleep. The wounds at Olmedo, the assassins outside the gate at Lérida, the raging French, the reverses and betrayals of fifty terrible years, the blindness, the poverty, the death of wives, the sickness, the loneliness—none of that any longer mattered. Isabel would have the Castilian crown—and his boy had Isabel. He had won.

21.

Release

The rest, in a sense, is epilogue—at least for Henry. He lived five more years. But the great task, from the start so far beyond his capacities, bequeathed to him in his own turn by his father and don Alvaro de Luna—the shutting out of Aragón—now was lost: in short, the political contest of the two kingdoms which has been the arch and diapason of our book is over. Nor was what remains of his private story much else than a coda, a fall of dusk, a shed of inner leaves as the realm dissolves around him in utter anarchy and ruin.

Even the scholar most versed in the annals of the period admits the sorting of that final chaos of the reign a work "outside the grasp of any historian."[1] And where a general falters, what of the rank and file? Yet peering through the Stygian mists one does discern a thread, a certain context. Aragón was within the gates, the marriage had been consummated; nothing could cancel that. Perhaps there was still a chance, however, of slowing Isabel's way. It might be possible to set up again, as a deterrent, La Beltraneja's tumbled rights. And she should also be provided with a husband (a future husband, since she was only eight), one of sufficient bulk to minimize Fernando. Such is, in effect, the last major effort to which Villena—for it can no longer be pretended that Henry was anything more than his mute and willing puppet—now puts his hand.

But it was not to be immediately undertaken; the wedding in Valladolid had been too heavy a shock. News of the event was brought to Henry and Villena while they lay before Trujillo. At once they lifted their siege (instead of the intractable city, Henry gave Stúñiga the dukedom of Arévalo) and hurried north. Yet on the road Villena fell gravely ill: mortification at his defeat by Juan of Aragón quite broke his health. He veered east to his town of Ocaña —the empty cage. There he sought his couch. Henry himself got on to Segovia and sank into new lethargy among his lions and mandolins. For six full months matters hung fire.

None the less, and even from his sickbed, Villena's pen was busy; though his body languished, already his steamy mind was putting forth initial tendrils in search of some method to recoup his loss. They soon caught hold. A husband for little Juana? Why not the heir to France—that same Guyenne whom Isabel had so deftly eluded? An exploratory letter went to Paris, and the answer returned before November's close. Louis was *"très joyeux"*[2] about this latest plan for his brother (whom he heartily despised). Again he would dispatch the Cardinal of Albi, to work out and sign the contracts. But winter—and it was an especially cruel one all through Europe—intervened. Only in the late spring of 1470 did word come down that the emissary was on his way. Villena, still convalescent, had himself placed upon a litter and carried over the Guadarramas. Henry rode to Medina del Campo. In mid-August, hot and more irritable than ever, the Cardinal arrived.

If Albi's previous behavior in Córdoba had been no worse than condescending, what he unloaded at Medina was plain abuse: some of the Grandes were so incensed by the string of tasteless Gallic animadversions which he "fired off"[3] about his hosts and the dreary country they inhabited that they began to talk of killing him. Notwithstanding, under the strain and mutual hostility of those August weeks, the business of the marriage lines did manage to progress. By September most of the conditions had been settled, and they all moved on to Segovia, there to make arrangements for the public *desposorios*, the engagement. The Mendozas, at the stunning price of the dukedom of Infantado (Alba, like the Count of Plasencia, had just been raised to ducal rank, and they were not the sort to see themselves surpassed), agreed to relinquish both the child and the Queen. Delivery, with the betrothal to follow immediately, was appointed for October 25. Accompanied by the French mission and the court, Henry set out from Segovia. The Mendozas sortied from Buitrago. Halfway between, in the high valley of Lozoya, their *comitivas* joined.

The ceremony which ensued—Bermejo goes so far as to call it "ridiculous,"[4] and it does, pale simulacrum of Guisando as it is, have elements of the bizarre—took place in a mountain glen beside the Angostura, that curious little stream which, fittingly enough, runs nowhere. Of Henry's meeting with Juana (now hopelessly *déclassée* and probably black and blue from the beatings which Pedro, tired of her infidelities even to him, had taken to administering) we are

not informed: the chroniclers left it, as no doubt did he, in stony
silence. But transcripts of the official acts have been preserved.
Henry, flanked by Villena, had one of his councilors read a letter
patent. In it, Isabel was condemned for her disobedience and "lack
of respect"⁵ and young Juana reinstated; the nobles, "a hundred
times perjured,"⁶ were bidden to swear allegiance to her, and Cortes
convoked for the same purpose. That done, the Cardinal advanced
on Henry and the Queen, thrusting forth a crucifix: he had to be
quite sure that his master was not about to buy a pig in a poke.
Would they give solemn oath that the child there present was indeed a fruit of their commingled loins? Juana revived sufficiently to
take hold of the sacred object and get out an emphatic "yes." Henry,
with the same gesture, answered that he "believed"⁷ it to be so.
Satisfied, Albi beckoned to the proxy of Guyenne; the little girl was
brought forward on her mare. The Cardinal joined their hands and
pronounced the union legal. And then a strange thing happened.
The sky, hitherto blue and limpid, suddenly turned pitch black. A
wild wind from the crags (from Heaven?) bore down upon them.
Terrified, the company scattered. Hail fell. Young Juana fell from
her mount. No attention was paid her; finally a stableboy picked her
up and carried her, sobbing and forgotten, to the shelter of an oak,
there to await the passing of the storm. But it did not pass. It turned
instead into a raging blizzard. All of them were snowbound in the
mountains for three days.

Many were the "prognostications"⁸ of disaster for the French
alliance to which this untoward conclusion of its formal seal gave
rise. And evidence soon abounded that they might prove true. The
Cortes seem not to have met—or, if they did assemble, refused to
withdraw their loyalty to Isabel. Guyenne showed no signs of coming; he even failed to write. Finally Villena and Henry sent a repre-
sentative to Paris. His reply only heightened their anxiety. Louis,
he announced, now had a son—the future Charles VIII—who of
course displaced Guyenne in the succession. Moreover, the *novio*
had obviously lost interest in Juana: he was wooing the daughter of
the Duke of Burgundy. But Guyenne, as things turned out, never
married anyone. Before long Louis did away with him, some say at
a banquet after which the Duke's eyebrows and fingernails dropped
off, some by envenoming the Wafer given him at Mass. Whatever
the circumstances, he was dead and buried—and with him all possi-

bility of a French marriage for Isabel's young rival (nobody proposed to wait fifteen years for the mewling and puking Charles).

One groom was lost; another, and of equal or even greater substance, had to be found. Villena's threshing thoughts turned to the west. What of Alfonso of Portugal? That would be a prize, a bulwark, indeed. Ambassadors departed for Lisbon—where, after considerable persuasion, they arranged a royal meeting to discuss the matter, between Badajoz and Elvas. But it went bad from the beginning. Singed as he was by his recent fiasco with his cousin Isabel, Alfonso felt small inclination for a similar bout, at forty, with his yet untasseled niece. Moreover, as he reasonably pointed out, his presence on the scene as Juana's fiancé and champion (the plan now seems to have been—unlike the exporting of Isabel—to bring the bridegroom in) would expose him to all sorts of risks, of retaliations by the opposing faction; he would need strong Castilian towns and fortresses where he could make himself secure. He specified them. Unfortunately—or by design—the greater part of them were unavailable; Henry had given many of them to the barons, others already crammed Villena's maw. Shoulders were shrugged, heads shaken; the sessions rose. Alfonso and Henry exchanged regrets and polite farewells, this time for ever. Both retinues started homeward *"sin conclusión alguna."*[9]

With no conclusion: so too appeared, with every passing month, young Juana's fate. Portugal and France had shied away; betrothal to her was rapidly acquiring, in foreign eyes, those same proportions of the lethal as the cause of the Catalans. Yet a few scattered victims, if distinctly second-table, did remain, and Villena (for it was all one to Henry; the only thing he ever asked about possible suitors was whether they were musicians) now totted up their merits. The King of Naples—Ferrante, illegitimate offshoot of Alfonso the Magnanimous—had a son; to marry the youngster to La Beltraneja and set him up as Prince of Castile, in opposition to Fernando, would spread havoc through the House of Aragón. Ferrante's own stance, however, was much too shaky to permit such an affront to his uncle Juan; he hastily declined the proffered hand. And then Villena really reached rock bottom: he invited in, as groom presumptive, Henry Fortuna, child of that earlier Master of Santiago who had received his mortal wound at the first Olmedo. Presumptive, in all senses: Fortuna rushed to Madrid, along with his equally excited and "imprudent"[10] mother, and made an instant ass of himself by his pomposity and arrogance. Soon the whole court was mocking the fatuous guest. But what wrecked him, in the end, was his very sponsor. Villena had stipulated a reward of fifteen millions for his arranging the match, and Henry's *mayordomo* Andrés de Cabrera—perhaps because he had his own ideas about its destination—refused to authorize the payment of such a sum. Villena's interest in Fortuna evaporated. The stranded fop crept off, still with his mother, to her embarrassed nephew, the Count of Benavente. Cast on that niggard bounty, and "repentant of their rashness,"[11] they wilted to obscurity. Nor did Villena try again; the roster of useful bridegrooms was exhausted; his last weapon against Aragón seemed to have no edge. Broken in health, his touch for the first time beginning to fumble, he took young Juana to his castle of Escalona. There he put her in guard and left her, unwanted, apparently undisposable, a drag, an albatross—and perhaps already old enough, at ten, to make her first dim reflections about the melancholy truth, hammered home remorselessly by Castillo, that the sins of a mother are all too often visited upon her blameless child.

Down, down, the poor girl sank. And as she went, the splendid young matron—for Isabel had given birth to a daughter—rose; that Wheel of Fortune which so obsessed the fatalistic medieval mind pursued its slow but stopless course. The early months of their marriage, to be sure, found Isabel and Fernando in chancy straits indeed. But almost from the first the kiss of *buenaventura* seemed to be upon them; they possessed, in well-nigh irresistible abundance, native attractions long absent from the Castilian royal House— normalcy, rectitude, bearing, buoyant health. Moreover, they soon took conscious steps—all of them sanctioned, and some of them inspired, by Zaragoza—to draw both places and people to their cause. Accommodation with the powerful counts of Benavente and Treviño was maneuvered. The southern magnates, never partial to Henry, gave ready ears to their call. Beatriz de Bobadilla, Isabel's best friend, married Cabrera and thus secured for the young couple a strong ally within the very bosom of the opposition. "By spontaneous impulse"[12] Aranda renounced the ruttish Queen, its technical owner, and invited them in. So did Sepúlveda, key to the strategic passes of Somosierra. The Admiral raised Simancas in their behalf;

Fernando and Alba found means to occupy Tordesillas; the Basque provinces acclaimed them. International success trod fast upon the local (Fernando's true dower to Isabel, far more than a necklace of rubies, was Aragón's wide experience in foreign affairs). At Abbéville, in 1471, Charles of Burgundy conceded them a pact of mutual aid. England's Edward followed suit. And before that year was out they had a further champion of enormous weight both temporal and moral—Rome itself: Paul II died.

Paul's end may not have been so "horrible"[13] as Palencia paints it—locked accidentally in his bedroom without his medicines, screaming and howling, shriveling up to the size of a diminutive black doll and vanishing in a puff of sulfurous smoke. But one thing about it is certain: it did away with Rome's hostility toward Juan. In Peninsular matters Paul's successor, Sixtus IV, held just the opposite view. One of his first acts as Pontiff was to grant the dispensation for Isabel and Fernando, so long and vainly sought, which legalized their marriage. In addition, he named a Spanish prelate—Rodrigo de Borgia, later Pope himself—to be its bearer. Borgia was a Valencian, a native of Játiva; as soon as he landed he hurried to see Juan. Sovereign and vassal had a fruitful talk. Might they not win over the whole clan of the Mendozas, flower and panache of the Castilian aristocracy, by procuring a cardinal's appointment for its ambitious scion, Pedro González? Henry, unwittingly, stoked this nascent fire: he sent east that very person in official welcome. The two sybarites struck it off at once. They also struck their agreement, and when they reached Madrid there was little doubt of the direction in which the winds of both papal and Mendozan favor blew. Borgia pointedly ignored the Queen—now a virtual prisoner in the Convent of San Francisco. With his own hands he bestowed the Sacrament of Confirmation on Isabel's two-year-old child. Then he got on for fiestas—and final bargaining—in Guadalajara. Before he turned home toward Italy, Pedro González was in possession of his Hat—and Isabel of a precious private document (private, because of course—being Mendozas, being hypocrites—they still professed loyalty to the Crown) guaranteeing her the family's full support.

By the summer of 1472, in fact, the couple's outlook was so auspicious, their footing so secure, that Fernando felt it safe, at last, to pay a visit to his father. They met outside Pedralbes—and Juan's joy

at the reunion, if kept within his usual control, scarce needs re-
counting here: the reckless lad who had plunged off into the un-
known three long years past now stood before him—now truly
stood again "before these eyes"—a man *de hecho y derecho*, twenty,
shaven, mature, a husband and paterfamilias, Prince of Castile.
Brief though their time together was, it charged Juan with new
energy to aim a *coup de grâce* at the revolt of the Catalans. For that
unlovely saga, like everything else which we have been considering,
now draws to an end. The rebels' lot, of late, had steadily worsened.
Jean of Lorraine had died, and they could find no other leader. Louis
of France, hemmed in by the Triple Alliance, was unable to send
them further aid. To seal them off completely, Juan now hurried
north into the Ampurdán; its towns and cities yielded. Then, doubling swiftly back, he set up siege of Barcelona. Blockaded, hungry,
friendless, it faced, at last, the consequence of its folly. On October
16 a hangdog deputation trudged out and sought him in his tent and
unconditionally surrendered. He made a conqueror's entrance the
next day. Four snow-white horses drew his chariot; swags of imperial purple velvet draped it; he stood beneath a canopy of state,
grip firm upon the reins, his wizened head held proud and high.
And surely very few will begrudge his triumph. One does one's best
to disapprove of Juan of Aragón. One freely admits his faults, even
his sins: he lied, forged, cheated, tricked, betrayed. But, in the end,
it is impossible not to admire him; his indomitable will, his granite
courage in the face of nearly hopeless odds, defeat all censure. One
wishes one had been there beside the Rambla that October morning
in Barcelona to applaud him, to cry at least one *Viva* for the magnificent old scoundrel as he passed, as he rode on, erect upon his purple
chariot, through the fallen city, on and on down the wide straight
avenue toward the cathedral. We shall not see him again.

Farewells—they now throng in: the stage begins to empty, a new
cast is assembling in the wings. The little Admiral died, his hopping
and pecking done—but to large avail. Pedro Fernández de Velasco,
the ancient Count of Haro, wrapped his habit about him in the
convent at Medina de Pomar and turned his weary eyes to the wall,
the sunlit day when he had ridden forth from Briviesca to welcome
an Infanta of Navarre no more than a dim memory. Fonseca's bad
tonsils finally carried him off. But not only the older generation

disappears; much of Henry's youthful circle crumbles away. The knights of Alcántara made war on their Master, Gómez de Cáceres. Surprisingly, don Beltrán—that fading star, that fizzled rocket—rode down to help him. But the two former rivals were ignominiously defeated in an autumn battle among the Extremaduran asters, and Gómez, grieving for his ouster and the loss of all his foul-won titles, took ill and—not yet past his thirties—expired. Juan de Valenzuela suffered a similar fate. His own Order, sick of his *moues* and shrieks and flounces, rose against him; fleeing before them, he fell in a river and caught his death, poor thing. And late in March of 1473 a courier spurred up from Jaén with news of a further passing, a passing truly terrible.

Lucas had been murdered.

Much mystery—at times it looks almost like a conspiracy of silence—surrounds this ghastly event. The "Old" Christians may have planned it: in the religious conflicts which poisoned the whole century, Lucas—whose unfortunate taste, like Henry's, drew him ever to the disreputable—gave open aid to the *marranos*, the despised and outcast crypto-Jews. Or it may well have arisen from relations yet more perilous, more sordid: "workmen,"[14] "low fellows,"[15] "*canalla*"[16]—the chroniclers tread on tiptoe in their descriptions of the three assailants. But whatever the motive, the act itself is all too hideously clear. The season: Lent. Lucas, at the high altar of Santa María, knelt in prayer. He heard the footsteps behind him, heard them stop. He glanced around over his shoulder—and had only time to see the leering one-eyed face of the trio's leader and the fatal weapon, a heavy iron crossbow, swinging down upon his head. We can imagine, and certainly must hope, that he was instantaneously killed. The blow split open his skull; his brains flew out and sloshed on the predella. But the vengeful hoodlums did not stop with that. They drew their swords and daggers and fell savagely upon the quivering corpse; they hacked and pounded and sliced until "no resemblance to a human being remained."[17] There they left him—a shapeless mass of bloody meat: Miguel Lucas, Constable of Castile.

It nearly finished Henry. The grief, the shock, were bad enough. But a supposition that he long had thought of Jaén as a potential refuge, a place where he could flee if matters ever came to total disaster and live out his days with Lucas, is hard to avoid. Shorn of that one sustaining prospect, he now begins to make his last withdrawals, his final retreats; instinctively, like a tired child going home (for he never really changed, his sadness and loneliness and sense of alienation only deepened with the passage of the years), he turns again to the few pursuits which had ever given him any solace. He built a new cloister for the Segovian cathedral—so beautiful, so perfect, that when the present *iglesia mayor* was constructed in the next century, it was moved there stone by stone. In the purple solitude of the Guadarramas, on his knees, he tenderly planted little saplings with his great beefy hands. We glimpse him dismounting on his rides along the slopes of Monte Gobia at remote and sooty huts of alpine shepherds—to sit in gangling silence, to share a crust of barley-bread, perhaps to stay the night. But it grows increasingly difficult to trace him: the chroniclers have other interests now. As, in his youth, the epic of don Alvaro de Luna had cast him into penumbra, so here at the close the world's expectant eye is fixed on Isabel. Even during Segovia's famous Christmas holidays of 1473 (and we must limn them, however briefly, for they announce his doom) he shines only in reflected light.

Cabrera had been the impresario of those last fiestas of the reign. By then entirely won to Isabel and seeking means to bring about her reconciliation with the sovereign, he thought, as the Nativity drew on, to have found a chance: Villena, eternal obstructionist to concord, had departed to spend the season in Peñafiel. Without that evil genius, Henry proved willing enough to harken to the idea of a reunion—his private feelings for his sister had never been anything but warm—and Isabel more than eager to accept his invitation: fresh validation of her contracts at Guisando, clear stamp on her inheritance, might result. She rode down from Aranda on December 28. Henry welcomed her "with great love,"[18] and if he gently turned aside the business which she was quick to broach (ah no, they must enjoy the visit, "she would have her answer later"),[19] he did not hold back on hospitality. Nightly there were banquets in the tall and torchlit Alcázar: minstrels beneath the Moorish ceilings of azure and vermilion, roast boars and flaming Christmas puddings preceded by heralds and tambourines. At one of them he conquered his shyness enough to sing (Henry sang—in public), and Isabel danced before him: no doubt some ceremonious pavane or sarabande. On New Year's Eve,[20] in state, he conducted her through the garlanded city, walking modestly beside her and leading her palfrey —signal honor—by the reins. That very night she wrote encouragingly to Fernando, who had been stationed at nearby Turégano until they saw how matters went, and the next morning, his bars and eagles of Sicily aloft, he galloped in. Him, too, Henry received with utmost cordiality, and the fraternal bonhomie, the balls and dinners, went on. Oddly—for it was Henry's birthday, his forty-ninth—there is nothing recorded in the way of entertainment on January 5. Did nobody remember? Apparently not. (Only one person had always faithfully observed it: oh Lucas, Lucas.) For the following day, however, the Epiphany, much was planned—another progress through the city, the whole court attendant, then a banquet at the Bishop's palace with Cabrera as host. And it bore an official air. Perhaps full bestowal of the succession was at hand: the Magi had offered gifts.

But it all came down; at what everybody had thought might be the climactic moment it failed, it broke and fell. In that new procession Henry went mounted, the radiant Princess and her husband riding on either side. They made the circuit of the walls, of Segovia's five great gates. They came back to the *casas episcopales*, close against the cathedral. Cabrera's feast was waiting. They went in and found their seats. Henry placed Isabel next to him, Fernando next to her; the Count of Ribadeo, whose hereditary privilege it was to dine on the Epiphany with the sovereign, joined them. They ate. They ate all afternoon. The tables taken up, and candles lighted against the winter dusk, they moved on to an inner chamber to listen to music, *"instrumentos y cantores."*[21] It lasted a long time. Henry was looking tired. When it finally finished, they returned to the hall. The tables had been freshly spread; they were served "a sumptuous collation."[22] The conversation buzzed. But suddenly it faltered, then completely stopped—Henry was rising. They all leaned forward; yes, now—the declaration. He started to speak. But all at once, instead, his face contorted. Wildly he clutched his side. He swayed, then collapsed into his seat. People crowded around, but he waved them off. He gestured to his servants—to come, to see him home. They tried to help him stand. He could not; he was locked, doubled up, with pain. They had to carry him out still in his chair. And surely, as they conveyed him in white-jawed agony

through the startled streets, he realized that a trumpet more imperi-
ous than any on the morning's march had sounded, that his own end
could now not be far off, that he bore inside him something which
would take him to the grave.

What was it? Clinical diagnoses after five centuries leave much to
be desired. Even at the time, analysis—let alone any treatment—
must have been hampered by his reticence, his extreme secretive-
ness; probably he never let the physicians so much as examine him.
Obviously it involved—and very seriously—his kidneys: he urinated blood from that day on. There seem to have been intestinal
complications, for henceforth he is seldom without dysentery and
nausea. Diverticulitis—with a possible perforation of the bladder?
Cancer? Bright's Disease? Let others guess; our interest here has
been in ills beyond the reach of medicine or scalpel. Only one thing
is certain—poison (although in time a resuscitated and desperate
Beltraneja so shouted) it was not: strange dosage that would strike,
abate, then strike again and again and finally require a year to do
its work.

For it was to be a slow dying—and all shadowed and clouded,
now, by physical suffering in addition to the other, so long familiar,
of the heart. His initial attack did moderate, although for many days
he had to keep his room. There the young Princes paid him a futile
visit: he was still too sick for any serious talk. And after the arrival
of Villena, who came as soon as he learned what was going on,
everything fell apart. How could he have been so foolish? he up-
braided Henry. Some repair of the damage wrought by this stupid
show of favor—of weakness—must be effected at once. With such
of the nobles as he yet was able to influence, he laid plans to seize
and imprison the young guests. Palencia (or so he said) heard a
discussion of the project while he "happened"²³ to be hiding in a
closet and warned the intended victims. Fernando galloped off immediately, in a rage. Isabel's counselors urged her to go with him.
But in her customary "great stamina of spirit,"²⁴ she chose to stay:
she was determined not to leave Segovia, no matter what the dangers, until she could ride out of it Queen of Castile. At that, she
developed a fever toward the last of February. And if even her
vigorous young system could little withstand the strain and mounting intrigues, the battered monarch's less. He was "simply not up
to it,"²⁵ he told Cabrera. In the middle of a dark March night, and

as we have so often seen him do before, he called for a horse—and fled.

Nobody knows where he went; for over a month he vanishes. When he finally does emerge, what brought him out was, characteristically, a mission of peace: the Count of Benavente had captured Carrión de los Condes, the Mendozas—since the bones of their ancestors there lay enshrined—assembled their kin and marched north into the greening Maytime wheatlands to wrest it back, and we see him briefly, wan and still unsteady, on the plain before Becerril between the confronted feudal hosts, disbursing more than seven millions (money—the only way he had ever found of pleasing) to avert a clash. But the effort clearly cost him a severe relapse, for when the curtains part once more some six weeks later—on June 24, San Juan—to provide us with another fleeting picture, it reveals him again most wretchedly reduced, is ominous to a degree. As he was riding in that afternoon from El Pardo to Madrid a violent attack of pain, accompanied by nausea, overtook him. He could not go on, could not keep his saddle. Santa María del Paso, however, stood near—the great Gothic monastery which he had built on the spot where Beltrán de la Cueva, in what must by then have seemed like another world, seemed centuries past, had put up his canvas castle and plucked his golden "J" and set the fire which consumed the realm. He dismounted and tottered in. Long hours he remained there *"mal de sus gómitos,"*[26] wracked by uncontrollable vomits. Only late at night could he get slowly along to Madrid. His servants supported him into the Alcázar. Although he was informed that Villena had been waiting since afternoon to see him, he could not, would not, face anyone at all. He went up by a back way to his bedroom. Tomorrow, he sent down word to the Marqués.

Villena himself, in this Walpurgis Night of horror and destruction, still ailed: he ran a stubborn temperature, all of his teeth— except one—had fallen out. But that single fang gleamed as hungrily as always, and his errand while he waited impatiently for Henry the evening of San Juan is not difficult to guess. He wanted Trujillo, had wanted it for some time. Now that the Master of Alcántara was dead, it had proved easy enough to work out a bargain with Alvaro de Stúñiga, the new Duke of Arévalo: exchange of Stúñiga's own nebulous claim upon the city for a nomination of his young son as the Order's head. Yet to have Stúñiga yield his rights to Trujillo and to persuade its *alcaide*—Gracián de Sesé—to deliver it were very different things. Royal letters were useless; Gracián had torn them up before. Henry's actual presence was needed, and to that end, as June concluded, the Master went to work. Henry wearily protested: Extremadura, in midsummer? And feeling the way he did? But Villena had never been noted for his consideration of others; he pressed relentlessly on. And finally he had, as usual, his way: to avoid further friction and unpleasantness, Henry gave in. Late in July of 1474 the two of them departed.

They must have made a strange sight as they rode off toward the western horizons—the toothless Marqués and the specter of a sovereign. For Henry now looked little more than that: his flesh was melting away, his big bones stuck out, his eyes, twitching and squinting from almost constant pain, bulged larger than ever above his sunken cheeks. And once they were there everything proved even more trying, more exhausting, than he had dreaded. The land around Trujillo was *malsana*, infected by plague. A pall of dust hung over it. In the immense and whited silence the bronze sun throbbed, the stunted cork trees writhed. Their business made no progress: in spite of Henry's advent, Gracián was full of what he regarded as *"legítimas excusaciones"*[27] for not giving in. Well, bribery then, said Villena. They withdrew to Santa Cruz, a cheerless village eight miles off, with no shade or water, to be about it. The *alcaide* did begin to bend a little, at that. But his terms were difficult, more than Villena cared to grant. The negotiations dragged on. It grew hotter and hotter. Henry was stricken with a fresh attack of dysentery. Finally he could stand it no longer; he had to leave the awful place. He got up and dressed for the long bleak journey back to Madrid (Segovia, with Isabel so firmly fixed there, in a way seemed no longer really his). He went in and found Villena and told him. Very well, replied the Marqués. Let him leave, if he wanted; goodbye. For his own part, he intended to see the matter through, to stay.

He stayed to his death. At the end of September, when he and Gracián had almost reached an understanding (Sanfelices de los Gallegos for Trujillo), he came down with a severe sore throat. None of the doctors' ministrations had any effect. An abcess appeared and ripened; rapidly he went from bad to worse. Soon he was unable to eat, could scarcely swallow. His fever soared. Four times they cut in through his neck and lanced the abcess; four times it returned. And finally it grew so large and hard—"solid as stone"[28] —that they could operate no more. On October 3, the day set for Gracián's arrival and a definite decision, he was sinking fast: his fever beyond control, his breath stertorous, an eye gone blind. Yet nothing could dissuade him from the conference. He had his attendants lift him, dress him, carry him into the *sala* and tie him, close to a corpse already, in a chair. He ordered the curtains drawn—that the room might be *"escura,"*[29] that Gracián might not discern his desperate condition and perhaps pull back: his ultimate deceit. It worked. In darkness, in mortal agony, he drove the bargain home: when Gracián departed, he left him Trujillo's keys. But they profited him little; he died the following day. His servants stripped him of his jewelry, even of his clothes. They rifled his chests and confiscated his cash. Then, fearful themselves of discovery, they rolled him up in a dirty carpet and stuffed him into a wine cask— "where he stank," in the lapidary words of Gutierre de Cárdenas, "as much as when he was alive."[30]

Villena's death brought universal joy. The reader, too, may experience a certain relief: try as one will (although perhaps no very strenuous effort has here been made), not a single redeeming trait can be found in this distasteful man. Yet the event does cause us to tarry for some wry and valedictory thoughts. It is curious, and ironic, that a person who came in every way so short of Luna should have worked, by his passing, a similar effect: in sum, that again the sovereign only briefly outlived the favorite. It is more than ironic that Henry, no sooner freed, pitched headlong from one bondage into another—an "insensate"[31] passion for a scheming, empty, beautiful young man. And it is most ironic of all, it edges the grotesque, is an unlucky lifetime's parting jape, that the object of this last infatuation should have been Diego López Pacheco, Villena's son.

Yet so the case fell out. Diego—unstable at best—was not well that October; apparently no one except Henry chose to bear him the word from Santa Cruz. He went immediately. Diego was in bed; Henry sat down beside him. He attempted to cushion the announcement as best he could. Soon, however, as he stayed on, his tongue began to stammer, his language to take a dangerous, a revelatory, turn. It "sweetened";[32] it slipped from "consolation"[33] into "flattery."³⁴ Nobody so attractive should ever feel lost or lonely. Did he need affection? Here he had it—a second father: perhaps still more. And finally, sitting there on the bedside of a naked youth "in flower,"³⁵ it proved too much for him. All of a sudden his heart went up in a wild and helpless blaze.

It is dreadful to witness—to watch him writhe, so near his end, in the grip of yet another unworthy and ruinous attachment. It was dreadful, if in a different way, for everybody else. Villena's boy: had he lost his mind? And it very nearly looks so. He gave no heed to the spreading gossip, to the havoc wrought by such emotions on his disintegrating frame, to the fact that Diego, truly his father's son, was set to dangle and exploit him; his lifelong thirst for love, and now in something on the verge of panic, now before it was for ever too late, cried out to be appeased. He groveled; he sought the flame. Every morning, at dawn, he hurried over, taking his mandolin. Diego continued to receive him abed. He sat beside him all day. He played and sang and stopped to hold his side and sang again, his clog of inarticulate yearnings unloosed at last in the ancient aubades and villanelles. Nor were the offerings, as Diego no doubt made sure, exclusively vocal: Henry's illimitable generosity is on display, if in a rather tawdry showcase, for a final time. What did he want? He would give him anything he could. Madrid? Yes, of course; it was his. Lieutenancy of the Alcázar? By all means. But an inch, an ell: soon the stakes were going higher, very high. Santiago? Santiago itself? Ah, there might be trouble with that.

Trouble to spare: hardly was Villena's corpse discovered and hauled from its wine cask when a bitter fight for the vacant mastership had broken out. Everyone wanted it—Medina Sidonia, Alba, Benavente, the Count of Paredes, Alonso de Cárdenas; even Beltrán de la Cueva put in his splintered oar. These were powerful men, said Henry, men perilous to cross. Diego sulked. Well, then, of course he would see what he could do. At once he ran into adamantine opposition: outrageous, unthinkable—somebody so young and inexperienced for so exalted a post. But, "all his avenues of reason blocked by ardor,"³⁶ he plunged on. He wrote, in vain, for a direct appointment from the Pope. He even stooped to a lie—Henry, whose word had always been more precious to him than emeralds: in Santa Cruz, he asserted, Villena had renounced the mastership in Diego's favor. That nobody believed. And then he had what impressed him as a fine idea. (Who lacked for counsel? He could make his own decisions now.) One of the Order's electors—Gabriel Manrique, Count of Osorno—seemed undetermined about where to throw his weight. Let Diego seek his support. Osorno, had either of them stopped to notice, was almost too ready for a meeting. He asked Diego to dinner, in an isolated hamlet, Vacialmadrid, twelve miles from town. An odd place, true, but no matter; Henry sent Diego off. The real oddity awaited. Osorno, "in secret,"[37] was planning to enter the race for the mastership himself—and to get at least one competitor out of his path. While they ate, a band of his henchmen rushed in. They seized Diego and bound him. They flung him on a horse. Posthaste they all rode away with him to Osorno's castle of Fuentidueña and locked him up.

Henry went almost crazy. A blunder, another of his blunders— and, this time, look what it had cost. How had he ever thought himself equipped for large affairs? He strode about in a torment of guilt, of grief, of shame. So great was his agitation, his distraction, that he twice dictated the same note of jumbled warning for the Countess of Medellín, Diego's aunt. But we need no documents to bear witness to his state of near hysteria: seldom though contemporaries agree on anything to do with Henry, in their descriptions of that disastrous afternoon the chroniclers, for once, are in accord. He was *"fuera de sí"*[38]—beside himself. He beat his breast and emitted frantic "lamentations."[39] He "refused all comfort";[40] in his anguish *"se le dobló su mal"*[41]—his illness struck him with new force. And finally he broke completely down. He sent everybody out. He dropped in a chair and covered his face with his hands and "bitterly wept."[42] He could not stop. On and on he sat, past dusk and into the night, still uncontrollably sobbing.

Whence sprang those terrible tears in the dark room of the Alcázar? From the occasion only? They seem too deep, too long, for that. Perhaps they flowed for the columned and dotted tally of his other failures and mistakes, his fifty years of hopes and good intentions gone amiss. Or they may have been not for himself at all (he was ever humble) but from a yet profounder source, some vast and welling sorrow—*sunt lacrimae rerum*—for the woe at the world's breast, for all the misery seen or sensed around him which his own had made him like a harp to catch and, catching, vibrate. We can never know; he shed them in solitude, his servants only heard. And perhaps, in the end, nothing much matters but their outcome. For when they were fully spent, all poured and uttered, a wondrous thing, a thing strange and close to miraculous, had taken place: they had cleansed him, scoured him, healed him—in spirit—at last. The frenzy was gone. The strain was over. His foolish passion for Diego, swept down in the devouring flood, had disappeared. He came himself again from the shadowed chamber: mute, sober—and now composed against his fate. He would seek no more, engage no more, not even touch: the final resignation. One task, of course, was still to be accomplished. He must free Diego; so honor, since he had caused the damage, required. But that would put the term to it, to everything. Then he could die.

His physicians were horrified at his plan of the long journey to Fuentidueña. But he brushed their objections aside. He steeled himself to plead for help—the Mendozas, Carrillo, the new Count of Haro (inheritor, also, of the Constable's baton). Together they traveled to Osorno's somber old castle and encamped before it. Henry left the sorry traffic—the bargains and bribing—to his companions. He seems to have spent most of his time cantering about, but very slowly now, in the environs. And if he needed anything to calm him, to prepare him, further, it was those rides: during the first fortnight of November, after the mournful oboes of the autumn wind give over and before the snow, there comes in the fields around Fuentidueña a brooding hush, tinged with sad semitones of mauve and silver, which singularly draws the heart to peace. He rode, he watched and waited. He waited, constantly weaker in the advancing cold and open elements, almost twenty days. And then, once he saw the business reaching an end and Diego's liberation assured, he waited no longer. The others could finish; his conscience was discharged. He put on his frayed *bonete* and pulled it far down on his brow and painfully mounted and started back, alone, to Madrid, toward what can only have been for him—and certainly he knew it, and as certainly welcomed it—a meaningless obliteration, an eternal night.

He rode, collapsing, though the Latina gate. He went to his bedroom, he shut the door. And now full winter settled in. The Manzanares froze. Owls huddled under the eaves; in the *caballerizas reales* the horses shivered and stamped. Snow finally fell. It fell on the Alcázar, on the Tower of the Lujanes. It fell on the ancient Convent of San Francisco—where Juana herself was to die some six months later, willing to Pedro her last pitiful possessions and begging, vain to the end, that she not be buried in the ground lest worms should gnaw her beauty. It whitened the *plaza mayor*, and few footsteps broke the powdery expanse: the town was fast emptying, the courtiers were streaming up through the high pass of La Tablada to Isabel. Probably he would not have received them, had they stayed. In his silent room he lay and gazed from the window and let the memories, the pictures, drift over him—eliding, gliding, tossing and intermingling, yet surely, surely, at last all steadying and leveling out to one and taking wing as strong and straight as a bird: Segovia, Segovia, Segovia. To sleep beneath that tranquil, star-strewn dome. To waken early, without suffering, and hear the bells of San Esteban, San Facundo, San Martín. To ride the yellow plains in the blue air, to walk and dream along the sedged, the murmurous, Eresma. It was just beyond the mountains, just on the other side. And they seemed so close, in the pure Castilian air. But far enough, too far. He would never cross them again.

Go there today; look off northwest to the Guadarramas from the loggia of the Royal Palace—it stands on the site of the medieval Alcázar—and you will see the very view that filled his dying eyes. For now he indeed was dying. On Friday, December 9, he had a fearful hemorrhage; when it finally stopped, it left him prostrate and rent. And after that the pain gave him no more time for memories; he could only lie there and breast its ever-mounting waves. He met them, bore them, in tight-lipped fortitude: half Moslem he undoubtedly was, half man perhaps, but with the rare exceptions when we have seen him driven outside the limits of human endurance he was all patience and stoicism, from first to last. Thus he lay through Saturday, and into Sunday—pallid, motionless, limp. But on Sunday afternoon he roused and stirred; he tried to lift himself. What did he want? they asked him. To see his animals at El Pardo, he said: that would "strengthen"[43] him, possibly cure him. So, anyway, he told them. One is free to have one's thoughts, to suspect that his real desire was to stretch out on the earth and die among those poor dumb creatures who had always been his kindest and truest friends. Even that small comfort, however, was not granted him. He did struggle up, did manage to dress and get down to the courtyard and mount. With a handful of attendants he rode away and along the river, bent low and clinging to his horse's neck. But when he was nearly there, already in sight of the lodge, the pain became intolerable; it struck through his side like a flaming sword. He cried one great despairing cry and toppled from the saddle.

They supported him back, between them. They put him on his narrow bed without undressing him, without bothering to pull off his Moorish boots (he wears them still, in Guadalupe). Someone threw a "wretched tunic"[44] across him. Who was it? Who was any-body? Faces, vaguely familiar, swam and dissolved around him; a few of the nobles, lured by the report of his fatal hemorrhage, had journeyed in to pick the bones. They were leaning down, shaking blurry fingers at him, demanding, almost threatening. Did he intend to make no testament? What of the falling crown? Was the Queen's daughter his? Was she really his—or whose? He had to declare, they insisted. But he did not, would not; the answer to that riddle—if he knew it—he took with him to the grave. The attending priest, Fray Juan de Mazuelo, fared just as ill. In the thickening haze he also was bowing over, admonishing, offering a crucifix. Repent, repent, he urged. Confess; come to the Sacrament. But he saw his exhortations failing of effect. He faltered, he stopped. And to him, as to the barons, Henry "made no reply."[45]

"*Ninguna cosa respondió*"! It has the true Henrician ring; it could be his epitaph. Nor did he ever speak again. He turned his head away. The nobles shrugged and departed: they would get nothing further there. Fray Juan dismantled his portable altar and soon followed. Servants went down and barred the palace gates. It was clearing: no wind, and the air gone boreal, sharp as knives. But Henry by then was beyond all wind or weather. He lay on his back, immobile, with glazing eyes. They waited. Nine o'clock arrived and passed, ten and eleven. The cold grew so intense that his laboring breath came out in puffs of smoke. Midnight sounded from the tower. As its distant strikes subsided, they heard the first of the rattle in his throat. All at once his arms began to flail. He started to lash about, wildly and ever wilder. Delirium set in; his mouth convulsed and foamed; his eyeballs rolled. It lasted half an hour. Then, suddenly he sank back—and so remained. Shortly after one there was no more breath to see.[46]

Even his grooms and squires, at the end, apparently deserted: Palencia tells us that "*gentes alquiladas*,"[47] paid help brought in, performed the final tasks. Their work was brief—so wasted was his body that it needed no embalming. They straightened the twisted limbs; they carried him downstairs. They set up a trestle in the *sala* and placed him, just as he was, on some bare "old boards."[48] They lighted candles around him. Then they, like all others, were off.

Let us, at least, stay with him a little longer; let us keep his vigil through the frosty night. Yet with the dawn, with the filtering pale light between the shutters, it is time for us as well—since now there is truly nothing more that can be done in his behalf—to rise, to leave him. But gently, gently again, as we first met him, when he was only a child. And even as one goes out, even with hand on door, it might be well to pause and turn and cast upon him—waxen in guttered wax, the bony arms beneath the raveled tunic folded, the ugly face at rest—a final, meditative look. For more than a tired and hapless man had died that winter night. Spain's Middle Ages themselves lay dead on those bare boards. An era, a world, were over: the same chill dawn was coming in Segovia, and as young Isabel rose to greet it, as she drew her martened robe around her and leaned from her casement and watched the tall square towers grow gray, grow faintly pink, then as at last the sun burst forth above the snowy mountains and scattered gold and diamonds across the wakening city at her feet, a new day, too, was breaking for the kingdom, a day which was triumphantly to free it from the rue and fraction we have sought to chronicle and bring it on—healed, rectified and welded— to might, to majesty, to sway of half the globe, to unimaginable splendor.

But that is another story.

❋ Notes

1. THE UNCLES, pp. 3–9

1. A niece of Henry II.
2. Any attempt to evaluate the money of a bygone age in current terms is foredoomed to abysmal failure. In a very general way, it can be said that the fifteenth-century ducat or *dobla* was worth roughly two dollars, the florin one, and the *maravedí* perhaps half a cent. (All references in the text to "millions" are of *maravedís*.)

2. SCENES FROM CHILDHOOD, pp. 10–19

1. Alonso de Palencia, *Crónica de Enrique IV* (tr. Paz y Meliá), 4 v., Madrid 1904–1908; I, p. 13. Referred to hereafter as "Palencia."
2. *Ibid.*, p. 147.
3. [Fernán Pérez de Guzmán], "Crónica del Rey Don Juan II," in *Biblioteca de Autores Españoles*, Madrid 1953, v. 68, pp. 273–695; p. 519. Referred to hereafter as "*Crónica Juan II.*"
4. *Ibid.*, p. 525.
5. *Ibid.*, p. 529.
6. *Cf.* Luis Suárez Fernández, *Nobleza y Monarquía*, Valladolid 1959; p. 106: "*rentas minúsculas.*"
7. *Crónica Juan II*, p. 535.
8. "*Acromegalia.*" Gregorio Marañón, *Ensayo Biológico sobre Enrique IV de Castilla y su tiempo*, 2nd. ed., Buenos Aires 1953; p. 72.
9. Diego Enríquez del Castillo, "Crónica del Rey don Enrique el Cuarto," in *Biblioteca de Autores Españoles*, Madrid 1953, v. 70, pp. 97–222; p. 101. Referred to hereafter as "Castillo." "Enríquez" would be proper. But with so many others of that name in the volume, I have sought to avoid confusion.
10. Padre Juan de Mariana, "Historia de España," in *Biblioteca de Autores Españoles*, Madrid 1854, v. 30–31; XXXI, p. 164.
11. Palencia, I, p. 94.
12. *Ibid.*, p. 276.
13. [Pedro de Escavias], *Hechos del Condestable Don Miguel Lucas de Iranzo* (ed. Carriazo), Madrid 1940; p. 48. Referred to hereafter as "*Hechos del Condestable.*"

3. A Wedding in Valladolid, pp. 20–28

1. *Crónica Juan II*, p. 565.
2. *Ibid.*
3. *Ibid.*, p. 566.
4. *Ibid.*
5. *Ibid.*
6. *Ibid.*, p. 567.
7. [Gonzalo Chacón], *Crónica de Don Alvaro de Luna* (ed. Carriazo), Madrid 1949; p. 269. Referred to hereafter as "*Crónica Luna.*"
8. Appendix to Enríquez del Castillo (ed. Sancha, Madrid 1787), p. 129.
9. *Crónica Juan II*, p. 567.
10. *Ibid.*
11. Castillo, p. 101.
12. *Crónica Juan II*, p. 567; Palencia, I, p. 8.

4. The King Is Captive, pp. 29–39

1. *Crónica Juan II*, p. 575.
2. *Ibid.*, p. 578.
3. *Ibid.*, p. 580.
4. *Crónica Luna*, p. 153.
5. *Crónica Juan II*, p. 563.
6. *Ibid.*, pp. 569, 574.
7. *Ibid.*, p. 617.
8. *Ibid.*
9. *Ibid.*
10. *Ibid.*, p. 623.

5. The Plains of Olmedo, pp. 40–53

1. *Crónica Juan II*, p. 625.
2. *Crónica Luna*, p. 158.
3. Palencia, I, p. 57.
4. Pedro Carrillo de Huete, *Crónica del Halconero de Juan II* (ed. Carriazo), Madrid 1946; p. 463.
5. *Crónica Luna*, p. 166.
6. *Ibid.*
7. *Ibid.*, p. 163.
8. The Julian calendar was still in effect. Furthermore, Spanish time has been set forward by one hour since the fifteenth century. Thus 5:30 on May 19, 1445, corresponds in modern reckoning to 6:30 on May 30.

9. J. Paz, "Versión oficial de la batalla de Olmedo," in *Homenaje ofrecido a Ramón Menéndez Pidal*, Madrid 1925, I, pp. 839–842; p. 841.
10. *Crónica Luna*, p. 170.
11. *Ibid.*
12. *Ibid.*, p. 171.
13. *Ibid.*
14. Carrillo de Huete, *op. cit.*, pp. 464–465.
15. *Crónica Juan II*, p. 629.
16. Palencia, I, p. 58.
17. Paz, *loc. cit.*
18. *Crónica Luna*, p. 174.
19. Palencia, I, p. 60.
20. *Ibid.*
21. Mosén Diego de Valera, "Capítulo CXXIV de la 'Crónica abreviada de España,'" in *Memorial de Diversas Hazañas* (ed. Carriazo), Madrid 1941, pp. [299]–337; p. 316.
22. *Crónica Luna*, p. 173.
23. Palencia, I, p. 60.

6. Two Marriages, pp. 54–63

1. Diego de Colmenares, *Historia de la Insigne Ciudad de Segovia*, Madrid 1640; p. 364.
2. Castillo, p. 101.
3. *Crónica Juan II*, p. 664.
4. *Cf.* Luis Fernández de Retana, *Isabel la Católica*, Madrid 1947; p. 29.
5. Valera, "Crónica abreviada," *op. cit.*, p. 314.
6. *Crónica Luna*, p. 269.
7. *Ibid.*, p. 271.
8. Palencia, I, p. 76.
9. *Crónica Luna*, p. 296.
10. *Ibid.*, p. 351.
11. *Ibid.*, p. 395.
12. *Ibid.*, pp. 383–384.

7. A Divorce, pp. 64–70

1. "Colección Diplomática de la Crónica de Enrique IV," in *Memorias de don Enrique IV de Castilla*, v. 2, Madrid 1835–1913; p. 62. Referred to hereafter as *"Colección Diplomática."*
2. *Et seq.* to "good, chaste, honorable ecclesiastical person," *ibid.*, pp. 62–64.
3. Marañón, *op. cit.*, p. 75.

4. Jerónimo Münzer, *Viaje por España y Portugal, 1494–1495* (tr. López Toro), Madrid 1951; p. 108.
5. Colmenares, *op. cit.*, p. 378.
6. *Ibid.*
7. Palencia, I, p. 168.
8. *Documentos Referentes a las relaciones con Portugal durante el reinado de los Reyes Católicos* (ed. De la Torre and Suárez Fernández), v. 1, Valladolid 1958; p. 24.
9. *Colección Diplomática*, p. 130.
10. *Ibid.*
11. *Ibid.*
12. *Crónica Luna*, p. 434.
13. *Ibid.*
14. Palencia, I, p. 136.
15. *Crónica Juan II*, p. 692.

8. SOUTHERN GAMES, pp. 73–83

1. Mosén Diego de Valera, *Memorial de Diversas Hazañas* (ed. Carriazo), Madrid 1941; p. 6. Referred to hereafter as "Valera." ("Mosén" was simply a term of address, somewhat on the order of "Esquire.")
2. Castillo, pp. 103–104.
3. *Ibid.*, p. 103.
4. *Ibid.*, p. 105.
5. *Ibid.*
6. *Ibid.*, p. 101.
7. Palencia, I, p. 61.
8. An unusual case. Almost always the chief obstacle to determining the size of medieval Spanish armies is the flexible definition of the "lance" —a military unit which could range from five (in the northern regions under French influence) to the single mounted knight (in parts of Andalucía).
9. Palencia, I, p. 182.
10. Castillo, p. 107.
11. *Ibid.*, p. 106.
12. Luis Suárez Fernández, "Los Trastámaras de Castilla y Aragón en el Siglo XV (1407–74)," in *Historia de España* (ed. Menéndez Pidal), Madrid 1964, v. 15, pp. 1–318; p. 225.
13. Castillo, pp. 104–105.
14. Palencia, I, p. 190.
15. *The Travels of Leo of Rozmital* (tr. and ed. Malcolm Letts), Cambridge 1957; p. 90.
16. Palencia, I, p. 86.

17. *Ibid.*, p. 176.
18. *The Travels of Leo of Rozmital, loc. cit.*
19. "Des bömischen Herrn Leo's von Rozmital Ritter-, Hof-und Pilger-Reise," in *Bibliothek des Literarischen Vereins im Stuttgart,* Stuttgart 1844, v. 7; p. 172.
20. Juan Torres Fontes, *Estudio sobre la "Crónica de Enrique IV" del Dr. Galíndez de Carvajal,* Murcia 1946; p. 96. Referred to hereafter as "Galíndez." This important volume prints, for the first time, the entire chronicle of Galíndez—a Councilor of Isabel the Catholic who attempted a synthesis of Castillo and the *Crónica Castellana* (a contemporary version of Palencia), buttressed by such subsequent data as he had been able to find.
21. *Ibid.*, p. 99.
22. Valera, p. 27.
23. Castillo, p. 107.
24. Palencia, I, p. 190.
25. *Ibid.*, p. 191.
26. *Ibid.*

9. NEW FACES, pp. 84–98

1. Palencia, I, p. 193.
2. Marañón, *op. cit.*, pp. 44–45.
3. Palencia, I, p. 14.
4. Valera, p. 19; also Galíndez, p. 103.
5. Palencia, I, p. 197.
6. Castillo, p. 112.
7. Palencia, I, p. 194.
8. Castillo, p. 112.
9. Galíndez, p. 144.
10. *Ibid.*
11. *Ibid.*
12. Marañón, *op. cit.*, pp. 89–90.
13. Palencia, I, p. 221.
14. Castillo, p. 112.
15. Galíndez, p. 144.
16. *Ibid.*
17. *Ibid.*
18. Palencia, I, p. 227.
19. Castillo, p. 109.
20. Palencia, I, p. 208.
21. *Ibid.*, p. 201.
22. *Ibid.*

23. Galíndez, p. 122.
24. Palencia, I, p. 237.
25. Galíndez, p. 140.
26. Palencia, I, p. 273.
27. Castillo, p. 109.
28. Valera, p. 41.
29. *Ibid.*
30. *Ibid.*, p. 157.
31. *Et seq.* to *"disciplina militar,"* ibid., pp. 43, 61–62.
32. Palencia, I, p. 246.
33. *Ibid.*
34. The letter is most readily accessible in Tarsicio de Azcona, *Isabel la Católica*, Madrid (Biblioteca de Autores Cristianos) 1964; p. 35.
35. Valera, p. 42.
36. *Ibid.*

10. FIRST FAREWELL, pp. 99–109

1. Valera, p. 48.
2. Palencia, II, p. 217.
3. *Hechos del Condestable*, p. 22.
4. *Ibid.*, p. 24.
5. *Ibid.*
6. *Ibid.*
7. *Ibid.*, p. 26.
8. *Ibid.*, p. 28.
9. *Ibid.*
10. *Ibid.*, p. 29.
11. *Ibid.*
12. *Ibid.*, p. 32.
13. *Ibid.*

11. DON BELTRÁN, pp. 110–117

1. Palencia, II, p. 430.
2. Galíndez, p. 210.
3. Palencia, I, p. 298.
4. Castillo, p. 113.
5. *Ibid.*
6. *Ibid.*
7. Münzer, *op. cit.*, p. 108.
8. *Colección Diplomática* (but erroneously given as of 1464), p. 325. Correctly dated and in its entirety, the document is printed in Antonio Paz y Meliá, *El Cronista Alonso de Palencia*, Madrid 1914; pp. 13–19.

9. *Colección Diplomática*, p. 323.
10. *Ibid.*
11. *Ibid.*
12. Valera, p. 62.
13. *Ibid.*
14. Palencia, I, p. 389.
15. *Ibid.*
16. *Ibid.*

12. UNCERTAIN FRUIT, pp. 118–126

1. Fernando del Pulgar, *Crónica de los Reyes Católicos* (ed. Carriazo), 2 v., Madrid 1943; I, p. 5. Referred to hereafter as "Pulgar."
2. Castillo, p. 119.
3. *Ibid.*, p. 120.
4. Palencia, I, p. 354.
5. Castillo, p. 120.
6. *Ibid.*
7. *Ibid.*
8. *Ibid.*, p. 121.
9. Pulgar, I, p. 6.
10. Valera, p. 70.
11. Castillo, p. 122.
12. *Ibid.*

13. VILLENA DEFECTS, pp. 127–141

1. Valera, p. 67.
2. *Ibid.*, p. 68.
3. *Ibid.*
4. *Et seq.* to "imperial cloak," Castillo, p. 123.
5. *Ibid.*, p. 126.
6. *Ibid.*, p. 124.
7. *Ibid.*, p. 127.
8. Palencia, I, p. 371.
9. "Coplas del Provincial," in *Révue Hispanique*, Paris, V (1898), pp. 255–266; stanza 37.
10. Valera, p. 84.
11. Colmenares, *op. cit.*, p. 374.
12. Philippe de Commynes, *Mémoires* (ed. Calmette), 3 v., Paris 1924–1925; I, p. 138.
13. *Crónica Incompleta de los Reyes Católicos, 1469–1476* (ed. Puyol), Madrid 1934; pp. 50–51.
14. Palencia, I, p. 374.

15. Commynes, *op. cit.*, I, p. 136.
16. *Colección Diplomática*, p. 280.
17. *The History of Comines* (tr. Thomas Danett, 1596), 2 v., London 1897; I, p. 133.
18. Palencia, I, p. 375.
19. Castillo, p. 129.
20. *Ibid.*, p. 133.
21. *Ibid.*

14. THE LOCKS OF THE STORM, pp. 142–161

1. Colmenares, *op. cit.*, p. 374.
2. The remark of Juana's physician about "wagering his head" that if the King were in Aranda she would soon enough be pregnant again, purveyed in a letter to Henry come to light not long ago and flourished about so triumphantly as evidence of his virility, seems to me to prove nothing at all—except the common tendency of courtiers to flatter. (First printed in Fritz Baer, *Die Juden im Christlichen Spanien*, Berlin 1936, p. 322, but perhaps more easily consulted in Azcona, *op. cit.*, p. 41.)
3. Castillo, p. 121.
4. *Hechos del Condestable*, p. 151.
5. Castillo, p. 131.
6. Palencia, I, p. 387.
7. *Hechos del Condestable*, p. 192.
8. *Ibid.*
9. *Ibid.*
10. *Ibid.*, p. 195.
11. Castillo, p. 101.
12. Palencia, I, p. 231.
13. *Ibid.*, p. 394.
14. Castillo, p. 132.
15. *Hechos del Condestable*, p. 189.
16. *Ibid.*, p. 199.
17. Castillo, p. 133.
18. Palencia, I, p. 417.
19. Castillo, p. 133.
20. *Ibid.*
21. *Ibid.*, p. 134.
22. *Ibid.*
23. *Colección Diplomática*, p. 496.
24. Galíndez, p. 212.
25. Colmenares, *op. cit.*, p. 375.

26. *Ibid.*
27. *Ibid.*
28. Castillo, p. 135.
29. *Ibid.*
30. *Ibid.*
31. *Ibid.*
32. *Ibid.*
33. *Ibid.*
34. Suárez, *Nobleza y Monarquía, op. cit.,* p. 151.
35. Castillo, p. 137.
36. Galíndez, p. 220.
37. *Et seq.* to "all Christian princes," *Colección Diplomática,* pp. 328–333.
38. Castillo, p. 138.
39. *Ibid.,* p. 139.
40. *Ibid.*
41. *Ibid.,* p. 140.
42. *Colección Diplomática,* p. 326.
43. Galíndez, p. 225.
44. *Ibid.*
45. *Ibid.,* p. 224.

15. A PLATFORM AT AVILA, pp. 162–173

1. Archivo General de Navarra, *cajón* 160, n. 39.
2. Galíndez, p. 230.
3. Castillo, p. 141.
4. *Ibid.,* p. 140.
5. Galíndez, p. 233.
6. Castillo, p. 143.
7. *Ibid.,* pp. 143–144.
8. Palencia, I, p. 457.
9. Galíndez, p. 236.
10. My statement in *The Castles and the Crown* that Carrillo said Mass was entirely mistaken, and based on faulty sources.
11. Valera, p. 98.
12. *Ibid.,* p. 99.
13. Galíndez, p. 239.

16. THE DOUBLE CROWN, pp. 177–192

1. Castillo, p. 145.
2. *Ibid.*
3. Palencia, I, p. 462.

4. Valera, p. 106.
5. *Ibid.*, p. 102.
6. Castillo, p. 145.
7. *Et seq.* to "dilation," Valera, p. 104.
8. *Ibid.*, p. 105.
9. Galíndez, p. 248.
10. Palencia, I, p. 491.
11. Castillo, p. 150.
12. *Ibid.*
13. *Ibid.*, p. 151.
14. *Ibid.*
15. Palencia, I, p. 478.
16. *Ibid.*, p. 538.
17. *Ibid.*, p. 539; Galíndez, p. 267.
18. Valera, p. 116.
19. Castillo, p. 151.
20. Galíndez, p. 260.
21. *Cf.*, for example, Suárez, *Nobleza y Monarquía, op. cit.*, p. 156.
22. Valera, p. 118.
23. "Coplas sobre el mal gobierno de Toledo."
24. *Cf.* J. Lucas-Dubreton, *El Rey Huraño (Enrique IV de Castilla y su época),* 2nd. ed., Madrid 1941; p. 164.
25. So reads the manuscript itself, in Munich's Bayerische Staatsbibliothek (Codex Monacensis, Germ. 1279, fol. 153v.), for this wildly misquoted and mistranslated passage.
26. Castillo, p. 158.
27. *Ibid.*
28. *Ibid.*

17. OLMEDO AGAIN, pp. 193–211

1. Joseph L. A. Calmette, *Louis XI, Jean II y la révolution catalane (1461–1473),* Toulouse 1903; p. 541.
2. *Cf.* Jaime Vicens Vives, *Historia Crítica de la Vida y Reinado de Fernando II de Aragón,* Zaragoza 1962; p. 233.
3. *Cf.* Suárez, "Los Trastámaras de Castilla y Aragón en el Siglo XV (1407–74)," *op. cit.*, p. 277.
4. Castillo, p. 162.
5. *Ibid.*, p. 166.
6. Galíndez, p. 297.
7. *Ibid.*, p. 298; according to Palencia (II, p. 85), "those who enjoyed the sad privilege of his intimacy."
8. Castillo, p. 163.

9. *Ibid.*
10. Palencia, II, p. 62; Valera, p. 128; Galíndez, p. 299. The chroniclers' accounts of the battle are contradictory not only to each other but even in themselves (Castillo has Pedro de Velasco in two places at the same time), and Galíndez's later effort to sort them out merely compounded the confusion. No one has attempted a study of the engagement for almost five centuries. My own is entirely open to correction in the light of any possible discoveries.
11. Palencia, II, p. 66.
12. *Ibid.*
13. *Ibid.*, p. 67.
14. Galíndez, p. 302.
15. Palencia, II, p. 70.
16. Castillo, p. 167.
17. *Ibid.*, p. 166.
18. *Ibid.*, p. 167.
19. *Ibid.*
20. Registra Vaticana 519, fol. 252v.

18 . A SUPPER OF TROUT, pp. 212–226

1. Palencia, II, p. 91.
2. Galíndez, p. 309.
3. *Ibid.*, p. 304.
4. Castillo, p. 169.
5. Palencia, II, p. 83.
6. Castillo, p. 169.
7. *Ibid.*
8. *Ibid.*
9. Palencia, II, p. 101.
10. *Ibid.*
11. *Ibid.*
12. *Et seq.* to "eloquence," Valera, p. 133.
13. Palencia, II, p. 102.
14. *Ibid.*, p. 103.
15. *Ibid.*
16. *Ibid.*, p. 108.
17. *Ibid.*
18. *Ibid.*
19. Galíndez, p. 313.
20. Palencia, II, p. 93.
21. Castillo, p. 165.
22. *Ibid.*

23. Colmenares, *op. cit.*, p. 397.
24. *Et seq.* to "glories," Azcona, *op. cit.*, p. 114.
25. Castillo, p. 170.
26. *Ibid.*, p. 169.
27. *Ibid.*, p. 195.
28. Galíndez, p. 315.
29. Castillo, p. 170.
30. *Et seq.* to "estate and honor," *Hechos del Condestable*, pp. 367–368.
31. *Ibid.*, p. 369.
32. *Ibid.*, p. 368.
33. *Ibid.*, p. 371.
34. Palencia, II, p. 151.
35. Galíndez, p. 316.
36. Castillo, p. 172.
37. *Ibid.*, p. 178.
38. Galíndez, p. 330.
39. Valera, p. 137.
40. Galíndez, p. 331.
41. Valera, p. 137.
42. *Ibid.*, p. 139.

19. WHAT THE BULLS SAW, pp. 227–238

1. She finally married Ferrante I of Naples, illegitimate son of her uncle Alfonso the Magnanimous.
2. *Cf.*, for example, Pulgar, I, p. 9.
3. Only those to Murcia are known. But similar ones must have been sent to all the cities constituent of Cortes.
4. Pulgar, I, p. 10.
5. Palencia, II, p. 156.
6. *Ibid.*
7. Castillo, p. 178.
8. *Ibid.*
9. Palencia, II, p. 175.
10. *Colección Diplomática*, p. 103. The entire bull is here printed. It contains not a trace of evidence for the grotesque and totally unrealistic theory, held by Isabel's grandson the Emperor Charles V and referred to in several of the chronicles, that Nicholas's dispensation was granted on the basis that if Henry had no child by Juana in a certain number of years the new marriage would be invalid and he must return to Blanca. For the statement of the Imperial councilors, *cf.* Paz y Meliá, *op. cit.*, pp. 337–338. (Here, too, appears the equally incredible charge that the baby's nose was broken upon her birth to make her resemble Henry.)

For the chroniclers, Galíndez, p. 101; Valera, p. 179; Pulgar, I, p. 13; *Crónica Incompleta de los Reyes Católicos, 1469–1476, op. cit.,* p. 56; Pedro de Escavias, from Chapter CXLVII of his "Repertorio de Príncipes de España," in J. B. Sitges, *Enrique IV y la excelente señora llamada vulgarmente La Beltraneja,* Madrid 1912, p. 391.

11. *Et seq.* to "royal arms," *Colección Diplomática,* pp. 562–566. Many scholars—particularly those of the school, currently fashionable, which is cold to Isabel—consider this famous "Pact" of Guisando a forgery, produced later to support her claim to the crown. But the dismissal as falsified of anything that does not happen to fit in with one's theories is much too easy a way of writing history. Admittedly, the original has never been found. Two copies, however, are in existence. And the case for their authenticity would seem to be strengthened by the recent discovery of a verbatim transcript of one of the clauses in a contemporary hand (published in De la Torre and Suárez, *op. cit.,* pp. 58–59).
12. Castillo, p. 179.
13. *Ibid.*
14. Palencia, II, p. 183.
15. *Ibid.*
16. *Ibid.*
17. *Et seq.* to "once, twice and thrice," Juan Torres Fontes, "La Contratación de Guisando," in *Anuario de Estudios Medievales,* Barcelona, II (1965), pp. 399–428; pp. 420–422.
18. Palencia, II, p. 189.

20. "Flowers of Aragón," pp. 239–255

1. Both of these children, Andrés and Pedro, were brought up in Guadalupe and Toledo's Santo Domingo el Antiguo—classic dustbins for royal missteps. Andrés, the older of them, became a monk. I have not succeeded in tracing the other.
2. Valera, p. 137.
3. *Ibid.,* p. 136.
4. Castillo, p. 181.
5. Pulgar, p. 33.
6. *Ibid.*
7. *Ibid.,* p. 28.
8. Valera, p. 149.
9. Vicens, *op. cit.,* p. 246.
10. Paz y Meliá, *op. cit.,* p. 80.
11. *Ibid.,* p. 85.
12. *Ibid.*
13. Although Villena had recently made over his marquesate to his son

Diego, and therefore should now be called either "Pacheco" or "Master of Santiago," I continue to use the name by which he has been known throughout the volume. In the Index, however, the distinction is observed.

14. *Colección Diplomática*, p. 619.
15. Galíndez, p. 342.
16. *Ibid.*, p. 344; Valera, p. 154.
17. *Hechos del Condestable*, p. 396.
18. *Ibid.*, p. 398.
19. Castillo, p. 184.
20. *Ibid.*
21. *Ibid.*, p. 187.
22. Palencia, II, p. 222.
23. Valera, p. 160.
24. *Et seq.* to "decrepitude had need," Vicens, *op. cit.*, p. 259. The letter is also printed, with minor variations, in Paz y Meliá, *op. cit.*, pp. 92–93.
25. Probably by Carrillo or the Nuncio Veneriis. The theory of a private dispensation *in foro conscientiae* imparted by Veneriis, attractive though it be, is now generally discounted.

21. RELEASE, pp. 256–275

1. Suárez, "Los Trastámaras de Castilla y Aragón en el Siglo XV (1407–74)," *op. cit.*, p. 301.
2. *Lettres de Louis XI roi de France* (ed. Vaessen and Charavay), 10 v., Paris 1883–1908; v. 4, p. 64.
3. Castillo, p. 201.
4. A. Bermejo de la Rica, *El Triste Destino de Enrique IV y La Beltraneja*, Madrid [n.d.]; p. 239.
5. *Colección Diplomática*, p. 619.
6. Palencia, II, p. 337.
7. Castillo, p. 204.
8. *Ibid.*
9. *Ibid.*, p. 211.
10. Palencia, III, p. 94.
11. *Ibid.*, p. 131.
12. *Ibid.*, p. 35.
13. Palencia, II, p. 431.
14. Pulgar, I, p. 53.
15. *Hechos del Condestable*, p. xliv.
16. Lorenzo Galíndez de Carvajal, "Anales breves del reynado de los Reyes Católicos," in *Biblioteca de Autores Españoles*, Madrid 1953, v. 71; p. 539.
17. Valera, p. 244.

18. Castillo, p. 217.
19. *Ibid.*, p. 218.
20. But not by medieval reckoning. The calendar year was dated from Christmas; a contemporary reference to "December 26, 1450," for example, should therefore be read as "December 26, 1449." Castillo's statement that Isabel came to Segovia after the New Year—treated by Vicens with such scorn for its inaccuracy—is entirely correct.
21. Galíndez, p. 445.
22. Castillo, p. 218.
23. Palencia, III, p. 189.
24. Pulgar, p. 57.
25. Azcona, *op. cit.*, p. 199.
26. Paz y Meliá, *op. cit.*, p. 161.
27. Castillo, p. 220.
28. Paz y Meliá, *op. cit.*, p. 166.
29. Valera, p. 277.
30. Paz y Meliá, *op. cit.*, p. 166.
31. Valera, p. 283.
32. Palencia, III, p. 256.
33. *Ibid.*
34. *Ibid.*
35. Mariana, *op. cit.*, p. 179.
36. Pulgar, I, p. 60.
37. *Ibid.*, p. 59.
38. Valera, pp. 282–283.
39. Palencia, III, p. 282.
40. *Ibid.*
41. Castillo, p. 221.
42. Valera, p. 283.
43. *Ibid.*, p. 292.
44. Palencia, III, p. 300.
45. Valera, p. 293.
46. Castillo alone among the sources has Henry die serenely. Accounts of his last hours and of his final dispositions (if any) are an irreconcilable chaos; inevitably, they were based upon the narrators' political and personal interests. On the whole, I have followed Palencia.
47. Palencia, III, p. 302.
48. *Ibid.*

❈ Bibliography

Although most books about Isabel the Catholic necessarily deal, in their early reaches, with the reign of Henry IV, no attempt has been made to include that extensive material here. A general bibliography of it can be found in my *The Castles and the Crown*.

Pablo Alvarez Rubiano, *Pedrarias Dávila*, Madrid 1944.

Lope de Barrientos, *Refundición de la Crónica del Halconero* (ed. Carriazo), Madrid 1946.

Eloy Benito Ruano, *Los Infantes de Aragón*, [Madrid] 1952.

A. Bermejo de la Rica, *El Triste Destino de Enrique IV y La Beltraneja*, [Madrid] n.d.

Joseph L. A. Calmette, *Louis XI, Jean II y la révolution catalane (1461–1473)*, Toulouse 1903.

———, *La question des Pyrénées et la Marche d'Espagne au Moyen-Age*, Dijon 1947.

Angel Canellas López, "El Reino de Aragón en el Siglo XV (1410–79)," in *Historia de España* (ed. Menéndez Pidal), Madrid 1964, v. 15, pp. [319]–594.

Pedro Carrillo de Huete, *Crónica del Halconero de Juan II* (ed. Carriazo), Madrid 1946.

Charlotte Rose de Caumont de la Force, *Histoire Secrète de Henri IV, Roy de Castille*, La Haye 1695.

Alfredo Cazabán, "Injusticias de la Historia: Quién fué y cómo fué D. Beltrán de la Cueva," in *Don Lope de Sosa*, Jaén, II (1914), pp. 357–365.

[Gonzalo Chacón], *Crónica de don Alvaro de Luna* (ed. Carriazo), Madrid 1949.

"Colección Diplomática de la Crónica de Enrique IV," in *Memorias de don Enrique IV de Castilla*, v. 2, Madrid 1835–1913.

Colección de Documentos Inéditos del Archivo General de la Corona de Aragón (ed. Bofarull y Mascaró), Barcelona 1859, v. 15; 1862, v. 16.

Nuria Coll Juliá, *Doña Juana Enríquez*, 2 v., Madrid 1953.

Diego de Colmenares, *Historia de la Insigne Ciudad de Segovia*, Madrid 1640.

Luis Comenge, *Clínica Egregia*, Barcelona 1895.

Philippe de Commynes, *Mémoires* (ed. Calmette), 3 v., Paris 1924–1925.

"Coplas del Provincial," in *Révue Hispanique*, Paris, V (1898), pp. 255–266.

Crónica Incompleta de los Reyes Católicos: 1469–1476 (ed. Puyol), Madrid 1934.

"Cronicón de Valladolid," in *Colección de Documentos Inéditos para la Historia de España*, Madrid 1848, v. 13, pp. 5–228.

Baltasar Cuarteto y Huerta, *El Pacto de los Toros de Guisando*, Madrid 1952.

Georges Daumet, "Etude sur l'Alliance de la France et de la Castille au XIVᵉ et au XVᵉ siècles," in *Bibliothèque de l'Ecole des Hautes Etudes*, Paris 1898, v. 118.

Georges Desdevises du Dezert, *Don Carlos D'Aragon, Prince de Viane, Etude sur L'Espagne du Nord au XVᵉ siècle, Paris 1889.*

Documentos Referentes a las relaciones con Portugal durante el reinado de los Reyes Católicos (ed. De la Torre and Suárez Fernández), v. 1, Valladolid 1958.

"Documentos relativos a los reinos de Navarra, Castilla y Aragón durante la segunda mitad del siglo XV," in *Colección de Documentos Inéditos para la Historia de España*, Madrid 1862, v. 40–41.

Jörg von Ehingen, *Diary* (tr. and ed. Malcolm Letts), London 1929.

Diego Enríquez del Castillo, "Crónica del Rey don Enrique el Cuarto," in *Biblioteca de Autores Españoles*, Madrid 1953, v. 70, pp. 97–222.

[Pedro de Escavias], *Hechos del Condestable Don Miguel Lucas de Iranzo* (ed. Carriazo), Madrid 1940.

Francisco Esteve Barba, *Alfonso Carrillo de Acuña*, Barcelona 1943.

Orestes Ferrara, *Un Pleito Sucesorio (Enrique IV, Isabel de Castilla, La Beltraneja)*, Madrid 1945.

P. Ferrer, "Noticias sobre el testamento de Enrique IV," in *Revista de Archivos, Bibliotecas y Museos*, Madrid, IV (1874), pp. 440–441.

Manuel de Foronda y Aguilera, "Cuatro Documentos suscriptos en 1465 por el rey don Alfonso XII en Avila," in *Boletín de la Real Academia de la Historia*, Madrid, LIX (1911), pp. 427–434.

———, *Precedentes de un glorioso reinado, 1465–1475*, Madrid 1901.

Fernán Gómez de Cibdarreal, "Centón Epistolario," in *Biblioteca de Autores Españoles*, Madrid 1850, v. 13, pp. 1–36.

Mariano Grau, *La Ciudad de Segovia*, 2nd ed., Segovia 1951.

J. Gutiérrez Gili, *Alvaro de Luna*, Barcelona 1929.

Manuel Iribarren, *El Príncipe de Viana*, Buenos Aires 1951.

Antonio Jaén, *Segovia y Enrique IV*, Segovia 1916.

Félix de Llanos y Torriglia, *Así llegó a reinar Isabel la Católica*, Madrid 1941.

J. Lucas-Dubreton, *El Rey Huraño (Enrique IV de Castilla y su época)*, 2nd ed., Madrid 1941.

I. I. Macdonald, *Don Fernando de Antequera*, Oxford 1948.

Gregorio Marañón, *Ensayo Biológico sobre Enrique IV de Castilla y su tiempo*, 2nd ed., Buenos Aires 1953.

P. Juan de Mariana, "Historia de España," in *Biblioteca de Autores Españoles*, Madrid 1854, v. 30–31.

Jerónimo Münzer, *Viaje por España y Portugal, 1494–1495* (tr. López Toro), Madrid 1951.

Eduardo Nunes de Leão, *Cronicas del Rey Dom João I . . . e dos Reys D. Duarte e D. Affonso V*, 2 v., Lisbon 1780.

José Palanco y Romero, *Estudios del Reinado de Enrique IV de Castilla*, Granada 1914.

Alonso de Palencia, *Crónica de Enrique IV* (tr. Paz y Meliá), 4 v., Madrid 1904–1908.

J. Paz, "Versión oficial de la batalla de Olmedo," in *Homenaje ofrecido a Ramón Menéndez Pidal*, Madrid 1925, v. 1, pp. 839–842.

Antonio Paz y Meliá, *El Cronista Alonso de Palencia*, Madrid 1914.

[Fernán Pérez de Guzmán], "Crónica del Rey Don Juan II," in *Biblioteca de Autores Españoles*, Madrid 1953, v. 68, pp. 273–695.

Fernán Pérez de Guzmán, *Generaciones y Semblanzas* (ed. Domínguez Bordona), Madrid 1941.

Ruy de Pina, "Chronica d'el Rey Dom Duarte," in *Colleção de livros ineditos de Historia Portuguesa*, Lisbon 1790, v. 1–2.

Francisco Pinal y Monroy, *Retrato del buen vasallo, copiado de la vida y hechos de don Andrés Cabrera*, Madrid 1677.

Eduardo Ponce de León y Freyre, *El Marqués de Cádiz, 1443–1492*, Madrid 1949.

Fernando del Pulgar, *Claros Varones de Castilla*, Buenos Aires 1948.

———, *Letras, Glosa a las Coplas de Mingo Revulgo*, Madrid 1929.

J. Puyol, *Los Cronistas de Enrique IV*, Madrid 1921.

Juan Rizzo y Ramírez, *Juicio Crítico y Significación Política de Don Alvaro de Luna*, Madrid 1865.

Vicente Rodríguez Valencia and Luis Suárez Fernández, *Matrimonio y Derecho Sucesorio de Isabel la Católica*, Valladolid 1960.

Antonio Rodríguez Villa, *Bosquejo Biográfico de Don Beltrán de la Cueva*, Madrid 1881.

Garci Sánchez, jurado de Sevilla, *Anales* (ed. Carriazo), Sevilla 1953.

César Silió, *Don Alvaro de Luna y Su Tiempo*, 4th ed., Buenos Aires 1948.

J. B. Sitges, *Enrique IV y la excelente señora llamada vulgarmente La Beltraneja*, Madrid 1912.

Luis Suárez Fernández, "Aragón y Portugal en la Política de don Alvaro

de Luna," in *Revista de Archivos, Bibliotecas y Museos*, Madrid, LIX (1953), pp. 117–134.
———, "En Torno al Pacto de los Toros de Guisando," in *Hispania*, Madrid, XXIII (1963), pp. 345–365.
———, "Los Trastámaras de Castilla y Aragón en el Siglo XV (1407–74)," in *Historia de España* (ed. Menéndez Pidal), Madrid 1964, v. 15, pp. [1]–318.
———, *Nobleza y Monarquía*, Valladolid 1959.
Juan Torres Fontes, *Don Pedro Fajardo, adelantado de Murcia*, Madrid 1953.
———, *Estudio sobre la "Crónica de Enrique IV" del Dr. Galíndez de Carvajal*, Murcia 1946.
———, *Fajardo el Bravo*, Murcia 1944.
———, *Itinerario de Enrique IV*, Murcia 1953.
———, "La Contratación de Guisando," in *Anuario de Estudios Medievales*, Barcelona, II (1965), pp. 399–428.
The Travels of Leo of Rozmital (tr. and ed. Malcolm Letts), Cambridge 1957.
Mosén Diego de Valera, *Epístolas*, Madrid 1878.
———, *Memorial de Diversas Hazañas* (ed. Carriazo), Madrid 1941.
Viajes de Extranjeros por España y Portugal (ed. García Mercadel), 3 v., Madrid 1879.
Jaime Vicens Vives, *Fernando el Católico, Príncipe de Aragón, Rey de Sicilia, 1458–1478*, Madrid 1952.
———, *Historia Crítica de la Vida y Reinado de Fernando II de Aragón*, Zaragoza 1962.
———, "Los Trastámaras y Cataluña (1410–79)," in *Historia de España* (ed. Menéndez Pidal), Madrid 1964, v. 15, pp. 595–793.
———, *Monarquía y revolución en el siglo XV, Juan II de Aragón*, Barcelona 1953.
"Vida del Serenísimo Príncipe Don Juan Segundo, Rey de Aragón, que compuso Gonzalo García de Santa María," in *Colección de Documentos Inéditos para la Historia de España*, Madrid 1887, v. 88, pp. 275–350.
Brito Vivar, *A Política de D. Affonso V en relação a Castela*, Lisbon 1919.
Jerónimo Zurita, *Anales de la Corona de Aragón*, 6 v., Zaragoza 1610.

❋ An Index of Persons

What a reader not acquainted with the customs of the country often mistakes for a Spaniard's middle name is, in reality, his patronymic. For that reason, in the following pages Juan Fernández Galindo will be found under "Fernández" and Diego Arias Dávila under "Arias." Only with the Mendozas (since they are almost universally known in that fashion) and with the chronicler Diego Enríquez del Castillo (for causes explained in the Notes) have I allowed myself to vary from this rule. Nobles and prelates are indexed under their family names, with cross references from their titles; the page entries for the Count of Plasencia, as example, are under "Stúñiga" and those for the Bishop of Jaén under "Peleas." With the exception of Juana Enríquez, royalty are listed by given name alone.